Playing
at
Being Bad:

The Hidden Resilience
of Troubled Teens

140201

Michael Ungar, Ph.D.

Pottersfield Press, Lawrencetown Beach, Nova Scotia, Canada

National Library of Canada Cataloguing in Publication
Ungar, Michael, 1963-
Playing at being bad: the hidden resilience of troubled teens/Michael Ungar.
ISBN 1-895900-52-2
1. Adolescent psychology. 2. Problem youth. I. Title
BF724.U54 2002   155.5   C2002-903591-0

Book cover design by Dalhousie Graphics

Front cover photograph by Findlay Muir

Quote on page 89 from *Daughters of Feminists* by Nancy White
in her CD *Momnipotent: Songs for Weary Parents* 1990

Pottersfield Press acknowledges the ongoing support of the Nova Scotia Department of Tourism and Culture, Cultural Affairs Division. We acknowledge the support of the Canada Council for the Arts which last year invested $19.1 million in writing and publishing throughout Canada. We also acknowledge the finanacial support of the Government of Canada through the Book Publishing Industry Development Program for our publishing activities.

Pottersfield Press
83 Leslie Road
East Lawrencetown, Nova Scotia, Canada B2Z 1P8
Web site: www.pottersfieldpress.com
To order, phone toll free 1-800-NIMBUS9 (1-800-646-2879)
Printed in Canada

Canada Council Conseil des Arts   Canadä
for the Arts   du Canada

Contents

Acknowledgements

My work over the years has been supported by many people, the most important of whom is my partner, Cathy. My children, Scott and Meg, have lent their support as well, patiently teaching me each day about what it means to be a child in today's world.

There were many others who had a big part to play in shaping my thinking about the material I discuss in this book. My own mentor as an adolescent, Steve Vineberg, started me along the road which led to my present career and interests, while Annette Werk, Margaret Bishop, Norris Turner, and Earla Vickers helped me hone my clinical skills.

Of course, it is to all the young people and their families whom I have met over the years through my formal and informal practice to whom I owe the greatest debt. Though they remain anonymous, they were both tolerant and helpful shaping my understanding of the lives of troubled young people.

Thanks also to Yvette Doucette for her comments on a first draft, and to Julia Swan, Jackie Barclay, and Rhonda Brophy for their editorial work. Finally, a heartfelt thanks to my many colleagues, notably Pat Warren, Eli Teram, John Picketts, and Ross Klein for assistance with my research and bringing this work to press.

In order to protect the privacy of all the individuals with whom I have had the privilege to work, the reader must know that the stories I share in these pages are both real and fictionalized, based on bits and pieces of lives lived, cobbled together from anecdotes common to many young people and their families. All of the composite sketches of youth and their families that appear are substitutes for individuals whose identities must, of course, remain confidential. None of the people portrayed actually exist as I described them. Though some readers might think they recognize in these pages someone in particular, the resemblance is more coincidence than fact. Perhaps, if the stories sound familiar it is because throughout my career in a number of communities, big and small, I have met hundreds of youth who shared much in common with one another. My hope is that readers find here stories which ring true for them and those for whom they care.

Introduction

> There is something I don't know
>   that I am supposed to know
> I don't know *what* it is I don't know
>   and yet am supposed to know,
> And I feel I look stupid
>   if I seem both not to know it
>   and not know what it is I don't know
> Therefore, I pretend I know it.
>
>   R.D. Laing, *Knots*. New York: Pantheon (1970)

Last night the evening news carried a story about eight teenagers who attacked a male jogger in his twenties in a park a mile from my home. At a dinner party with friends I hear about their daughter's grade nine graduation party where girls offered sex to the boys in exchange for $20 bags of dope. My colleague's 18-year-old son was charged by police after he attacked another man in a downtown bar, stabbing him in the back for no apparent reason. Girls who attend the private school next to my office amble past my window, smoking, with their pleated tartan uniforms pulled up to look like mini-skirts. A fast food outlet near my home has had to hire a security guard to make sure adolescents don't loiter. At the busy intersection in front of the offices of the local social services department, two street youth, one an anorexic young woman in jeans and running shoes, the other a pony-tailed young man with a pit-bull he keeps tied beside the road, meander between four lanes of traffic offering to clean the windshields of stopped motorists.

Some of these young people will become involved with services designed to help them. Others will simply continue to frustrate their families and communities. I once felt certain that the troubled children and adolescents with whom I worked had problems I could fix. They came to me for treatment with lists of charges against them and even longer lists of diagnoses that described them and their problems in great detail. It was comfortable thinking that as a therapist I could be helpful even if most of what I knew to be true about these young people I'd learned from other adults. These children were dangerous or deviant, delinquent or disordered. They had been violent with classmates, or threatened police, slashed their wrists, stolen cars, burned down houses, become pregnant, run away, or been suspended. They were often sexually active, hyperactive, demanding, troubled, and in such a state of turmoil that they had long past overwhelmed the emotional resources of their parents. Almost always, it seemed, they were running with the wrong crowd. I still believe I can help these young people and their families, but I have found I am most successful in my interventions when I rely more on youths' own descriptions of their lives and their explanations for why they do what they do.

For the past twenty years I have been working mostly with what are called "high-risk" youth and their families as a social worker, family therapist, child and youth care worker, and researcher, learning from them what it means to survive by whatever means possible. While many of these youth have not been from stable homes, a surprising number have. Strange, but even kids born into families that share many of the advantages of ordered communities and good incomes find themselves scarred by the emotional and physical abuse they experience at home, school or among peers.

Whether from good homes or bad, wealthy communities or poor, the deeply troubled youth whom I meet through my work tell me they play at being bad because that is the simplest way to feel good. They discover outside their homes opportunities to express their pain, alternatives to the chaos of their biological families, or sometimes just the sheer excitement that frenetic young lives relish.

These children have left me wondering how it is that over and over again, we adults come to the wrong conclusions about what we think we see when we observe what appears to us to be one youth leading another into trouble. Where we see only an endless stream of misery that loves company, very troubled children and adolescents tell me we adults have it all wrong. They tell me we need to look closer at our children's lives, their peer relationships, and the pathways they travel to both health and illness when confronted with adversity. Psychiatrist Terri Moffitt and her colleagues who have studied these pathways tell us that less than 5 percent of our children will persist with troubling behaviours into adulthood. While encouraging news, we have yet to understand developmentally what it is that anchors this minority to deviant and disordered lifestyles.

Increasingly, we see children like those I mentioned above commanding our attention for all the wrong reasons. They are the ones who appear on the six o'clock news, handcuffed or worse, dead. They are every parent's nightmare, and greatest shame. Instead of being told, however, what we can do to help, we are left blaming children, and just as often their families, without understanding why these problem behaviours hold such attraction.

This book is about helping these young people *before* they become statistics. It's for all of us, parents and professionals, who are frustrated and afraid. Unlike most books, though, it relies on some unconventional sources of wisdom: troubled kids themselves and their peer groups. Together, these youth and I were like archeologists exploring hidden caverns in search of an elusive quality we called "health." The youth themselves proved the best spelunkers, guiding me deep inside their worlds, forcing me to reconsider everything I believed about what makes a child healthy.

There are many different ways to understand health. Studies have documented that children with high self-esteem, a sense of belonging and meaning in their lives, proper care, and a safe environment are the ones most likely to be healthy. We also know that children need an ever expanding web of relationships as they grow, and opportunities to feel competent and in control of some aspects of their lives. William Pollack in his book *Real Boys* has helped to document this weave of relationships in the lives of young males. Samuel Osherson did much the same when he interviewed more than two hundred men about their experiences of love and connection with their partners, children, mothers and fathers. Mary Pipher, in *Reviving Ophelia,* took a long look at the lives of young women, building on the work of feminist authors like Jean Baker Miller and Carol Gilligan who have shown that women's development (and perhaps men's too) takes place through connections with others, and not as previously thought by asserting one's own independence.

But teens need more than just connection. They also need boundaries, rules and the feeling that someone gives a damn and is going to keep them safe and help them succeed. After all, we know from the work of developmental psychologists like Britain's Michael Rutter that when stressors build up in a child's life, good problem-solving skills, opportunities to grow, and strong attachments will get them through life's tumultuous moments.

While all these aspects of health are important, strangely, many of our youth experience health in ways we adults insist are unhealthy. We are not always able, and frequently as communities are unwilling, to listen to youth explain the choices they make when charting a course towards feeling good about themselves. Instead, we insist they achieve health in ways acceptable to us, though at times meaningless to them.

Many of the young people who find their way to my office laugh at the image promoted by their caregivers of a world which looks like a Disney streetscape. While we wish we could provide our children with such muted conformity and order, many teenagers argue that such a world is void of challenge or meaning. Many more know they will never have access to such a fairy-tale existence, and instead spend most of their lives in communities where the only opportunities to feel good about themselves may come from breaking the law, or acting crazy.

The youth with whom I work may have solved for us an age old riddle. For centuries we have made adolescence a problem, threatened perhaps by the raw idealism and unlimited potential that takes hold during our teen years. We have all wanted to know what makes our children act out in ways that puts them in harm's way without ever looking seriously at the role we play as adults in our adolescents' search for identity. Authors like Nancy Lesko say that adolescence is nothing more than a creation of adults who feel threatened by this youthful exuberance and therefore characterize children as untamed, savage, and something other than we are supposed to be. Teenagers have become our collective scapegoats.

Even if we accept this notion of adolescence as a developmentally distinct period, a phase during which we lack self-control, for all our hard efforts we haven't yet succeeded as well as we should with the resources we have committed to keeping teenagers safe. I always get this uneasy gut feeling when meeting for the first time a young person who arrives at my office with a foot thick file. In it are frequently five, ten, or even more assessments, stacked like rungs on a ladder, climbing nowhere. While I might be frustrated, I can practically hear the howls of anger echoing from the folders from children and parents who have had to tolerate these multiple intrusions into their lives.

What Have We Missed?

The sad truth, and what is seldom said publically, is that most of the counselling, placements, time in jail, stints on psychiatric units, and group therapy stop very few of these children from returning to their peer groups and doing more of the same. If one wades deep into the reams of academic studies which have examined outcomes for troubled kids who get treatment, one would find that many who never receive therapy do very well, and that many who get all the help we can provide wind up permanently dependent on our systems of care. At a recent international conference of family therapists, a panel of distinguished experts told their audience that there is only limited evidence for the effectiveness of most of what professional helpers do. Too often professionals assume that if people appear to be getting better then it must be because of the treatment provided. Those that don't get better are called "resistant" and told their problem behaviours would change if they just agreed to participate in the programs that are offered.

As parents, teachers, mental health practitioners, and journalists, we have all missed the obvious. Dangerous, deviant, delinquent, and disordered children are in a frantic search to find some way to feel good about themselves. They don't always want to change, though they do want to be healthy, happy and live life to its fullest. David Gregson, a west coast counsellor for drug addicted youth, talks about his clients as "normally very abnormal." The phrase couldn't be better chosen. The behaviours that so frighten us adults are often the best troubled kids could manage from a bad set of choices.

Many times, children and youth *achieve health through their problem behaviours*. Understanding what our children find attractive about acting out makes it easier for us to help them stay safe. When we see how youth find health amidst chaos, we are better able to offer them opportunities to experience themselves in ways that are every bit as powerful but more socially acceptable. These offers only work when they bring troubled youth the same *benefits* they find along the dangerous, deviant, and delinquent paths they have already chosen to travel.

Problems as pathways to health? Delinquent behaviour as a survival strategy? It is hard to believe but the evidence is abundant.

A Journey to the Source

Ten years ago, I felt like Alice going down the rabbit hole. When I first started asking children about the positive aspects of their problem behaviours, it was disorienting. Then downright scary. I still carry that dis-ease deep inside me even as I have discovered the hidden resilience of many young people. It can be a bit jarring to discover resilience, or health, hidden inside the kind of problem kids we see on the news. In the upside-down landscape of possibilities in which many of these kids live, bad can be good, jail can be a place to feel safe from one's family or community, drug abuse can be recreation, and violence can be a road to acceptance and self-esteem.

Most parents will never have to find out their kids think this way, because most of our children find other ways to survive. But for those who aren't so lucky, I'm reminded of the old Isley Brothers' tune during which we all crouch on the dance floor and begin to quietly "shout." We keep raising our voices a "little louder now," again and again, until we are standing and waving our arms above our heads, yelling "shout" at the top of our lungs. If the youth in these pages speak rather loudly, it's so that other children who are silenced can be heard.

Anna and Melissa

Anna showed up twenty minutes early for an 8:30 morning appointment. She is one of the many parents I have met over the years through my clinical practice who arrive in desperation, as if at sea in a leaky boat with nothing but a tin can for a bailer. I remember her gaze, a mix of distraction, which comes from too much caffeine and a lack of sleep, and an intensity, which reminds one of the panicked sailor scanning the horizon for hope of landfall. Decidedly absent from the room was Anna's 14-year-old daughter, Melissa, who was supposed to join us that morning.

Anna sat with me, wringing her long thin hands, her wedding ring still there from a marriage she'd ended two years earlier. Her ex-husband had been an alcoholic who passed through her life leaving nothing but lonesome evenings and a clutter of bills. The morning we met it was one of those crisp sunny fall days when the air has the vitality of a north wind. Here on the east coast, a wind like that carries with it a lick of salt that can make eyes tear.

Anna told me about feeling anxiety and helplessness, emotions she'd come to expect in a world which was always one accident away from ruin. This time, though, it was her daughter who was depleting Anna's few resources to cope. She'd come to feel lately there was nothing she could do to keep Melissa safe. She told me how she'd watched Melissa leave the house at nine o'clock the night before. Though there was school the next day, Anna had been unable to stop Melissa from going out. No amount of threats or tears convinced her daughter to come back. Even worse, she told me she had watched helplessly as Melissa was joined on the street by teens two and three years older than she, boys and girls whom Anna knew were doing drugs, and who had already been in trouble with the law.

There is no quick way to help a child like Melissa, or to calm her mother's fears. Eventually, Melissa would come home and stay, and the relationship that took hold between mother and daughter would be an anchor of security in both their lives. But first, since Melissa wasn't there to speak for herself, I asked Anna if she could remember what it was like for her when she was a 14-year-old adolescent. Who were her friends, and what attracted her to them? Anna was absolutely certain she could remember what it was like to be Melissa's age: the anxiety which comes from a desperate need for acceptance, and the mythic peer pressure to do what others told her to do. She was too embarrassed during that first interview, however, to share with me details of what she said were the many "mistakes" she'd made when younger.

While I sat and listened to Anna tell me about her daughter's behaviour, I couldn't help but wonder: if I was to go down the rabbit hole again, and ask Melissa about her life on the street, and at home, might I not find a very different story to tell about what happened the night before? Anna was right, though. Melissa's behaviour was inviting trouble. But to get her to change, I needed to understand from Melissa's point of view what was drawing her to the street. I was curious about the spirited defiance Melissa had shown as she walked out her mother's door. How did this sprightly 14-year-old manage to evoke the attention of much older youth? And why was it so necessary that Melissa defy her mother, putting herself in harm's way?

Both Anna and I agreed wholeheartedly that a child Melissa's age shouldn't be roaming the neighbourhood late at night, but where Anna wanted to "take control," I suggested a more cautious approach might be needed. Youth who play hard at being bad are not likely to toe the line when told to do so.

Adult Help

"Nobody's ever been any help. I don't need help. I don't have a problem." Sarah made her point over and over again. She was convinced no one was listening. She was thirteen and, like Melissa, felt she should be treated like an 18-year-old. She was self-assured enough to let me and her parents know that in spite of what we all might think, she was doing quite well on her own, thank you very much. Maybe she was. More likely she wasn't.

Already at her young age, she'd managed to get herself *back* into custody for a series of property crimes and breaches of her probation order. It was hard to imagine this girl with the jet black hair and an impish grin ever doing much harm to anybody. She was all of ninety-eight pounds, her clothes a loose fitting sack that hung about her lanky

5-foot 10-inch frame. She talked incessantly about anything and everything. She seldom sat still. She'd fidget through our conversations, though she had an uncanny knack of staring at the television for hours in the hyper-stimulation-induced euphoria of a Nintendo game. Hand on the controller, her whole body would be the soldier in battle, the jet fighter, even the little Mario figure moving from one near death adventure to the next. Perhaps she found there on the screen a story as vivid as her own. Unfortunately, I never thought to ask.

Instead, shortly after we'd been officially introduced by the youth worker responsible for ferrying her through her time in custody, I sat down with Sarah and asked her, "Can you tell me a bit about your life, what it's like being in here, about your friends, your family?" Such simple questions allow youth to take me along on a voyage of their own choosing and at their own pace. It doesn't matter what they talk about first; our lives are like tapestries woven with multicoloured threads that intertwine in endless patterns. If we are patient, everything eventually gets revealed.

In fact, sometimes it's better if I don't have too much information about a child I'm getting to know for the first time. Those foot-thick files can make us deaf to what a child wants us to hear. Besides, a little information is a dangerous thing. It can make us think we understand a person: it can finesse us into making assumptions, give us categories in which to slot behaviour without really understanding the ins and outs of a life as it is lived. Oftentimes, the kids prove us wrong anyway, or at least they will if we give them half a chance. Sarah was one of those kids.

She lived, she told me, with her mother and father on a small farm. Though she'd spent most of her early life in the city, her parents had decided to move back to where her father grew up and try to make a go of it fishing part-time and operating a small hobby farm. While her parents were doing well, Sarah had been getting into trouble for some time. She'd never had that many problems in the city, but in a new community, where many of the neighbours kids were already drinking by her age, and where the kids felt isolated but still plugged in to the wider world, it was a bad mix of Hollywood expectations and rural realities.

Being so young, and so out of control, Sarah was getting noticed. Her parents were embarrassed by their daughter's behaviour, having made a good life for themselves now that they were back home. They didn't want their kid drifting into trouble like many of the other county kids. When we'd first met, they told me how Sarah roamed about with "wild types" four and five years older than herself. They worried she'd be pressured into doing drugs (which she'd already tried), and that her school work would slip further. They'd already had her seen by a local pediatrician who had prescribed Ritalin to cope with what looked to everyone to be a sure case of Attention Deficit Hyperactivity Disorder.

Sarah had accepted with a wry smile this identity as the hyperactive, impulsive kid who couldn't control herself. She told me she was drinking "heavily" and with great confidence said she was destined to be a criminal. She could give me little explanation as to why she'd chosen this lifestyle over any other, but it was clear that she loved it. Time in custody just added an extra bit of mystique to who she wanted to be and returned her to her community wiser in the ways of being a delinquent. Far from a deterrence, time inside was part of a challenge that she had set for herself.

But Sarah had her strengths too. There was a fiercely loyal spirit in the girl that woke up at the first sign of an attack being mounted against her friends or family. As long as she wasn't having to defend herself or others, Sarah was a joy to be around. She could sing beautifully, she could tirelessly kick a soccer ball, she was always up for any outing or adventure, and she shined when she and her youth worker had time by themselves to talk or play games. It was hard not to imagine a puppy happily chasing its tail when watching Sarah bounce through her life.

This happy-go-lucky façade made it easy to like Sarah. But there was a darker side that worried all of us who knew her and were trying to get her to change. Safely placed inside a jail, we didn't have to worry about her breaking into our cottage, lighting a fire at school, or f'ing off at us on the street. She was sober, taking her medications, amused, well cared for with plenty of structure, in a safe and predictable routine for as long as she stayed in custody. Our struggle, and hers, was how to achieve self-esteem, a personal sense of power and meaningful relationships in ways that didn't involve playing the delinquent.

Three Different Children

Youth who come from both good homes and bad homes have shown me that their behaviour is always the way they exercise control over the identity they carry and the acceptance they receive for who they want to be. Kids whose lives are in chaos, and who are drifting toward deviant and problem solutions to life's challenges, tell me they start down these dangerous paths for one of three reasons.

Traumatized kids, from any home, whether wealthy or poor, in good neighbourhoods and safe communities, or in war torn, crime ridden inner cities, who are abused, neglected, or witnesses to violence and degradation, are often deeply affected by what they see, hear and experience firsthand. While not all traumatized kids come through horrific experiences and turn to drugs, violence or self-destruction, becoming labelled as deviant, disordered, or dangerous, many that do explain their problem behaviours as their best ways to cope with the pain of their recent pasts. I would prefer children had more choices and didn't need to bolster their self-esteem, find social support, feel loved, or soothe the pain inflicted on them by putting themselves in harm's way. Sadly, though, for many of these traumatizd youth, this is what they do. Efforts to prevent them from choosing these problem behaviours start with understanding why they do what they do and, strangely, the positive things they experience when they act out.

Disadvantaged kids are, in contrast, those who come from environments where they don't have access to the resources they need to sustain health even though we assume those resources are there for all children. These kids don't have good job prospects, they don't have the gadgets and clothing that can make them feel like they belong, they don't have the social address, or the right skin colour, or sexual orientation, or abilities, to easily find a place of respect in their broader communities. Instead, lacking health and just as often hope, these youth find a healthy status through the one door still open to them, the street culture of deviance, risk-taking and delinquency.

Lucky kids are the ones we are most baffled by. These are the invisible problem children who often appear to have all that they need to be healthy. They are well-cared for in many respects, yet still are dissatisfied with their lives. As their caregivers, we don't understand why children who appear to lack for nothing turn out bad. We knock ourselves out so that our children have safe and stable homes in which to grow. Yet, increasingly, I am seeing these lucky youth inside the institutions in which I work. I call these youth lucky because that is how we think of them: lucky to have loving parents, even if they are latchkey kids; lucky to have stable homes, even if they are fed up with the order and safety that removes any healthy risk-taking from their lives; lucky to live in safe homes and communities, but without opportunities to live life more chaotically and resist the sameness of everything and everyone around them; lucky to have hope for the future, but little power to decide what that future will look like; and finally, lucky to live in a picture-perfect world, when what they miss is something more substantial, away from the mass marketers and manipulation of adults. These lucky kids are the least understood because they are the ones who seem to explode without warning from their middle-class roots, embarrassing their parents and communities who hang their heads in disbelief when their apparently healthy children commit unthinkable acts of destruction.

All three types of kids tell me they are playing at being bad when they act out in ways that give them some say over who they are. This is a tragedy, that large numbers of our youth turn to dangerous, deviant, delinquent and disordered behaviours to cope with their feelings and meet their needs for a powerful identity. As a therapist, a father, and a member of my community, I wish these children could find what it is they are looking for in ways that are more socially acceptable and less self-destructive. My wishes aside, for many youth their choices are just that, a decision they make, not necessarily consciously or purposefully, but a decision nonetheless that puts them on a path towards health.

I have found my best success working with deeply troubled youth occurs when I accept that what they are doing makes sense to them and solves other more pressing problems in their lives. Without this understanding, and blinded by the bias that comes with age, I misunderstand the behaviour of problem youth and remain at the margins of their lives.

Traumatized kids have shown me how disordered behaviour and time spent on psychiatry wards is an effective strategy to be something other than just another abused kid who couldn't stop the violence. Disadvantaged kids exploit the few opportunities they have to prove themselves, demonstrating everything from an entrepreneurial spirit to bookish street smarts by selling drugs, committing thefts or demonstrating in-your-face attitudes towards those who hold power over their lives. Meanwhile, the lucky kids who grow up in cultural wastelands seek through their deviant behaviours the excitement and challenge neutered from their lives. For all three groups, the roots of their pain may be different, but their solutions are all too frequently the same. All three see their problem behaviours as their salvation.

Five Strategies

Sarah said nobody could help her. I believe what she really meant was she liked the way her life was going. For many of the kids I meet, their families and communities are both willing and able to provide opportunities for their children to grow up accepted and healthy. Yet kids still turn to their troubled peers and deviant behaviours to feel good about themselves. This shouldn't surprise us. Study after study of street youth in countries such as Thailand, Poland, Colombia, and Australia, and here in the United States and Canada, have shown that peer groups often mean the difference between exploitation and survival for kids who are rejected or discarded. Though not all the youth met in the following pages fit this description (many having loving homes and "good enough" or exceptional parents) it is sadly true that for some children the street is the only home where they feel they belong.

I keep two things in my office when I work with children like Sarah and their families. The first is paper and pen so that I can record the wisdom of those whose lives I am privileged to share. The second is a garbage can so they can throw away anything *I say* that does not hold true for them.

I have discovered through these conversations over the years five strategies that adults can use with the troubled children and youth in their care to help them grow up safe and feel accepted without having to resort to delinquent and dangerous behaviours. Though I tend to see children after they have gone down these self-destructive paths, these strategies can be just as useful in preventing kids from starting problem behaviours altogether:

> Strategy One: Ask them "What is true for you?" Help children and adolescents become critical consumers of everyone's values, including those of their parents, peers or anyone else who would have them believe their truth is The Truth.

> Strategy Two: Encourage them to "Shop around." Children and youth need to become a part of different peer groups if they are to discover who they really want to be.

Strategy Three: Celebrate storytelling: Listen closely to the complex stories young people tell about themselves.

Strategy Four: Accept the unusual: Acknowledge the identity a child or youth chooses. Find the positive aspects of that identity and show whatever acceptance is possible.

Strategy Five: Stop blaming our children's peers. See children and youth as equal participants in creating their group identity.

Each of these five strategies can be used by parents, caregivers and professional helpers to make our relationships with children of value to them and us. I'm certain we can help teens like Sarah and Melissa turn their lives in a different direction, but not by offering them more of the same kinds of help we've already forced on them. We need to do things differently. In the chapters that follow, each of these strategies will be explored through stories of youth who struggled to be themselves both at home and beyond their front doors.

No one family, caregiver, or helper will likely try all five strategies at once. They nest one inside the other. Some are as much about a change in attitude as a prescribed course of action. These strategies need not be followed in sequence either. Start wherever you, or the young person, feels most comfortable.

These five strategies cannot, however, always be accomplished by a family alone. First, a child must still be willing to have a relationship. Sadly, some children and youth have drifted away from their families and live without any close attachments to them. Those relationships are reparable, but a parent or caregiver may need professional help to rebuild bridges to communication. Without dialogue, connection and time, there is little that can be done to help our children grow up safely.

When Problems Are Solutions

There are any number of reasons our relationships with the troubled children and youth in our care get derailed. Sometimes it's obvious, though more often the cause of the problems are vague, lost behind a thick bank of impenetrable fog. Johnathan, for example, has grown up in an upper-class home where he has had all the comforts two wealthy professional working parents can provide. He's fifteen and doesn't talk to his parents much about his life outside their home, though they tell me they try to find out what they can from other parents about the kids they see with their son. When Johnathan was charged with armed robbery they couldn't believe it was *their* son they met at the police station, *their* child who needed a lawyer, a probation officer, and treatment for his addictions. Suddenly they were sure their suspicions about Johnathan's friends had been right all along, and that those other kids were the reason their son was in trouble.

Peter, on the other hand, has spent all of his fifteen years growing up in a neighbourhood where most kids drop out of school long before grade twelve and where welfare cheques are more common than paycheques. His mother sleeps most days, and seldom knows or cares where her three sons are. Peter has lots of friends, but doesn't do drugs, doesn't even smoke, and has never been in any serious trouble. When Child and Family Services is called to investigate the home because Peter's youngest brother is showing up at school hungry, tired and in need of a bath, Peter meets the social workers at the door and explains his mom is just not feeling well. When he's not at home playing at being a parent, Peter's at school, or on the street, or down at the local youth centre, shooting baskets. Sometimes he prefers to hang out with the staff there helping out with the younger kids. Peter navigates the peer groups in his neighbourhood like a minesweeper, alert to trouble which is always close at hand. But this is the story Peter tells about himself. Those who check in on him from the community think he's on the streets far too much, and assume that he is in as much trouble, doing as much drugs, and skipping school every bit as often as his friends. Peter jokes that it would be easier if he was just another bad kid. He gets tired of convincing people otherwise.

Allison's life began much the same as Peter's, only she was taken from her parents by the department of social services and placed in one group home after another. She did everything she needed to survive in those homes, becoming one of the in-crowd, excelling at being a problem youth. She was doing as well as could be expected for a "group-home-kid" until she met Becky, a freer spirit than most, who asked her mother to let Allison live with them. At Becky's, Allison found a safe place to try and be someone different. Only problem was, social services had no faith that the kid they had come to know as a foul-mouthed delinquent was ever going to survive in such an unstructured environment. Realizing they had little choice, however, and faced with Allison threatening to run away, they finally agreed to her placement in the unlicensed foster home. Everyone, except Allison, was surprised when she returned to school, got off drugs, and voluntarily put herself on the pill.

A Puzzle

We have been trying to listen to people's accounts of their problems for years, starting with Freud who put people on a couch and let them free associate. The problem has been, though, that Freud and his followers have never looked at how *their* interpretations of what they think they hear are rooted in who they are as people. What they believe about their patients says much more about how they as helpers see the world than about what the patients experience. Incredible as it is to us today, Freud never believed his female patients had actually been sexually abused, though they talked about early sexual experiences forced on them by parents and others. Freud dismissed these stories as fantasies, as easily as we dismiss the stories told by youth who seek time in jail, enjoy their deviant peer groups, and enjoy the numbing effects of drugs. If we are to help, and prevent kids from turning to these problem behaviours, we need to first shed our prejudices in order to hear what children tell us.

Michel Foucault, a French philosopher and sociologist, offers us a much better way than Freud's to understand the experiences of others. He talks about mental health, deviance, and disorder as things those in power define for others. Those who lack power become victims of the control imposed upon them when they are judged by experts to be "unhealthy." Kids who act bad get known as bad kids, though we conveniently forget that what we say is bad today may not have been so bad when we were young. What we define as deviance is a product of our time and the way we think about youth.

When I was growing up, bullying on the school playground was something schools dealt with themselves, or conveniently overlooked. It now contributes to a diagnosis of "conduct disorder," an unfortunately vague label that means nothing except that a child won't do as he or she is told. But being a bully today is also much more likely to lead to involvement with the criminal justice system or a mental health professional. In many cases we have welcomed this change, as we have become increasingly adept at protecting victims from acts of violence.

But we should not forget that when we criminalize bullying we are also contributing to the power bullies have. By dealing with these kids through more formal means, we tell them they are every bit as mean as they want to appear. Bullies tell me that our heightened vigilance and zero tolerance policies for school yard violence have made youth who see themselves as bullies become more, not less, lethal as they accept their title as dangerous and delinquent. Incarceration or suspension may protect victims, but neither strategy does anything but make the bully feel more powerful in a socially deviant way.

Listening to troubled children explain their world has not been our strength. We really want to believe that those kids who killed their classmates at Columbine High School, or the ones who choose to live on the street cleaning the windshields of passing cars, or the invisible kids who are wasting away on our neighbour's couch, uneducated and unemployed, that all those youth behave as they do because of something wrong with *them*. I'm no longer sure this is the case, nor that we have been offering them the help they need in ways that make sense to them.

Don't Believe What You Read

Despite the way we see youth today, a look at the numbers reveals that the vast majority of kids are doing better than ever. Youth crime is going down, teenagers are doing less drugs, are staying in school longer, are more aware of the global community, are more interested in politics, use birth control more than we adults ever did during our youth, and are even smoking fewer cigarettes. Yet it is the minority of really troubled and dangerous youth whom we watch with voracious appetites for the macabre each evening on the news. The "few bad apples" we see convince us our children are making worse choices than we made when we were young. For many distraught parents like Anna, our struggles as caregivers of these children leaves us blind to the latent health present in our most troubled youth.

Study after study has shown that problem youth, when given the chance to explain themselves, gain status, self-esteem, a sense of personal competence, meaning, a feeling of family and community belonging, hopefulness, and an appreciation for unique talents, all by being the worst kids, rather than the best. We have reserved the term resilience for a select few "superkids" and completely overlooked that the vulnerable "losers" who populate high-risk neighbourhoods cope in exactly the same way as their peers. For both groups, the way they search for health is remarkably similar. Only the specifics of their behaviour are different. Research has shown that youth in delinquent peer groups develop high self-esteem, have enhanced problem-solving skills, are well-attached to others, feel like they have meaning in their lives, and may actually suffer fewer mental health problems than youth who come from similar backgrounds but who remain as loners. Other studies have shown that youth inside and outside institutions are not all that different on many measures of mental health, such as feeling like they have a say over their lives and optimism about their future. Denying the health benefits of problem behaviour is not going to get us closer to our goal of changing kids living troubled lives.

The late Paul Steinhauer, a renowned child psychiatrist and advocate for children in care, believed deeply in the right of these children to tell their stories as they experienced them. His work over four decades helped to establish networks for children to share their experiences living apart from their families. Kids often tell me they feel like their worlds have different rules from those of their parents. In their search for health, high-risk children and youth rely most on their peer groups to nurture and maintain an identity which is positive, powerful and widely accepted. It is for this reason that much of this book is devoted to understanding what really happens in adolescent peer groups. Troubled kids who spend time with other troubled kids, even in family street groups, wannabe gangs, and gangs, report that they feel greater self-esteem, more say over their lives, and learn better problem-solving skills inside the group than out. "Dysfunctional" peer groups can exert a positive influence on the lives of high-risk youth who may have few other opportunities to feel really healthy. Needless to say, such a controversial idea is not much comfort to a parent like Anna in the midst of a crisis. It does, however, open up a world of possibilities for interventions with high-risk youth.

As parents and caregivers, we can offer our kids opportunities to find their own unique paths to resilience. Resilience is typically thought of as individual characteristics of a child, or the child's family and community, that help a child exposed to substantial amounts of risk rise above his or her adversity and live a healthy life.

Allison's new peer group, which she found through a chance meeting with Becky, offered her an easy path to a different story about herself. Peter's life story demonstrates the way a child's entire community can be an audience, bearing witness to his or her strengths and talents, or completely ignoring them. For Johnathan, a peer group with different values from those of his family provided him an elusive sense of belonging he never found at home. Or as Melissa discovered beyond her front door, street culture can be a place to experiment with feeling powerful and in control when denied these feelings elsewhere in her life. Behaviours that are troubling for caregivers all too often are the first choice of problem teens when they go searching for opportunities to practice the skills they need either to bolster a fledgling identity or to find a new more powerful one.

Parenting Today

As parents and caregivers to adolescents, our role is every bit as daunting and demanding as when our children are infants and toddlers. As Barbara Coloroso makes so very clear, what we do as parents is the same for the young child as it is for the older adolescent: we are there to help them make good choices. Our children need us desperately during their teen years even though they seem miles away both emotionally and physically. As the world becomes more complicated and change happens at lightning speed, I see adults all around me despairing that they no longer have a role to play guiding their children through these turbulent times. We see our children turning to manufactured pop idols more than their own elders for guidance. We may mistakenly come to believe we are no longer needed. I couldn't disagree more. We will need, however, a different approach to parenting if we are to keep up with the new "truths" our children are discovering.

The good news is that kids know they need help from adults. They've told me this in no uncertain terms and on numerous occasions in my office, frequently with their parents right there to hear the good news. But to be there for them will demand of us caregivers a different attitude, one that is more respectful of the way children and adolescents construct their worlds. For kids who are at-risk for more serious problems, the demands on their caregivers are that much more challenging.

I once told one of the youth I was working with how uneasy I was feeling when she succeeded in making me understand how healthy she was despite all the test scores which showed quite clearly she was very "ill." She sat there but a moment, fixed her eyes on mine, and smiled. "Get over it!" was her terse advice. I'm still working on it.

I find myself at times not wanting to believe what it is kids tell me because to do so shakes the foundations of what I have been comfortable believing. And yet, at the same time, I see all around me our failings as caregivers, and a proliferation of advice for parents which is seldom ever put to the kids themselves for comment. There's an old joke that says the problem with parenting books is that the kids never read them. That's not the case here. This time, the content comes directly from the kids.

What To Expect Next

The youth introduced in the following chapters are violent, suicidal, delinquent, substance abusing and behaviourally disordered adolescents whom I have encountered over the past twenty years in mental health, corrections and child protection agencies as well as through volunteer youth organizations and on the street in my various roles as both a professional and lay helper. Many started out as stellar students in grade school. Some showed great promise at sports earlier in their lives. And while others had a much tougher beginning, all share a path through life that for some reason veered towards trouble.

This, then, is not a book about "nice kids," though the more one gets to know these youth, the more one sees in them the shadows of other children we know who are drifting in the same direction. Many, but not all, of these children live on the edge of our society, inhabiting places we hope our children never encounter. Some also come from within the secure confines of middle-class or upper-class neighbourhoods. Many have loving and devoted parents. Many others do not. Collectively, the lessons they teach us as parents and caregivers are valuable whether our children are still part of a world which makes sense to us or have drifted into street cultures with their own sets of rules.

This book is meant to offer a message of hope. It is for parents, caregivers, professionals and anyone else who wants to understand children differently, to challenge themselves to see the resilience and strength hidden beneath our children's "deviance." It is also a book which offers us adults a way to approach high-risk youth that brings them closer without threatening their resilience.

Each chapter will provide a piece of the puzzle to explain *what* is really going on among troubled youth today. I have woven together chapters that explain the behaviours of children with chapters that discuss each of the five strategies for helping high-risk youth grow-up safe and healthy. I conclude with a look at what we as parents, caregivers, professionals and lay helpers can do together to influence positively the lives of troubled youth.

Chapter 1, "The Way Things Were," looks at what we believe about kids, about their peer groups, and about what puts kids at risk. Chapter 2, "Searching For Truth," then considers how we can use this knowledge to help children and youth discover what is true for them. Helping kids become critical consumers of all "truths" inoculates them against the influence of others who would prevent our children from thinking for themselves.

Chapter 3, "Lost and Found," examines how teens acquire and maintain healthy identities while challenging unhealthy ones through their problem behaviours. Chapter 4, "Shop Around," discusses the benefits youth find when they are encouraged to shop around and be a part of many different peer and community groups.

Chapter 5, "I'm Okay, You're Not," takes a critical look at what we call mental health and who has the power to decide if a child is healthy or not. Chapter 6, "Complex Stories for Complex Lives," shows us how to celebrate the complex stories youth tell about themselves and how they stay healthy.

Chapter 7, "The Healthy Deviant," looks more closely at youth who are dangerous, delinquent, deviant and disordered and shows how, ironically, they use these troubling behaviours among their peers to maintain their well-being. Chapter 8, "Acceptance," demonstrates the importance for us as adults to show acceptance for these behaviours, even while we work hard to change them.

Chapter 9, "Rough Seas," talks about the tough times many kids have trying to survive beyond our front doors. It explores the sad truths, which many teenagers confront on a daily basis that make a life full of problems all the more attractive as a way to cope. Chapter 10, "When The Blaming Stops," shows us how to stop blaming our children's peer groups for their problem behaviours as an important strategy that gets us closer to our kids.

Chapter 11, "Learning," points us forward and encourages us to have hope for our children, especially when we listen to what they have to teach us. It offers us a glimpse of what we can do *now* to help youth by weaving together all the resources of our communities into an approach that makes it easier for children and adolescents to navigate their way to more widely accepted definitions of themselves as healthy and resilient. The chapter summarizes what we now know about resilience among high-risk youth and looks at the implications of this new understanding for raising healthy children in communities without barriers to their participation.

Chapter 1
The Way Things Were

Most parents in the same desperate circumstances as Melissa's mother, Anna, whom I introduced in the introduction, don't want to believe that associating with a peer group that is known for its risk-taking behaviours could be adding something positive to their child's life. I have found when working with families that the best place to start when trying to understand and help these children is by asking their caregivers to recall their own adolescence. Unfortunately, time plays tricks on our memory. I meet parents who can remember only the "bad" and "stupid" things they did. I meet others who filter these out, embarrassed to share with their children and me the tough decisions they were confronted with during their teen years.

These lapses in memory are not a sign of early senility, or even intentional efforts to distort the truth. They are indicative of what a new wave of psychologists like Kenneth Gergen have characterized as the way we *socially construct* our lives, the very thoughts we have dependent upon the words our culture and community provide us with to describe ourselves and our experiences. Similarly, our memories are not ours alone, but *co-authored* through interaction with others, those with whom we are intimate sharing responsibility to write the story of our past. Events happen for sure, but how we remember episodes in our life and the meaning we attach to them has as much to do with the society in which we live and how it shapes our world view as the views of those with whom we interact closely. Our memories depend on the language which is available at a particular historical point in time that gives us words to describe our experiences. The language we have may or may not allow us to adequately describe what happened in our past, or what is happening to us now. For example, as difficult as it is to believe, the term sexual abuse only came into vogue in the early 1980s. Before then, survivors of abuse lacked a language to describe what happened to them. They knew something was wrong: they could describe what they had experienced physically, but they tended not to think of what had occurred as an abusive and criminal act. To put this another way, if we as adults think about adolescence as a period of strife, then we will remember our own adolescence in those terms.

For Anna, one of the bad decisions she remembers resulted in the daughter she now loved so dearly. Anna was seventeen when she met Melissa's father, Brody, an alcoholic 21-year-old with lovely deep brown eyes, a motorcycle, and a classic James Dean swagger. He convinced her she belonged with him. It was an easy sell to a girl who had nothing else going right in her life. After she became pregnant, their relationship ended. He said the baby probably wasn't his anyway and that she was a "slut for sleeping around" behind his back. Anna's life is as tragic as it is cliché. Not that Anna shed so much as one tear in the telling of the story. She had a beautiful daughter and couldn't give a "rat's ass" for Melissa's dad. She just didn't want her daughter to do what she had done. She was sure that the only reason she had become involved with Brody was because all her peers were sexually active and she was fed up with being the lone virgin, or so she said. At thirty-one, these bitter memories were all that remained of those years when becoming an adult meant having sex. She was certain she was pressured by her peer group into doing something which she says now she didn't really want to do.

The Myth Of Peer Pressure

Strangely, I have never met a teenager who, if given an opportunity to talk about his or her life, explains what he or she is doing at that moment as the result of peer pressure. I meet many youth who, like the adults who care for them, will say they did something in their past because of peer pressure. They will tell me exactly what they think I want to hear. But if I ask these same kids questions like: How did you decide what to wear today? Are you a follower or a leader? What kinds of decisions do you make for yourself? How are you different from your peers? and What's unique or special about you? we end up having a very different conversation.

Youth of all ages will, if they think I'm really listening, tell me all about how they make decisions independent of their peers. They will tell me that if it appears to us adults that all teenagers look and act alike it is because we aren't seeing the differences between them. If they are dressed like their friends, or act like them, it's because they have decided for themselves that is the best way either to get noticed or accepted. It's darn near impossible, in my experience, to get children to admit that they are dressing or behaving the way they are because of peer pressure. They will buy into the myth of peer pressure if it pleases their audience, but when it comes to explaining day to day what they are doing and why, I am told peer pressure plays no part. I'm inclined to believe them.

It took some time, but Anna and I eventually re-visited episodes of her troubled youth. Instead of talking about the tragic end of her relationship with Brody, we talked about its beginning. Suddenly, as if the sunlight outside had swept in on the breeze, Anna's tone and posture changed. She shed years there in front of me till I could see her clearly as her daughter. Anna told me shyly how when Brody had chosen her to be his girlfriend he had paraded her in front of all his friends. She had ridden with him often on his bike, and she had stood comfortably in his shadow. It was as close as she had ever come to feeling like the fashion model she imagined herself when she was a teen. There were other boys interested in her too, ones who didn't drink, who didn't ride a bike, who were her age, and who were still in school, but Brody was the one who made her feel most special.

Our myth of peer pressure is so much a part of popular culture that we can hardly hear what kids are telling us. Study after study continues to ask children about peer pressure, never stopping to question whether it is all an adult fabrication in the first place. However, when international studies show that kids actually increase their self-esteem in their peer groups and that minority children are actually healthier when they act out with their friends, when they drink and do drugs, then we explain away the results. Instead of asking the tough questions about why some children enhance their health through association with deviant peers, we instead try and suppress these associations. We naively assume that children will find other more acceptable relationships, and change their behaviour, if we take them away from these other problem children. We miss the important lessons our own work teaches us: that even problem peers and their nasty behaviours bring with them some positive benefits to the youth who participate.

It's too obvious that kids in desperate circumstances would of their own volition migrate toward problem peers. The more we understand this, however, the better able we will be to offer these kids alternatives that fit well with how they see their world. James Coyne, a Fellow of the American Psychological Association, has been researching the impact of genetic testing on women at risk of developing cancer. Contrary to popular medical opinion, these women do not experience more stress or depression when they are given the information they request. In fact, Coyne and his colleagues found that the biggest stress in women's lives was the intrusive psychologists who insisted on providing counselling prior to sharing the results of the tests. High-risk youth are similar. When we listen closely to them and what they say they need, and deliver that assistance in ways that make sense to them, then we are more likely to get it right and provide youth with diversions that actually work. It sounds simple, but in practice we have been hesitant to privilege the voices of youth (or women, for that matter), especially when we don't like what they have to say.

This should come as no surprise to many of us adults who frequently act out in ways similar to our youth, but demand respect for the way we exercise control over our words and deeds. When we act out, seeking adventure to break the monotony of ordered lives, we gamble, pub-crawl, compulsively shop, and stray into extra-marital affairs. These behaviours bring us something we can't find elsewhere in our lives, even as each compromises us in some way.

We can't believe there was a time in our own lives when we were sure we were beyond the reach of social pressures. No sooner does the latest teen trend hit our neighbourhood (raves, gangster rap, folding scooters, school shootings), than we are quick to jump to the erroneous conclusion that teens all act similarly because of social pressures to do so. How can peer pressure not exist? Didn't we all experience it? Don't some of us have memories of being hopelessly influenced by other children? And finally, don't we see even today all around us gangs of youth all apparently cookie cutter reproductions of each other with the same culture, dress, habits, and attitudes? What we as adults see, however, is not what youth themselves experience. They are no more controlled by peer pressure than we were at their age.

Instead, they explain, they use opportunities available through their peer groups to gain status, to bolster their self-esteem and to remain healthy. If that means revelling in the identity they help to author for their peer group as a "bunch of bad kids," then so be it. They argue that it's better to be good at being bad, than just a plain old loser. They purposefully overlook all the dangerous and painful things that might happen while in those peer groups, denying the many negative consequences to their associations because the benefits are both valued and needed.

"Not my child!"

Our popular culture persists in trying to find scapegoats who can be blamed for our children's troubling behaviours. All those problems our kids have today have to be someone's responsibility. But the cause of deviance is not easy to discern. A recent book by Katharine Kelly and Mark Totten examined the lives of nineteen individuals who had committed murder while teenagers. Another book by John Hagan and Bill McCarthy recounts interviews with 390 street youth in two North American cities. There are many other similar volumes. The findings are inconclusive at best. Problem children grow up in rich homes and poor; some have suffered abuse and some have not; some are mentally ill, others score at the upper end on tests of well-being. True, some factors predict deviance better than others (experiences of abuse and poverty are two factors commonly associated with later problems in life), but the research on suspected causes could, and has, filled libraries. Blaming children's peers, or parents for that matter, reduces complex problems in ways that seldom lead to informed and effective interventions, much less help for parents who have to cope day to day with their troubled teen. But then, if we are looking for a simple answer, who better to blame for our children's problems than other children?

Jeanine and Philip are two struggling parents whom I got to know through my work. Philip, who's of African descent, has twenty years of service with the military police, while Jeanine, whose roots are Irish, has spent most of the last twenty years raising her family and running a small business as an interior decorator. They have five children, the older of whom have followed an almost predictable pattern of delinquent behaviour. I came to know the family when their second oldest son, 17-year-old Shawn, following his older brother's lead, was placed in detention for stealing cars and possession of drugs.

This was not the first time I had worked with children of law enforcement personnel. Their shame is understandably much greater than that of other parents when they find out it's their kids who are in trouble with the law. For Philip, the embarrassment of having to, for the second time in his life, go to a young offenders facility to pick up one of his sons was almost too painful to express; yet, despite the shame he felt, he went. He was long past being angry by the time he arrived to take Shawn back home for a period of time while waiting to go to trial. Philip just looked drained. This was a problem completely beyond his control. Not so for Jeanine. For her it was a rallying call to arms. If before she had been the meddlesome mother who saw to it that the boys obeyed the rules (Shawn's description of her), now she was frantic that Shawn obey the conditions of his release to the letter of the law.

Shawn told me that Jeanine and Philip argued for hours over who was to blame for what he had done – Jeanine saying Philip was too lenient with the boys, Philip telling her she was more like a cop than him. When they couldn't get anywhere with blaming each other they turned their attention to Shawn's friends, most of whom came from another part of town and were known to school officials and most of the local police as children with "problems." While Jeanine and Philip were certain their boys' friends were leading their sons astray, they were not convinced that anything happening at home was contributing to their sons' problems.

I have long since stopped trying to muddle through these messy arguments over who is to blame for what. Quite frankly, though there are many psychological theories that could explain Shawn's behaviour as the result of his peers or his parents, I was much more interested in Shawn's explanation for why he was in jail. Shawn told me he enjoyed his lifestyle as a thief and drug user, and that for him and his friends doing a little time in custody was "no big deal." He knew that being there was much more of a problem for his mother and father. His only problem, as far as we could both tell, was that the more trouble with the law he got into, the more his parents placed restrictions on him and the more they nagged.

While I won't blame a child's peers for what he or she does, I am always very curious to know how it came to be that a child like Shawn, from his background, chose to hang out with a group of kids for whom going to jail is not an embarrassment. As parents, we almost never ask our kids about their choices. We may appear to ask the question, but frequently what we say is laced with a heavy dose of criticism which shuts down communication before it begins.

In later chapters, I will go into more detail how children like Shawn explain their choice of peer groups. What's important here is that Shawn's parents saw problems where Shawn did not. For Shawn, his lifestyle brought with it everything he felt he needed to feel good about himself. Somehow, through his delinquent acts, and later during his incarceration, he said he had discovered a way to be more in control of his life than when he spent time at home.

We don't need to be a trained marriage and family therapist to ask ourselves and our children, "Is there is a problem here? And whose is it?" Typically it is the adults who come to me for help who suffer most acutely the problems created by their children, problems for which their children accept no responsibility, nor for which they want to participate in seeking better solutions. Parents arrive in my office full of fear and anxiety, anger and sadness, and all for good reason. But the problems they identify are seldom the ones shared by their children. In fact, one of the reasons children abandon their homes is because the home is saturated with problems for which they feel no ownership.

Problems can be like elephants in the living room. They take up a tremendous amount of room and make an awful mess. And they have a way of ruining every reasonable opportunity to share quality time together. Besides, anything that big needs lots of attention and feeding. Everybody has to do their part, and indeed, whether children admit it or not, they, just like their parents, have a relationship with the elephant. Nobody's problem is theirs alone when living together as a family.

When children get fed up with problems at home they escape to the street. When they get fed up with problems with their peers, they escape back home, or to work, or school, or they try new peer groups. What kids tell me is that they are searching for ways to feel some sense of personal well-being. They are not blindly following their peers into problem behaviours, but very consciously looking for the best way to express their personal resilience to the stress and strain of the lives they live.

Misguided

Debunking a myth tends to be experienced by people as unpleasant, as if one of the foundation stones of how we think of our world is torn out from under us. There are many with a vested interest in keeping alive the myths, like peer pressure, we tell about our children. I have debated on radio talk shows the misguided attempts by law enforcement officials to deal with youth by increasing the number of police patrolling the streets. The message youth are given when they become the target of police interventions is that they are every bit as mean and dangerous as they thought they were. I have seen the public equally duped by cigarette advertisers who have launched campaigns to stop tobacco use among teens by trying to convince them that smoking is an "adult" decision they should wait to make. Nothing could be more of an enticement for teens to smoke. A recent decision by the Canadian Medical Association to condemn such campaigns has brought this to the public's attention. The problem, however, persists. Smoking and other behaviours which have the potential to harm young people (such as early sexual activity) are packaged by marketers as things adults do, making them more, not less, attractive to youth.

Teens search for ways to proclaim their maturity and status to a world that sees them either as naive and incompetent, or potentially dangerous and misguided. Guided by the myths we hold about teens as weak-kneed followers and misguided fools, we intervene with youth in ways that make our problems with them even worse: more police, more control, more punishment, indeed things that give delinquent teens more status as problem children.

It is status that they want. Recently a group of researchers in the United Kingdom found that as cell phone use has increased among teens, rates for smoking have gone down significantly, especially for teens who have their own personal phones. The researchers believe that both activities satisfy the same needs and occupy a similar niche in the lives of youth. With almost 70 percent of youth in the U.K. having a cell phone, it is to be seen if smoking will lose its appeal altogether. Such news makes perfect sense when we listen to adolescents themselves. In their search for status, it doesn't really matter if a cigarette or a cell phone is the means to the ends sought. The point is that teens will select whatever behaviours help them to feel good about themselves from the choices provided.

Is this any different from how we as their parents behave? As urbanites career through city streets in four-wheel-drive SUVs, one can't help but wonder if this drive for status is every bit as alive in us adults as it is in our children.

Behaviours don't always make sense, but their meaning and status are something to which we all contribute. This truth seems to elude us when we preach to kids to stop smoking, stop having sex, stop fighting, or stop drinking. What options have we left them to feel powerful while growing up in worlds that would convince them they are otherwise?

We need to find ways to reach youth like Shawn that provide them with the same benefits they derive from the behaviours we hope to extinguish. Try as we may to change our kids, we will fail unless we understand how successful their coping strategies are *from their perspective*.

Risk and Resilience

There are many risks confronting our children, both those surviving on the fringes of society, and those who still live in their family homes and share lives with their caregivers. Risk factors include both personal characteristics of a child as well as things happening outside the child that make it more likely he or she will experience problems later in life. However, as Ann Masten, a well-known developmental psychologist explains, saying someone is "at risk" or "high risk" says nothing in particular about the individual, only that he or she resembles a group of other children who, on the whole, grow up and have more problems. Your child may be at risk, may live each day in circumstances similar to the children whose lives are documented in these pages, but still be healthy and avoid the pitfalls into which their peers tumble.

A way of thinking about this is to imagine each child as a traveller trying to get from one city to the next. Some children make progress quickly, others meander for a time, perhaps never arriving where their caregivers had hoped. The risk factors we face, or the absence of them, makes the trip more or less hazardous, more or less direct, and may even determine if in the end a child arrives at his or her destination at all.

While we cannot say with any certainty what will happen for one particular child, we can predict how successful the child's voyage will be by studying groups of children with the same risk factors and watching their progress over time. Put another way, we can make an informed guess about how a particular high-risk child will end up. The individual always has some capacity to demonstrate his or her personal power and decide the path he or she travels through life. When speaking about a *particular* individual's risk factors, we more correctly talk about the child's personal vulnerabilities. We might also want to talk about the same child's personal competencies, factors which lessen the chances that the risks he or she faces will have a negative impact on his or her life.

This shift to a focus on resilience amidst risk was pioneered by Norman Garmezy and his colleagues in the early 1980s following studies of children in both war-torn countries and more stable Western communities. More recently we have witnessed an explosion of popular literature examining the lives of resilient individuals: Frank McCourt's Pulitzer Prize-winning novel *Angela's Ashes*, Quincy Jones' *Q*, Eric Weihenmayer's *Touch the Top of the World*, and Denise Chong's graphic *The Girl in the Picture: The Story of Kim Phuc* all show the indomitable spirit of children who rise above adversity. Research shows that as many as two-thirds of youth exposed to difficult life circumstances will grow and thrive without serious intervention. When talking about high-risk youth, then, I am talking about youth growing up in threatening environments or children who show characteristics typical of troubled youth that make us expect the child's personal vulnerabilities will outweigh his or her strengths. Many of these children will, however, surprise us.

As we will see, determining what is a sign of strength and what is a sign of weakness is all in the eye of the beholder. Children who are at high risk for future problems may exploit the risk factors in their lives to their advantage. We cannot really say much about how risk factors will affect a child unless we understand how the child copes day to day with his or her lot in life. As previously mentioned, one of the risk factors long thought to be a negative influence in the lives of teens is their association with other problem kids.

Growing Up With a Myth

My doubts about peer pressure and other such myths of childhood began when I was a teenager. I'm now in my late thirties, a safe distance from those chaotic years of self-discovery. But I remember as if it was last week the anger I felt when adults, especially my parents, told me year after year as I was growing from a child to a young man, "Think for yourself" and "Don't do what everyone else is doing."

I knew, or thought I knew, like every other child, that peer pressure existed and threatened me with a life of complacency, in which I would become a "follower." That word was thrown at me, as it was at my peers, as the ultimate insult to those of us growing up in the fiercely independent culture of our middle-class neighbourhoods. I was like most of the other teens who were my friends at a time when gangs weren't the media and mass marketing phenomenon they are now. We all felt vaguely uneasy about appearing to be too much like each other. We wanted to all buy the same clothes, talk the same way, be part of whatever was popular at the time, but we did all this, so we thought, at the peril of our individuality.

It's ironic, looking back, that while we were being told not to be followers with our peers, we were being told to "fit in" as much as possible with the adults we relied on for our future success. If we were to survive and grow up healthy, there was only ever supposed to be one way to behave. We sat dutifully at desks in rows in sterile classrooms as our bodies, which were full of energy and alive with an hormonal maelstrom, raged and stretched. We literally twisted ourselves into shapes that we were told were right for us.

This type of conformity was never called peer pressure, because it didn't come from our peers. It was sold to us youth as simply "the right way to do things." I find this strange as we have tended to condemn unquestioned group thinking. But then again, we only condemn thoughts that are at odds with our dominant value system. Paulo Freire, the Brazilian social activist and popular educator, spent his career encouraging peasants subjugated by oppressive social and economic forces to reconsider their view of themselves as less than those who held power. He accomplished all this by teaching basic literacy that offered people the language they needed to describe their lives differently. Educators who have worked with adolescents and offered them a similar anti-oppressive language to document their lives, as is occurring with young gay, lesbian, bisexual, and transgendered youth, have found that young people are capable of authoring new and innovative stories about themselves that are far healthier than the ones others tell about them.

Each family, each community, has a variety of stories they tell about their youth. Unfortunately, each is meant to guide young people in how to behave. When I was growing up, there was of course still room for individuality. We could "be" whatever we wanted to "be," as long as that meant a good job, a family, children and a buy-in to the global economy. The emphasis was on being some "thing," not the process by which we became some "one."

The End of the Myth

The term peer pressure, as commonly used, describes the pressure peers exert on one another to do something, whether the individual wants to act that way or not. It is a surprisingly simple idea, which might explain why it has had such a huge following among everyone from parents to academics. Oftentimes the idea of peer pressure goes completely unquestioned, talked about and written about as if everyone knows it must exist. Behind the façade, individual efforts to survive by associating with people other than one's family are ignored or denigrated. Nobody really wants to believe that those peer relationships that trouble caregivers offer many youth a pathway to personal resilience and an escape from troubled homes and sterile or threatening communities.

I am now certain that peer pressure does not exist. *It is a myth adults use to explain the troubling behaviours of youth that result from an adolescent's search for personal and social power.* This may be a challenging statement for many of us growing up in a time of "trenchcoat mafias," "neo-nazis" and "the Craft." It appears too obvious to us that kids are being influenced by each other just as we are certain we were influenced by our peers when we were younger. But while the pressures on our youth to conform appear to come from within their own peer groups, it is also a time when adults more than youth are telling children how to behave. MuchMusic, the Internet and the global economy are exerting every bit as much influence on youth as their peers. As Victor Malarek, well-known journalist and child advocate, has commented, "We have effectively merchandised the souls of our children." But these forces, like a child's peer group, are still only part of the smorgasbord of choices from which a child chooses his or her identity.

Challenging the concept of peer pressure means asking ourselves what a healthy identity is and, more importantly, who decides which identities are healthy and which are not. I've found that the youth who can teach us the most about identity building are the ones who have had contact with mental health counsellors, social services, and community and correctional systems. They have been told over and over that they have multiple "problems," are "dysfunctional" by community standards, and display signs of diagnosable "disordered" behaviour. Yet it is precisely this group of youth who have the most to teach us about how teens use their peer relationships and problem behaviours to construct health enhancing identities which oppose the unhealthy labels *adults* give them. While I am certain that the pressure to conform exists, that doesn't mean that kids succumb to what others tell them to do without consciously deciding, "What's in it for me?"

Pressures to conform are put on young people much more by the adults in their lives than peers. These expectations of our youth are embedded in the fabric of our social institutions. In places where young people interact with older people such as schools, community centres and at McJobs, they are told exactly what kind of behaviour is expected of them. We have assumed that in teenagers' peer groups, the same social process is at work, with the group telling our children how to behave. If we listen closely to youth themselves, they show us that this is not what happens.

Within the peer group, a teen has more power than in places where adults run the show. Teens can negotiate with their peers for an identity which is partly of their own choosing. I say partly, because power is not shared equally among all youth. Some youth are better able to negotiate an acceptable and high status identity than others. Any wonder that children's author Robert Munsch has sold more than a million copies of an anti-fairy tale called *The Paper Bag Princess*? In Munsch's tale, Elizabeth, a beautiful princess with expensive princess, clothes is to marry Prince Ronald. At least that is until a dragon smashes the castle, burns all her clothes and carries off Ronald. Angry, she puts on the only thing not burnt, a paper bag, and chases after the dragon, eventually outsmarting him and rescuing her prince. But Prince Ronald will have nothing to do with Princess Elizabeth. He tells her, "You are a mess! You smell like ashes, your hair is all tangled and you are wearing a dirty old paper bag. Come back when you are dressed like a real princess." Elizabeth, to her credit, and the credit of all young people like her, tells Ronald he is a "bum" and decides not to get married after all.

Certainly, some teens like the mythical Elizabeth have more luck, more talents, more money, more self-confidence, or just better genes. Whatever the case, building a healthy identity takes resources, both the internal and external kind. Some youth, like Peter, the young responsible son of a mother coping with depression, whom I introduced in the Introduction, simply bring to their peer groups more strengths.

That wasn't the case for Melissa who, despite hanging around with a cohort of delinquents, really wanted to be part of a group of kids known as "preps." For all Melissa's wishing to be seen as one of them she is sorely disadvantaged coming from a one-parent household that survives on social assistance. In Melissa's world, until she can find a way to get her own money, she will remain an outsider to the rich kids. To them she is just another "charity case," as she put it. Besides, growing up in a disadvantaged environment, the question remains, even if she could find the money, whether she would have the social skills to play the prep, or even feel comfortable in a culture different from her own. Maybe, just maybe, playing the delinquent is easier.

Several years ago I managed to get free tickets for several of the youth with whom I was working to see a main stage production of *A Christmas Tale*. Not surprisingly, for most of these teenagers who came from low-income housing projects, it was their first time in a posh theatre, sitting amongst people who intimidated them for no other reason than who they are. I remember sadly how Amanda, a talented and bright young woman who lived in disparaging conditions in low-rent housing with her alcoholic parents, had nervously agreed to come along. She had shown up dressed very appropriately for the occasion in a navy coloured dress and a white blouse, her long red hair pinned. When I asked her at the intermission if she was enjoying the show, she looked at me accusingly and said that she felt really uncomfortable. "I don't belong here," she hissed at me. "I'm not like these people." Try as I might to convince her otherwise, Amanda would not believe that no one else thought her out of place.

To my knowledge, Amanda never did find her way back to the theatre. The last time I met her she was twenty years old, a single mother with two young children, visibly anorexic, and involved with a 35-year-old alcoholic in jail for manslaughter. The world she had drifted back to was the one she could most comfortably negotiate. There she knew the rules and though that world made me feel uncomfortable with its violence and drugs, it was where she had come to believe she belonged.

The Stories We Tell

The myth of peer pressure is no different from other myths about "bad" kids who make bad choices. According to Joseph Campbell, who has spent his life travelling the world collecting and comparing the stories different cultures tell, myths are simply the stories we share that make our world a predictable and orderly place in which to live. For their power, myths depend on an almost imperceptible seepage into our language, leading us blindly from one assumption to the next. Take for example another familiar myth: Work hard and you'll get ahead. In the coastal community where I now live, where fishing is still a large part of both the culture and economy, this myth is shared through the countless stories passed along from generation to generation. David Weale, a storyteller who collects these bits of folk wisdom, tells a story that goes like this:

> Two fishermen from the Miminegash area were returning to harbour after a most unsuccessful day on the water. One of the men began to lament about the poor catch and low prices. "Jesus, Mary, and Joseph," he grumbled, "we've been at this all spring and scarcely a cent to show for it."
>
> "Oh, don't be complainin'," chided the other man, "just be thankful we've got the work."

When I hear this story, I imagine an older fellow chiding a younger one, playing out between them the same kind of misunderstanding between the generations that I find so familiar in the work I do. Like the myth of peer pressure, or the other mistaken beliefs we hold about why kids act bad, the myth of hard work being worthwhile has tended to go unquestioned in my community even when times are tough and work scarce. For many of the youth I work with who come from families and communities where money is tight and opportunities few, the "hard work" myth holds even less truth.

Understanding how myths maintain their tenacious hold on what we think requires some appreciation for how language itself works. Myths are reflexive, meaning that as we tell stories, those stories shape what we perceive as reality. Without these words and phrases, we would be hopelessly lost to tell anyone about how we experience the world because we would have no way of *thinking* about what has happened, much less a language to describe our experiences to others. Most of us imagine language as being somehow inside us. We like to believe the child learns to express what is already a thought inside his or her head. This is not actually the way language works. Without a word to describe an experience, *the experience does not exist.*

For example, The Red Cross, like many other organizations, has been trying to prevent the abuse of children by going into schools and educating teens about what abusive behaviour is. They literally give children a whole new language to describe their experiences. In the anonymous evaluation forms completed after these workshops, I have seen teen after teen wrestling to describe old experiences in new ways. What some children would have described as reasonable "discipline" is more properly understood as "physical abuse" once they have been given a different language to name their world. For others, the workshops help them sort out their confusion between a caregiver's "love" and "sexual touching," which is a form of "sexual abuse." Where before vulnerable teens might have accepted their abusers' definitions of their experiences, education can help them find a new more powerful language to express themselves.

Understanding the way myths about troubled kids are sustained requires an appreciation for one other important concept: power. While we all contribute to the meaning of words, and indirectly to the authenticity of the myths we tell, the decision as to which myths are accepted as true depends on who has the most say over which stories get told. As the tale of the two fishers and the more serious self-disclosures by victims of abuse make clear, it is typically people who are older and more powerful whose descriptions of our world are the most convincing.

If peer pressure is just a myth that is used to justify our adult misinterpretations of what kids do, then how can we explain the apparent conformity between one teen and the next? How is it possible that they can all "look" and "act" alike if teens aren't responsible for forcing identities on one another? How do teens construct their identities, anyway, if peer pressure is not part of how they decide who they are? A teenager's identity is built through relationships with peers, family and his or her community, but the dynamic way in which this construction takes place has largely been ignored or misunderstood by those who work with youth. There is another better way to understand what we adults are seeing.

Drifting Towards A Healthy Identity

It might be strange to think of Johnathan as inspiring admiration or having much to teach parents about parenting when he is in jail for armed robbery. But Johnathan has managed to put himself exactly where he intended. The forensic psychiatry unit, designed to treat young offenders with perceived mental health issues, in which I once worked is housed in a newer cement-block building, painted in the muted pastels thought to induce calm amongst residents. Spartan in its decoration, it is clean and efficient in design. Residents "rooms" have magnetic locking doors. Each youth has his or her own small cell with a window made of unbreakable glass. A wire mesh outside reassures them they are in detention, even if it's not a jail. Each living unit, or "cottage," houses ten adolescents and is staffed by two youth workers each shift and a social worker for each unit. The atmosphere is friendly, but strict. Privileges that on the outside might seem inconsequential become very important inside. A chocolate bar or an extra bowl of Kraft dinner, an extra few minutes for a phone call or the freedom to walk by one's self around the enclosed courtyard are jealously guarded prizes handed out to youth only when merited. It's a place that I often thought would drive me crazy if I'd been a resident.

Not Johnathan. He told me that he liked the sense of predictable security while a patient there, knowing all he had to do was get up at 7:00 a.m., do chores, eat, go to school, play some sports, meet with his therapist, sit in his room for a bit, and go back to bed. There were few choices to be made, and no one to put him down. The other kids on his unit might have tried to get him going but Johnathan just ignored them. He was friendly, but shuffled through his day with a moody aloofness that kept others at a safe distance. Inside, Johnathan attended school regularly and was likely to pass his grade, a major accomplishment, he said.

His parents visited, as did his girlfriend. They sat in the cafeteria under the constant gaze of a guard armed with a radio, a panic button and years of experience anticipating when a conversation will become an all-out argument. Both his parents came dressed in jeans and designer t-shirts, looking relaxed in the same way they might on Fridays at the office when they purposefully dress casual and make a donation to charity. They sat across from their son on plastic chairs and drank weak tea and instant coffee from Styrofoam cups. They brought Johnathan new clothes, and news of home. And they kept asking him "Why?" Johnathan shrugged his shoulders and said nothing. When he was alone with either a youth worker or in session with myself or one of my colleagues, and we asked him the same question, he'd only say that he liked it better in jail than at home or on the street.

He was, though, very frank when he talked about his crime. He knew he would get caught. A black balaclava could hardly hide his identity when he shot out the window of an electronics store with his own hunting rifle and stole several expensive CD players. The store was just minutes from his home. He didn't even really need the money. He said he was fed up with going nowhere and needed an escape.

He had lots of friends on the outside. His parents had paid for him to join any sport he wanted and for a time he'd played hockey. He wasn't half bad, either. He used to attend school and was accepted by some of the regular kids as their peer. Despite his mediocre academic performance, he is a remarkably good chess player. He appeared on the surface to have lots of ways to define himself as a healthy young man. But Johnathan also has a father who makes a point of telling his son he's an "idiot" every chance he gets. At least, that's how Johnathan tells it. His dad says his son is too sensitive and that he rarely speaks to his son about his friends, schooling, or attitude. Still, Johnathan's story is hard to dismiss. He shows so many of the signs of an emotionally abused child and insists he has endured these put downs since he very young. His mother has stood by doing little to protect her son, likely afraid, I believe, that she would be the next target.

There are other youth I meet who do not choose such drastic behaviour to escape an abusive home. Johnathan could have turned to sports, or school, or suicide, all popular "choices" among his peers. But jail was a better solution, he said, because it let everyone know just how "screwed-up" he felt inside. It also brought the worst kind of attention to his family, and that was what Johnathan really wanted.

His peer group played its part helping him become a delinquent. He drifted towards them like a ship without an anchor. It just seemed a natural place to be for a big moody kid. He didn't start with robbing a store. He developed his career as a young offender in stages, first drifting away from long established friendships with friends who didn't break the law. Somewhere along the way he met his girlfriend who wasn't part of either peer group.

She and some of Johnathan's friends, at least the ones his parents allowed on his visitation list, came to see Johnathan each Sunday. They told him they would find it a drag being in a place like that, or asked him what it was like to be in with all the losers they would have nothing to do with at school. To them, Johnathan was still a part of their group, even if he messed up. It was interesting watching Johnathan navigate back and forth between the "winners" and "losers" in his life. He remained noncommital to either, though accepted by both.

His girlfriend is much like him. She is attractive in the way of moody teenaged girls. Dishevelled hair, black wardrobe, heavy eyeshadow and a withdrawn attitude. Watching them together you could see that she thought Johnathan was more interesting when he was placed in a jail and then a psychiatric hospital for his strange behaviour. I can guess it drives her family crazy that they continue to date. Johnathan said she was waiting for him to get out, though he told her it's all right if she didn't. When he talked about her he always creased the corner of his mouth, as if there is something else more humorous to share, but he doesn't think I'd appreciate the joke.

Johnathan explained it was easier being a violent delinquent than staying at home and arguing for his right to be treated with respect. Sad, really, because Johnathan's parents didn't mean to hurt him. In their own way they tried to love him. In fact, within weeks of our meeting all together, his family were making changes that would make it easier for Johnathan to return home. It never worked really well, but it eventually worked well enough to make it possible for Johnathan to live at home again. Eight months after we met, Johnathan left a secure group home where he'd been transferred as part of his sentence. I remember being by the security desk at the front of that facility the day he was being checked out. He had three green garbage bags of clothes at his feet. His hair had been buzz cut, he wore tattered army surplus pants, and a wallet on a chain hung from his hip. He didn't smile as his dad picked up two of the bags and shook hands with staff. But he did look to see if his favourite youth worker had come from the unit to say good-bye. Security radioed a message back and the worker ambled down. I couldn't tell exactly what was going on inside Johnathan's head, but in his eyes he looked slightly afraid as he shook hands and turned to leave. Maybe the fear was just mine. I wasn't quite sure what he would have to do next time to catch our attention. I don't think he knew either as he walked out through the double-locking doors.

I needn't have worried. He went back to school, found a job, and when I checked in with him and his parents months later, he was hanging around mostly with his old friends. He and his girlfriend had broken up, at least for the time being.

I have come to understand through the lived experiences of youth like Johnathan that at-risk adolescents drift towards mental health in a way that is part chance and part an expression of their own personal power or "agency." Professional helpers have studied endlessly the origins of mental health problems, what is called their etiology. We have spent much less time on the etiology of mental health. The young people I meet tell me that the power to control the labels which attach to them is the fulcrum upon which an adolescent's mental health teeters.

Having a large and diverse group of friends can add greatly to this control. Together a group of kids can scream louder "This is who I am." They are likely to be heard better than one kid acting alone. It's for this reason that peers play such an important part in the mental health of teens.

Building Mental Health . . . All Together

Think of the colour red. Was the colour you imagined the red of candied apples, the deeper maroon red of blood, the subdued red of dried autumn leaves, or perhaps the commercial red of a new sports car? Even a word as simple as red is not likely to get agreement when two people negotiate its exact meaning. We can, on such a simple point, agree to disagree.

Agreeing on what words mean becomes remarkably more complicated when we try to understand the names high-risk youth use to describe themselves. Adults frequently misunderstand the meaning young people attach to the labels they adopt. The mistaken assumption is that words like "delinquent" or "street kid" mean to the kids what they mean to us caregivers. Youth are either unwilling or unable to correct us. They politely or obstinately refuse to share with adults what they really mean when they use certain words to describe themselves. Experience has taught them that adults are either condescending or mocking when they should be listening.

It is especially difficult for us adults to accept the self-descriptions of youth when the words they use are an affront to who we are, our values, and our cultural norms. It was difficult to get Johnathan's parents to respect Johnathan's choice to be locked up, and to understand that their son liked what being there said about him. When we first started meeting, they were polite and listened to *me*, the therapist. Later, they took the time to listen to their son. Much of the work I do clinically is simply negotiating with parents opportunities for their children to speak and be heard, then convincing the kids that their parents have actually heard what they said.

Too often, however, there are no adults with whom to negotiate. In Allison's case, as a permanent ward of the court, there had been so many dislocations in her life that her caregivers had become the endless staff assigned to watch over her in the institutions where she was placed.

Another teenager I worked with briefly, Alex, had a parent, his mother Doris, but she truthfully had more than enough to deal with without worrying after her son. She tried to be there for him, but in many ways could not provide what he needed. Doris is a sole parent surviving on meagre welfare handouts and coping daily with the effects of her early sexual abuse and years as an alcoholic. Now sober, Doris is a survivor in so many ways, but in her son's life, she is of little or no influence. That's unfortunate, as she has much to teach her son about surviving. For my last meeting with them both I had gone with Alex on a home visit during a temporary release from custody. He was happy to be going home, to get back to his own room and spend some time with his video games. He was close to his mother in the awkward way of teenaged boys, especially those who have had only a mother's sole presence over the years. We met in their upstairs duplex, a cramped derelict unit in a part of the city where many of the kids I work with live. Doris's boyfriend was there, stoic but polite. He watched television and stayed apart from the to-ing and fro-ing of Alex and the jail staff who accompanied him.

Together we chatted over tea at the kitchen table, a dull melamine yellow and black speckled vintage piece with chrome legs and black plastic caps to protect the greying vinyl on which it stood. The table reminded me of the retro-chic decor of some of my friends' apartments. Only here the table was the authentic article, a '50s piece thrown "out" to the poor to furnish their homes. Doris smoked, offering her 15-year-old son a cigarette. He picked up matches from the counter behind him, offering his mother a light before drawing heavily on his own cigarette to get it lit. This might have been Alex's home, but beyond a video game, cigarettes, some simple food, and his mother, his life was beyond these walls.

We talked about what was going to happen when Alex returned home in a few months. Doris wanted him home but knew it was unlikely she could keep him out of trouble. Alex would roam back to the streets and his friends. She wished she had more to offer but had nothing better to give Alex than what he could find elsewhere. A poor kid, living in a poor neighbourhood, already beyond the control and hope of an education system that had failed to connect with him, Alex had nowhere but the street to turn to if he was going to find something powerful to say about himself.

A month after his discharge, I spotted Alex among a group of youth hanging out near a fast food burger place I was at with my own children. He looked comfortable, even though he had to hunch over in his lightweight jacket to stay warm in the cold evening breeze. Out of the corner of my eye I saw him jostle another youth, then light a cigarette and laugh. It was like I was watching a movie.

That's how I often feel when I meet these kids outside the institutions where I work, like I have somehow been allowed in to a special viewing of a movie only the two of us are privileged to see. The plot always feels so predictable. I know so much about the main character and his or her vulnerability that I am seldom afraid of the potential danger these kids pose to others in their communities. Instead, I find myself admiring their spirits, which are so adept at surviving and thriving where I'm sure I would wither and perish. Here was Alex where he needed to be to feel some sense of himself as part of something important. Maybe one day the winds of chance will blow him elsewhere, I thought to myself, but for now this was his place of safety. At the time I didn't think I had anything else to offer him. His peers seemed content to pick up where the rest of Alex's community had left off.

In his own way, Alex had found a measure of mental health that was denied him elsewhere. But he would never convince the professionals who helped him, or his family, school or community, that he was actually pleased with the identity he had found out there on the street.

Who defines what mental health is, and is not, depends a great deal on who has the most power in the way the concept of health is understood. Like many other terms we use, mental health is a social construction. This means that what we accept as the definition of mental health depends on the social, cultural and historical context in which we use the word. R.D. Laing, a famous and rebellious psychiatrist, gave the example years ago of how at most times in history acting on murderous impulses is a sign of mental disorder. However, the combat soldier who behaves exactly this way is likely to be considered perfectly healthy and his or her courage lauded. In other words, in some circumstances, a particular behaviour can be seen very positively, while in other circumstances the same behaviour is condemned.

The distinction, then, between healthy functioning and unhealthy functioning does not just depend on how one behaves. It depends far more on the power brokers in society at a particular point in time who try to secure their position by convincing others that how they see the world is the right way. Those with the most power, like mental health professionals (and even amongst these people there is a pecking order and turf wars!), politicians, and those with money, are the ones best positioned to take a leading role in this collective conversation, or discourse, about what is and is not mental health. Alex, Johnathan, Melissa and Allison have almost no voice in this discourse.

The more power one has, on one's own or in a group, the more likely one is to label one's own experience of the world as mentally healthy, while labelling the experiences of others as signs of illness or deviance. Recall the story of the two fishers and their disagreement over the value of a hard day's work. Who are we going to side with: the one who says it's healthy to work a long day for almost no pay, or the one who thinks that's a foolish waste of time?

When it comes to peer pressure, those with power, usually adults, label as unhealthy youth who appear to act in ways they disagree with. Frequently, these youth are called "delinquents." Coincidently, the term delinquent is another label we use which is synonymous with poor mental health. Teens themselves, arguing from a position in society where their voices are largely silenced, beg to disagree. Even J.K. Rowling's delightful character Harry Potter teaches us this. Placed with his Aunt and Uncle Dursley, a family of Muggles, people without magical powers, Harry, a powerful magician, never knows he has remarkable talents until on his eleventh birthday the truth of his identity is revealed by a giant named Hagrid. Harry is transported to a private school named Hogwarts School of Witchcraft and Wizardry where he meets a new peer group, some who appreciate him for who he is, some who despise him for it. I find it most interesting that his uncle objects so vehemently to Harry becoming a magician. He can't see Harry's special abilities. To Dursley, magic is nonsense and a threat to the orderly life he lives.

Teens experience their peer groups as a place where they choose to act in ways that enhance their personal and social power. They choose to conform to norms established in their peer groups because being seen to belong to the group adds to their individual status. Most of the young people with whom I work are searching for their own special Hogwarts. They seem to understand that in such places they are both actors and acted upon. Each child's participation in the peer group adds one more voice to the group's collective identity, making the group and everyone in it a little more widely accepted, a little stronger.

Back to the Future

Thinking back to my own adolescence, I am beginning to remember those years differently. Suddenly, I have been able to recall that I held many of the same beliefs as the kids with whom I now work, only I'd forgotten over time what it was *really* like growing up.

I was born and raised in the suburbs of Montréal, a large vibrant city of three million at the time. My world, like that of most children, was geographically very small and largely isolated from the social and economic upheavals that were affecting my parents. By age thirteen, my concerns were like those of other teenaged boys. I wanted to have as much fun as possible, which meant understanding and, hopefully, exploring my sexuality, buying and fixing up old motorcycles and cars, and playing pick-up games of hockey or football on our street or in a neighbourhood park. By age sixteen, weekend evenings were taken up watching *Saturday Night Live*, experimenting with drugs, drinking, finding someone with a car to go out cruising, trying to meet girls, and then when all that failed to amuse us, trying it all again in the hopes of better results.

I think back to my teen years as a time when my friends and I were pushing life to the limits of what we knew. Though we were all middle- and working-class kids, we were able to quite clearly see differences between us and knew how we were different from other kids in the communities next to ours. We challenged the law but we seldom broke it; we got into some fights, but we avoided brawls where any serious weapons appeared; we drank and used recreational drugs, but we kept an eye on each other to make sure anyone who used (or abused) too often got some help. We weren't always successful at staying out of trouble. But we knew that somehow, *each of the things we did gave us an identity*. We wanted others to see us the same way we saw ourselves.

There were other groups I hung out with as well. They were artsy kids who were in plays, and who worked on the school paper. There were also those strange kids who dressed in old clothes bought at the Salvation Army Thrift Store who seemed to float through life freer spirits than the rest of us. They were into social causes, the environment, vegetarianism. While my old group of peers remained a part of my life, my circle expanded through my teen years and more and more I found myself with these other youth. That was when the trouble began.

By that time, I thought of myself as pretty different from many of my neighbourhood friends. In my late teens I read books by Leo Buscaglia, Richard Bach and Antoine Saint-Exupery. All said value myself as an individual and told me that those who loved me would want the best for me. In *The Little Prince*, Saint-Exupery writes, "Perhaps love is the process of my leading you gently back to yourself." These words, like my experiences at home and in my community, became discordant notes in a world I understood less and less. I had a story to tell about myself which didn't jive well with the story others told about who I was supposed to be. The authors of that other story, my parents mostly, were not trying to be malicious. They just wanted to ensure that I grew up and was successful. To them, my crazy friends threatened an otherwise secure future. Their anxieties and my frustrations ripped us apart as a family. They saw in me a blind follower; I saw in myself a free thinker. My friends reflected back to me best who I wanted to be while my parents seemed out of touch, even threatening.

My parents could accept me being with peers who they understood, but coming from a family that had climbed out of poverty, had established itself firmly in the lower-middle class, who had one motto from birth, "You will go to university," and who never thought much about the environment and peace, much less art, my new friends stretched my family's capacity for tolerance. It must have been hell for my parents watching me grow away from them and their world .

One summer in particular this conflict overwhelmed us. Once they caught on that I was hanging around with my artsy friends more than the neighbourhood kids, my parents became even more worried than usual about me. They started insisting I hang out with my old friends and practically bribed me to spend time with one young fellow whom I had met the winter before. His name was Gordon and he was loosely attached to my old peer group. Gordon was a lot like me. He was my same age, he dressed "normally," he was well-mannered and middle-class. Gordon's parents had respectable jobs. But Gordon also had a clandestine existence. He was heavily into drugs and drinking and many of the people I met when at his home were anything but like my parents and I.

At first I protested, told my parents I wanted to choose my own friends, then when it appeared that they were dead set against my becoming part of the artsy crowd I had previously chosen I said, "To hell with it" and joined up with Gordon and his crew. I decided to use them to further my own ends. They brought me life experience, made me feel like a rebel, challenged my parents' values, and gave me an in with a much more delinquent crowd than I had ever been a part of. Best of all, I relished the irony of being allowed to stay out later with Gordon than with my other friends. Having talked to many youth who complain, "My parents don't understand me or my friends," I am convinced that my story is not unique.

My double existence should have worked fine, but at some point it didn't feel right. I didn't really want to be known as a delinquent. Thankfully, I found my way back to peers who seemed more what I wanted to be. To my parents it looked like I had succumbed to peer pressure. At the time I doubted what I was being told by adults: that my friends were pressuring me to act the way I did. It has taken me these last twenty years and exhausting work with some remarkable and resilient youth, to find a way to express what I felt all those years ago: that my own path to health was better than the one my parents forced on me

Learning From Teens How To Parent

I am astounded by the amount of energy and money that goes into opposing the identities teens author for themselves, *even when they are not dangerous*. Barbara Coloroso, whose advice for parents I particularly like, has said that as long as a child's behaviour is not life threatening or morally threatening we should allow that child to make his or her own decisions. Coloroso encourages parents to fight the battles which really count, and otherwise let their children learn their own lessons in life.

This doesn't mean as caregivers we sit back and do nothing. On the contrary, we can openly express our opinion but needn't give our kids a lecture about all the consequences they might encounter.

Orange spiky hair and not taking a bath (or taking too many) may not be my idea of a good time, but for a child who is beyond our control anyway these are not the battles on which I want to expend my emotional arsenal. I'll bide my time for the big battles, the ones that count, which usually have to do with drug use, sexuality, curfews, and other risk-taking behaviours. And yet, parents spend endless amounts of time trying to control what children do with their bodies: when they sleep, what they eat, who they date, how they dress, when they study, their recreational activities, and of course, the friends they keep. Each time we go to war over these petty issues we chip away at the relationship we have with our children at a time when that relationship is most critical and most in jeopardy. Too often, the battles we are fighting need not be fought at all.

There are few truths in my clinical practice, but one I have encountered too often to ignore is that children are more like their parents than their parents (and children) realize. Parents tie themselves in knots worrying after children who tell me that what they hold to as their guiding truths are almost exactly the same things their parents believe.

My second observation over the years is that there are many frustrated and angry teens who would appreciate someone setting some limits for them so they will know they are loved. It's hard for many parents to believe, and even harder for them to actually put into practice, the power kids want their parents to use to keep them safe and disciplined. It is important we know as parents that our children are looking to us to save them from many of the more serious risks they face. While trying on a new identity with peers is one thing, becoming pregnant, addicted, jailed, or abused is not what most kids intend to have happen. I say most, because for some desperate children with whom I work, jail, pregnancy, even death, can be the solution they seek to the problems they confront. It's a difficult balance to find as a parent, to know when to offer a helping hand and when to leave a child alone.

If we too quickly step in as parents and make judgements regarding our children's choices, such as who they have as friends, we send the message they aren't capable of making their own decisions. While trying to save them, we damage their self-esteem and run the risk they will do exactly what we didn't want them doing in the first place. I know of nobody who listens really well to people who are critical of their every move.

Yet if we hold back and allow children to fall too far, allow them to encounter risks beyond what they can reasonably handle, and are not there to support them in finding solutions to their problems, then they feel equally abandoned and worthless. In such an environment teens are likely to turn to their peers for the support they want from their parents and caregivers. While teens tell me they prefer to have both friends and adults guiding them through life, many teens find their homes so full of conflict, or so lacking in opportunities to feel powerful and accepted, that their only real option is to turn to their peers for help. Parents don't want their homes to be battle grounds, either. They too feel cornered, misunderstood, and too frequently abused by their children. It's a vicious cycle of miscommunication, anger and blame all masking the love that winds up trampled underfoot.

It's what teens find out there beyond their front door that interests me. What happens among peers and in the community that helps teens nurture and maintain their mental health? While parents and caregivers have a role to play in keeping teens feeling good about themselves, their peers play an equally important role, one that has been largely overlooked.

Mirror, Mirror on the Wall . . .

In the fairy tale *Snow White*, the Queen looks deep into her mirror searching for affirmation that she is the "fairest of them all." The world of mirrors, like people, can be somewhat unpredictable. The Queen just can't accept the truth being reflected back at her, that there is another one more beautiful than she. Tragic as her conceit is, I am intrigued by the way the Queen sets out to prove the mirror wrong by destroying that which threatens her identity and status. When we have only one way of seeing ourselves we can become rather defensive when challenged. Any wonder the Queen resorts to heinous crimes to make her point and gets rid of Snow White?

It shouldn't surprise us that teens who feel like they have few options for a powerful identity will do anything, including behaving in ways that are criminal or deviant, in order to defend their tenuous health status. In such cases, youth act just like the Queen who tries to have Snow White murdered as a child. Youth will make preemptive strikes to avoid threats to their identity. Their best defence is a collective offence, often choosing to join with other youth who feel the same as they do, and together working hard at convincing themselves they're worth something. When in danger, birds of a feather need to flock together.

Though I know nobody has a magic mirror, we all have experiences with other people when it feels like we show them something special about ourselves in the hope that what is reflected back is every bit as precious as what we expose. Every parent has seen their child gleefully call out "look at me" or "look at what I did" as if the child's success depended only on it being acknowledged by the parent. In the case of vulnerable children, they have fewer of these opportunities to have mirrored back to them their uniqueness and talents. Socioeconomic factors and personal limitations, family problems, or experiences of abuse can make it less likely a child experiences the mirroring of caring adults, or is able to accept anything positive being mirrored back when it does happen. More often, these children have reflected back to them the message that they are the "ugliest of them all," the ones who are least likely to succeed and worse than their peers at whatever they do.

Troubled kids cope by challenging these identities that are assigned to them which threaten their well-being. Ironically, it is peer groups that offer vulnerable youth powerful self-definitions which are an alternative to the stigmatizing labels the broader community and their families assign them. Consider for a moment some of the words I have encountered during my clinical practice which are used by care-givers, parents and other adults to describe the high-risk children and youth with whom I work:

> loser
> charity case
> brat
> stupid
> victim
> slut
> drop-out
> thief
> little f___er.

Kids understand the threat these labels pose to their well-being. While they might use these words among themselves, coming from adults, these words sting and irritate already open sores.

Now add to these the labels professionals assign these youth and we quickly see why a child may not be getting the mirroring he or she needs to feel good. Some of the most common clinical labels I encounter in the files of the youth with whom I work include:

> conduct disordered
> parentified
> attention deficit hyperactivity disordered
> depressed

suicidal
borderline
antisocial
bi-polar
emotionally disturbed
dysfunctional
resistant
lacking impulse control
difficult

Many of the adolescents I have worked with have told me that interventions by professionals and their endless cycle of assessments do them more harm than good. Furthermore, teens who appear to have succumbed to demoniac pressures from peers are told by professionals in no uncertain terms that the likelihood is poor that they will shake off these clinical labels.

High-risk youth challenge these negative constructions of their identity by exploiting the experiences they have with their peers and communities. Unfortunately, life seldom presents such youth with the health resources we typically associate with resilience, such as academic talents, evoking personalities, or athletic prowess, along with the sports facilities, schools and welcoming communities in which to experience competence in these areas. Instead, many if not most of the youth with whom I work, and whom we see on the nightly news, must make the most of whatever health resources they can scrounge up. High-risk youth from resource poor environments will resist the labels of their caregivers by choosing to be known by much more powerful names such as:

leader
tough
gang member
dealer
sexy

survivor
stud
street kid
helper
drinker
fighter

In the limited ocean of possibilities available to at-risk youth there aren't always identities available that find widespread acceptance. Teens reason their own labels are a far sight better than the ones given them by adults. At least these names are of the child's own choosing, even if those choices are few.

At issue here is what we accept as a sign of mental health and, perhaps even more importantly, what we tolerate as normal. In general, my experience is that parents attribute to the peers of their children behaviours that they see in their children which they do not consider normal or healthy. This is a variation on the "not in my backyard" syndrome, only in this case it's the "not in my kid" way of looking at the world. It can never, we assume, be our children who are the ones contributing to deviant group norms. Sadly, many parents remain blind to the ways their children are engaged with their peers in defining the identity of their peer group. Our children, by their presence in these group, are both leaders and followers at different moments. Even as followers, they are important contributors to the meaning the group attaches to what it does. In order to create a powerful identity or story about ourselves, we need a stage full of actors, as well as an engaged audience.

Imagine the child who colours her (or his) hair purple, pierces her ears ten times, or navel, or tongue, and then goes unnoticed. This would be a serious problem. The child has no choice but to try again, only this time screaming his or her individuality even louder. The peer group becomes one forum in which a young person finds support for this identity story. Peers are used like amplifiers to add volume and power to an adolescent's communication. We might not pay much attention to one child whose behaviour is odd, but we will pay a great deal of attention to a number of individuals who challenge us to see their lifestyle as a healthy alternative to our own. One need only think of the youth culture of the '60s to know this is true.

Chapter 2
Searching for Truth

Earlier, I listed five strategies parents and other caregivers of high-risk children and youth can use to help those in their care remain safe and feeling good about themselves. These strategies are designed to help those responsible for these young people become a part of their children's lives in ways that prevent the dangerous, delinquent, deviant or disordered behaviours some of them use to survive. This chapter looks at the first and perhaps most important of these strategies, helping our kids discover their own truth.

Strategy One: Ask children and youth, "What is true for you?" Help them to become critical consumers of everyone's values, including those of their parents, peers or anyone else who would have them believe their truth is The Truth.

Nathaniel's mother, Tara, and stepfather, Joseph, are soft-spoken, gentle people. Both Native, they reluctantly chose to live off-reserve with their son, mostly because the opportunities for employment were better. Nathaniel, who had just turned fourteen when I met him, was brought to my office after having been jailed for a number of offences including break and enters and possessing and selling drugs. He liked to brag that he had committed many more crimes than the ones for which he'd been caught. It was a study in contrasts meeting Nathaniel alongside his parents. And yet, once we got to know each other, I could see how my first impression of Nathaniel had been wrong. Beneath the bravado lay a sensitive child with ambitions as great as those of his parents.

Though the family enjoyed a modest living, Tara and Joseph had made every effort they could to provide for Nathaniel. Tara attended a United Baptist church regularly. The family had many friends and a large extended family. There was no problem with either violence or drinking in the home. And though Nathaniel's father had left Tara and his son when Nathaniel was just two years old, Nathaniel seldom gave it a second thought that Joseph, his father for the past eleven years, was not his "real" father. When we met together, the family exuded love, order and calm, qualities that are not always there when parents meet their child's therapist in a building with wire mesh on the windows and double locking doors which keep residents in. Tara was confused, though, and Joseph deeply hurt. They both wanted to understand why Nathaniel was a child "doing everything wrong." It was hard to disagree with this frank appraisal of their son, given that he seemed determined to spend his entire adolescence either in jail or on probation. There was something in the lifestyle of the delinquent that drew Nathaniel like a Siren.

After I heard from both Nathaniel and his parents what each wanted to talk about, I suggested that first, rather than focus exclusively on Nathaniel's problems (which was going to get us nowhere as Nathaniel insisted he had none), we look instead at how much Nathaniel shared in common with his parents. Second, I thought it best we try to understand what Nathaniel was finding so attractive among his chosen peer group. In other words, I proposed we go on a treasure hunt. Amidst the debris left in the wake of Nathaniel's destructive behaviour, we were in search of some of what he held to be true for him and others like him. Together, we excavated a new story about Nathaniel, one which better represented the strange sense of order and attachment he found in his world and the power and personal sense of well-being his lifestyle brought with it. Eventually we would help the boy find ways of achieving these same feelings in socially acceptable ways. But until we understood better what it was exactly that Nathaniel was attracted to (his truth), we were hopelessly lost to know what would engage Nathaniel in the work of looking critically at the choices he had made.

We started with Nathaniel's parents. While I needed to get to know them too, it was more important that Nathaniel get to see what his parents valued and believed so he could take a closer look at how much he and they were alike. I also wanted to hear about the kinds of adversity Tara and Joseph had overcome in their own lives. It impressed me (and I think Nathaniel) that they were clearly two people who didn't get knocked down easily, had both survived histories of abuse and in Tara's case, overcome a drug habit that had led to a period of hospitalization ten years earlier. Both Tara and Joseph had for years been trying to build a better life for themselves and their son. They had nurtured a sense of home and place in their new community. They wanted most to be respected by their neighbours and refused to accept the negative labels forced upon them because of their skin colour.

Nathaniel wasn't that different. I knew him a little, but the people who looked after him in the facility where I worked and his teachers in the community knew him far better. I asked them about the boy. This information wasn't just mine to analyze with a critical and detached professional eye. I gathered it for the benefit of Nathaniel and his parents. The story these other caregivers told painted a picture not just of a problem child, but also of a likeable friendly boy who could be a pleasure to have around. Most days, they said, Nathaniel knew how to behave. He knew how to evoke respect from others. He knew how to play fair on the sports field. And he volunteered to cook and do extra chores when living in a structured environment. He was a charming young man who showed promise in his studies now that he was again engaged with them.

One can imagine the effect sharing this had on Nathaniel's parents, especially hearing this kind of praise from their child's jailors, therapists, and teachers. It was as if we were telling them their son was still theirs, that he was still like them in so many ways. Their investment of love, time and energy was paying great dividends despite evidence to the contrary (we were, after all, meeting inside a secure psychiatric facility). The delinquent behaviour was not Nathaniel's only story. It was only one part of who he is.

A conversation like this does not romanticize a child, or ignore the cold hard facts of the problems a kid like Nathaniel is facing. But it does get us adults and our children started on a path of discovery. The truth about Nathaniel was he still had a strong attachment to his home and family and the values he had acquired there. He was just using them elsewhere in his life, in places his parents would rather he never experienced.

Now that we knew that Nathaniel was like his parents, *that they together shared a common truth*, we needed to find out what it was about Nathaniel's dangerous and delinquent lifestyle that drew him. The answer was simple and obvious: power. Among his peers Nathaniel enjoyed the power afforded him by kids who get a lot of attention in their community, most of it negative. Nathaniel had found money, excitement, people to be with, and it was all handed to him with little effort on his part. To his mind, he'd become very successful. "I was holding $10,000 one day, and it was my responsibility to get it where it had to go!" he told me, referring to his activities as a runner for drug dealers. "I'm not going to worry about staying out of trouble until I'm at least seventeen or so, because juvenile time doesn't count for much. But I don't want to do adult time. That would be crazy."

"Ah ha!" I thought, here is the lynchpin which makes Nathaniel's life different from that of those other dealers. Nathaniel still *believed* that being a career criminal made no sense. He understood that being "bad" carried with it a measure of social disapproval which he clearly wanted to avoid. Our challenge, as his helpers and audience, was to discover how else Nathaniel thought he was different from his very delinquent peers. What were his private truths and how did he express them, or keep them hidden, when he was with his friends? There was a lot we talked about.

Nathaniel said he wasn't into robbing people he knew. He preferred property crimes against public buildings, stores and the like. He hated the idea of the drug dealers for whom he worked pushing to kids younger than himself. He thought anyone doing really hard drugs was a "moron." He knew he needed to go to school and knew he had the potential to go to college or university. He could see that many of his friends were going to have to be criminals all their lives because they had no other way to make a living. He told me, though, that he was in control of the amount of time he did in custody and other locked facilities, unlike some of the kids there who didn't have the "brains" to keep themselves out. And he fiercely believed that Native people like himself who started out in trouble could still make something of their lives. He idealized the Warriors who were involved in armed conflict with the government over treaty rights and land claims. He didn't want to be seen as a stereotypical Indian and was convinced that was not his future, any more than it was that of his parents.

The more we talked, the more Nathaniel grew in stature in the eyes of everyone who took the time to listen and engage with him. People stopped blaming Nathaniel's friends for Nathaniel's problems. Instead, we tried to arm Nathaniel, like a Warrior, with the tools he needed to stand up to people who would have him do things that might threaten what he believed. His parents and I wanted to get to know more about his friends, but not so we could put them down. We wanted to really understand his friends and the powerful identities he and his peers built for themselves through their deviance. Only then could we have an honest conversation with Nathaniel about what he believes and what, if anything, made him different from others his own age.

A funny thing happens to kids like Nathaniel when they get back home after time in custody. Frequently, they are given *less* responsibility, not more. It's as if parents are afraid to trust them when that is exactly what kids say they need most to feel like they belong at home. I'm not suggesting we just hand over money, abandon all rules, or make it easy for delinquent kids to return to criminal lifestyles. There are other ways we can find to show a child like Nathaniel he is trusted, respected and welcome. We can let him cook his own meals and prepare some dinners for us too. We can let him decide his own bedtime (though not necessarily his curfew) and provide him with his own spending money.

I have seen parents whose kids were practically living on the street feel compelled to make every decision for their child when he or she is once again forced to reside at home. It's as if caregivers conveniently forget that for days their child survived the dangers of street life, relying on his or her personal resources to keep safe. The true story about such children is that they are often very competent at surviving and proud of their street smarts. It is these traits which are at the root of a health-enhancing identity available to these children.

Fortunately, Nathaniel was given opportunities to assume greater and greater responsibility at home and in his community while in treatment and after discharge. He got a job he wanted as a busboy which gave him some legally earned spending money. He went back to school and though he attended erratically, he did well enough to complete his year. Nathaniel was lucky: there was a teacher who liked him and cut him some slack, allowing him to make up work, or providing the extra help he needed during lunch. Nathaniel's parents also made the effort to get him down to the local recreation centre more often. At least there Nathaniel could burn off some energy in a safe environment. If he was given a few bucks for some food, in general, that's how he spent it, rather than on alcohol or drugs. Most of all, his parents continued to believe in him. They knew their son could be something other than a criminal. They were now convinced he was at least thinking for himself and trying to be different from many of the peers he called his friends.

Through all this change, everyone held their breath. Every time Nathaniel was given a little bit of responsibility we all half expected him to return to his old ways. But remember, we'd already established that Nathaniel was more like his parents than they had suspected, and that what Nathaniel was really looking for was respect, maturity, responsibility and acceptance. We now understood the world according to Nathaniel. Grounding him at home, turning home into a jail, locking away all the valuables, never trusting Nathaniel to be out of sight, all solutions Tara and Joseph had tried before, had only made Nathaniel's street-based peer group that much more enticing. *Instead, we invited Nathaniel home*, and asked him to bring along the story he'd created for himself outside the home. Nathaniel was never more committed to being a delinquent than he was to any other way to be somebody special. He was just out shopping for some personal power. He loved having the opportunity to show his parents who he really was.

There is one important caution which must be made, though, to a story like Nathaniel's. While I can think of many kids like Nathaniel who successfully turned their lives around, children who are addicted to drugs and alcohol, glue or gas sniffing, or are seriously depressed and suicidal will not necessarily change. Though all the things we did to help Nathaniel will help these other children, more limits need to be negotiated with children who are a danger to themselves or others. The goal is exactly the same, to understand their world, but the timing is different. With those children we need to move forward a little slower. With them, the first step is to structure a world around them where there is less easy access to drugs or the money to buy them, and fewer opportunities to hurt themselves. We still need to understand the good things kids tell us they experience when abusing substances, or self-mutilating, but we won't be able to change anything – no matter how much we understand about their lives – until the addictions and other self-destructive patterns are under someone's control. For that work, forced treatment with a professional counsellor is often the only effective course of action when the child and his or her family cannot find that control themselves.

One Truth or Another

What we accept as the truth about the everyday worlds in which we live is, in fact, an elaborate social construction of meaning. We are embroiled in endless negotiations to see whose version of reality will be accepted as the truth. Kids are no different. As we saw earlier, a term as simple as "health" depends for its definition on who is using it. Violence, harassment, and theft are all traits we tell our children are unacceptable. And then we turn on the six o'clock news! Suddenly we realize that there are many people who would disagree with us. We might even see in the case of war and civil unrest justifiable "delinquent" acts. Nathaniel's understanding of what it means to be a modern day Native Warrior fighting for treaty rights is different from that of his White neighbours.

It's important to help teens explore these contradictions in meaning. It's important that we listen, really listen, to what they have to say. We needn't agree. In fact, the teenager who finds his folks at home mimicking his friends, passing themselves off as equally hip, is a teen who is likely to run out the door at twice the speed he or she did before. Listening to teens share their truth doesn't mean we have to agree with them, any more than I have to wear what others wear, or paint my house the colour of my neighbour's. We can agree to disagree.

Teens are particularly adept at identifying hypocrisy. It's a strength we will want them to cultivate, first at home with us adults, and then unleash outside the home with their peers. Developmental theorists have long known that during our teen years we naturally think of the world as neatly packaged into either/or categories. At that age, we are alert to inconsistency and hypocrisy, exploiting any slip our parents make to our advantage. It is a talent which grows from our cognitive development and we relish the opportunity to put it to use. Any couple who has had their teenager go back and forth between them, trying to trip them up in the confusion that ensues, knows that kids have an uncanny way of finding technical loopholes.

The problem, as Barbara Coloroso points out, is that we teach kids what to think, not how to think. A big part of doing the work of thinking is becoming critically aware of what we take for granted as our values and beliefs. Not everyone believes the same thing. As adults, we must be polite in our social circles, but we seldom extend the same courtesy of self-determination to our children. We expect them to be us in miniature despite what we say to the contrary.

The best way we can prepare our children to handle their peers is by allowing them to practice at home questioning *our* beliefs. Why does what we say carry the air of truth? How does one go about, respectfully, challenging that truth? When our children are under two feet tall, we teach them to not put their fingers in wall plugs. When they are teenagers we have a responsibility to teach them how to negotiate for power and control. They will need to know this because different people's constructions of reality carry with them different rights. Not everyone gets to express freely what he or she believes. Ask anyone who is gay, who professes a different understanding of God, or who wants to just live differently from his or her neighbours. Just try not mowing the lawn in front of your suburban home and you'll quickly see how conformity is enforced. This is not some form of mythic peer pressure from neighbours, but the imposition of state sanctioned power that reflects a collective order to which we all contribute disproportionate amounts of influence.

Some of us have more power than others deciding the rules by which we are governed. Derrick Jensen in his recent look at White male privilege, *The Culture of Make-Believe*, makes the point that democracy only really works when we all have the means to participate as equals. By any measure, age, finances, or education, our children are disadvantaged in the decision-making process. Troubled kids even more so. What they tell us, when we take the time to listen, is that they want to participate as equals but lack the means to gain access to the collective decision-making process legitimately. So they come in the back door, finding power though dangerous, delinquent, deviant, and disordered behaviour. I have found the best way to move youth away from these behaviours, and I do want to move them, is by offering them a front door to my world, by being open to hearing from them their truths.

A microcosm of this battle over beliefs can be seen readily in our teenagers' choice of dress. Even the most outlandishly individualistic teen fashion rebel still stays within gender norms, norms related to sexual orientation, and frequently social class. What is the right way to dress? For teens, like adults, that truth depends on whoever has the most power to decide the standard.

We must make sure our kids have this power. I want my children to dress themselves. I want them to try on different images. I want them to take risks, even if it's personally embarrassing for me and, maybe, even for them. I want them to shock. I want them to at least once be looked at like something they don't want to be: a criminal, a crackhead, a geek, a browner, a prep. It's only in the feeling of being labeled something we're not that we learn how to resist being labeled at all. A well supported failure is better than endless success which comes from activities that are risk-free.

What we are asking teenagers to do out in their communities is like feeding them to the lions, throwing them out into a chaotic world where even we adults struggle to convince others what we believe is right. We must equip children with the skills they will need to argue for acceptance of their realities. Kids need the relative security of close-knit peer groups to practice these skills. But first, they need the experience at home.

As caregivers, we can help teens construct healthy identities by encouraging them to be critical consumers of everyone's values, ours included. Instead of putting roadblocks between our teens and their peers, far better we dialogue with them about the conflicting realities to be found among different peer groups. I am not arguing that we push teens towards "negative" peer groups, any more than I am arguing we push them towards positive ones. We are simply coaches on the sidelines. The best thing we can do is help teens *evaluate* the different norms of each group they encounter. What I see parents doing instead is interpreting the reality of a peer group for their child. "Oh, they're trouble," "You don't want to get involved with them," or "Why don't you choose better friends?" These evaluations by parents are often wrong, and usually ineffective at helping their teens make decisions that help them chart a course towards resilience.

That's because as adults we assume we understand the subtlety of dress, language and behaviour of our children. We seldom do. What's more, trying to direct our child's choices doesn't work because we overlook our teenager's own role as a contributor to the very group culture we would have him or her reject. If parents had their way, there would be very little variety among children. Even a great artist like Michelangelo, who would grow into the painter of the Sistine Chapel under the rule of Pope Paul, was admonished by his father for not going into the family business, and instead becoming a sculptor and painter. Even as Michelangelo's fame and fortune saved his family from ruin, still, he never convinced them of the rightness of his path.

If we take a closer look at what's happening for our children, we often find that our teens are not who we think they are. Very few will ever be a Michelangelo. Their notoriety will come from being outcasts of another sort. In either case, though, their lives will be misunderstood by their caregivers.

For example, I meet teens whose parents say they are threats to themselves and others, but who astound me when they tell me they are the ones who keep everyone else in their peer group safe. In J.D. Salinger's American classic *The Catcher in the Rye*, Holden Caulfield fantasizes he has the power to save children who are playing carelessly in a field of rye in danger of falling from a cliff hidden at the field's edge. He daydreams, "I'm standing on the edge of some crazy cliff. What I have to do, I have to catch everybody if they start to go over the cliff – I mean if they're running and they don't look where they're going, I have to come out from somewhere and *catch* them. That's all I do all day. I'd just be the catcher in the rye and all."

It's no surprise that Salinger's book appeals to so many youth generation after generation. We are all a bit like Holden, earnestly hoping to make a difference and exercise some control over our lives and the lives of others. While such fantasy might lead us to label Holden as narcissistic, I prefer to accept the character as he is presented, at a crossroads between childhood and adulthood, searching for whatever means possible to play the game that his former teacher Spencer tells him is life. If we give youth the opportunities to figure out who they are and are not when among peers and their communities, then we open up space for them to assert their own truth and identity. They learn to play the game better. Frequently, the good in them rubs off on their friends, preventing the entire group from getting into too much trouble.

Dialogue for a Change

I encourage parents of risk-taking teens to talk to them more about their safety plans than about their problem behaviours. The 15-year-old who is arguing for the right to go to an all night party with friends much older than herself and where there will be lots of drinking would have a nearly impossible task convincing me to let her go. But it's her job to convince me. Her task is to build a safety net. "How will the party be supervised?" I'll want to know. "What happens if someone drinks too much? What about cars? Is anyone going to be driving? Is anyone going to stay sober?" And then there are issues about sex. Though it might seem like a crisis at the time, most girls (and boys) do not really want the pressures of keeping themselves safe in such a dangerous situation. They'd rather stay at home or have a smaller party they can better handle. But first they have to be able to say, "This is who I am."

Who they are has to be someone who does not take those kind of risks at fifteen. As the child develops a safety plan, she is also saying that she is different from her peers. She is becoming a critical consumer of their values. She is asserting her own way of having fun. If we're fortunate, and many parents often are, the teenager says to herself, "Gosh, there is a lot to think about if I'm not going to get hurt, pregnant or sick at this party." While such a coherent thought is unlikely, kids tell me that somewhere deep inside this is what they're thinking.

Of course, this doesn't always work. Sometimes teens decide the risks are worth it and the identity they get from being at that party is the one they want. At such moments parents will probably have to stand their ground and say, "No, you can't go." But that's not the end of it. Any child who is looking for that much stimulation is going to find it one way or the other. This whole challenge has given a parent a great deal of valuable information about what his or her teen needs and how she sees herself. It shouldn't be wasted.

To offer an adolescent like this a pyjama party with popcorn and a rented movie in lieu of the all night drunk is unlikely to move a stubborn teen away from her high-risk peers. Bungy jumping by moonlight might; attending an outdoor summer rock concert might; an all night horror movie spree at the local repertory theater might; a legitimate excuse to drink, such as hosting a formal end-of-school-year party for friends, might; something, anything with some risk, that pushes the limits of parental tolerance, and includes lots of friends, might satisfy the child's need for whatever she hoped to find through more dangerous behaviour.

As parents, respecting our children's paths to health means losing some battles along the way. Remember, the goal is to raise a healthy teen and declare the war won. As long as what a parent tries meets the same needs for a powerful, widely accepted identity as what the teen wanted to do in the first place, there is a chance a teenager will accept this other way of expressing who she wants to be. We should consider whether, after the child agrees with our plan, she will be able to hold up an image of herself to her peers which is every bit as powerful as theirs. "Hey, look at me," our child needs to say, "I'm having some fun too, and what I'm doing takes more guts, more class, more 'stuff' than just getting wasted."

These suggestions are just that, some thoughts. As I said in the introduction, I always keep a garbage can in my office. If things I say don't fit with a family's way of living, I always encourage them to throw my suggestions away. Better to try a homegrown solution that taps into their child's energy and the family and community's resources than borrow something from someone else. Each family is their own expert on what works.

Many Truths, Many Groups

Parents need to encourage teens to participate critically with a number of different peer groups. Fate and circumstance will take care of the selection. Then, when a child like Nathaniel comes home the real work of loving him begins. If the youth is still talking with his caregivers, they would do well to find out what their child enjoyed about being out.

We seldom stop to ask what made the night particularly exciting, or satisfying. I'd even ask the kid who winds up in jail this same question. In fact I often do. Not surprisingly, delinquent youth often tell me they had so much fun that going to jail was worth it. At such moments it's like a spotlight is turned on and it becomes clear we both live in different worlds. I'd say putting in an 18-hour work day might be worth it if I got a great deal of enjoyment from what I produced. But going to jail? I can't imagine anything worth paying that kind of price for. Neither can most parents.

Getting pregnant? Ditto. And yet, more than one teen I've met has told me she is happy about having a child while still a child herself. She's not alone. A number of researchers, including Kathy Weingarten and her colleagues at the Harvard Medical School, have documented these same feelings among young mothers who say that becoming a mother is one way they can mature faster and get more serious about school, work, and community, all the while becoming more like their own mothers, aunts, and other women whom they respect. Caring for a child, like mundane activities such as cigarette smoking and owning a cell phone, has the potential to address the maturity gap which plagues the lives of youth. Socially, our children are denied legitimate rites of passage through which they can try on adult roles and create a set of values that makes sense to them. Much of this construction of values takes place for teens out among peers. That's why we need dialogue. We need to help kids compare and contrast the truth they find in their own lives with the truth they find among their friends and families.

Ask youth: What do you like about hanging out with your friends? How did the evening (or morning, or afternoon) go? By asking questions this way, the assumption is that positive things happen when youth get together. I like to show support for children being happy. If by chance a parent gets a conversation of any substance going, the next evening or at breakfast the day following, one might ask the same questions but add, "Anything happening with your friends you don't like?" If you get an answer, try building upon it. "What did you do while they were doing those things?" It is absolutely amazing to me how time after time, if asked, teens will differentiate themselves from their peers. They will emphasize how they are unique, and be highly critical of what their friends are doing. But they won't do this if the questions they are being asked assume the listener knows better, or that the listener has already made a judgement about the relative value of what the kid is up to. In that climate, the teen simply defends what his or her peers are doing. He or she would never say what was upsetting or difficult, even if there was plenty to fit the bill.

When it appears a miracle happens and a youth lets out a hint that something occurred which made him or her feel uncomfortable, avoid the lecture. This is one of the most common patterns I see in parents of high-risk youth, the mini-lecture the moment children begin to tell their version of the truth. A youth says, "Some kids got picked up last night for drinking and driving, but I was back at the party," and the parent responds with a lengthy, "I told you to stay away from those no-good little ___s. See what happens when you hang out with them," and on and on.

But let's look back at what the teen said. The most important part was completely overlooked, and the opportunity of a decade missed. The youth said "*I was back at the party.*" Even if the teen was in the car, they may have said, "I wasn't driving." I worked once with a young fellow who had taken part in a break and enter, but told me very clearly, "I didn't get into trashing the place," as his friends had. An addicted youth I know explained that while he did drugs, "I don't get into the harder stuff." We miss these exceptional moments in which youth share their version of reality with us. Instead of jumping all over them because of our fears of what could have happened, we have an opportunity to help them evaluate the relative risks of their actions to themselves and others. My goal would be to move the youth away from needing to put him or herself in harm's way. I don't want to see children having to do these things to find a powerful identity. I want them, in contrast to the young mothers I discussed above, to find the respect they seek without the burden caused by life-changing decisions.

The child who doesn't get into a car with friends who are drinking is scoring brownie points in my book. I'll ask that child, What made you not get in the car and stay at the party? Are you worried about your friends now that they got into trouble? What's going to happen to them? and Any regrets about what you did? I met one young woman who, after a similar episode, felt guilty that she hadn't gone along and offered to drive even though she didn't have a licence.

If the conversation has miraculously sustained itself to this point, and there is some trust established between the child and parent, then a caring parent may want to say something about what he or she thinks about the situation. Of all the things a parent does, however, this is usually the least helpful. All youth but a hardened few know it would have been stupid to get into that car and let their friend drive drunk. But a parent who is really listening can also offer some supportive words of encouragement for a job well done. In so doing we model for our children how to be there for others and express ourselves. "I'm glad you didn't get into the car" is a simple way of saying so much. "It looks like you made a good decision." Add a hug and maybe the message will get through.

If children know how to keep themselves safe and practice at it from very young, then they will be ready to evaluate the relative merits of different truths. But they need to practice, and with different sets of friends and adults. Parents who shelter their children are fighting a losing battle. I prefer to inoculate a child by teaching good thinking skills, rather than try to customize an environment that is unlikely to contain a growing child.

Inviting Criticism of Adults

As mentioned above, the other way to develop these critical skills is to invite the child to become a wary consumer of his or her family's value. This is an especially difficult task for most of us as we tend to think of our beliefs as fixed and, even worse, rational. Raising a teenager should challenge this complacency. Singer-songwriter Nancy White sings a funny little song titled "Daughters of Feminists" in which she recounts the trials of liberated parents who, much to their chagrin, wind up raising conservative-minded children:

Daughters of feminists bruise so easily
Daughters of feminists hurt
Daughters of feminists curtsey and skip
Daughters of feminists flirt
They say, "Please mommy, can I do the dishes," or,
"Let's make a pie for my brother."
Are they sincere?
Are they crazy?
Or are they just trying to stick it to mother?

Sadly, the song has an element of truth in it. The more rigid a family's values, any values, the more difficult for a child to challenge what they are being handed. The more difficult it is to express one's self at home, the more likely a peer group with competing values will hold sway in a child's life.

Besides, our parenting styles are bound to change over time anyway. Anyone who has ever raised more than one child will say this. We ourselves become critical of our own values as our children present us with new challenges. "I'll never . . ." statements quickly get replaced with "Well, it's not that bad for them. . . ." It might feel like everything stays the same, but in fact, we too participate in a society which is forever rethinking what it calls "parenting." Our children too have a say over what is and is not good care, though their voice is often weak compared to ours. All this adds up to a never-ending story of clashing truths, truths which we import from our own families of origin and then reconstitute with about as much thought as we give to mixing orange juice from concentrate at breakfast. Our children have the difficult task of dismantling our truths and challenging us to rebuild them in ways we never imagined, just as we may have done on occasion with our own parents.

Chapter 3
Lost and Found

The teenagers I work with tell me that gaining control over how they are seen by others is the most important part of feeling good about themselves. When positive labels are scarce, however, being crazy or a delinquent can make as much sense as excelling at school. It all depends on what each behaviour means to the child.

In a recent study by Martin Gooden of Black and White American youth, a strange relationship was found between delinquency and self-esteem for the Black adolescents in the study. Black youth who did poorly at school, rather than feeling down on themselves about it, seemed to stop identifying school as a place they depended on to find self-worth. In contrast, Black youth in the study who were performing poorly at school and who were delinquent (breaking the law, truant, or violent) actually had much higher self-esteem than the kids who were just doing poorly in their studies. The same was not true for the White kids who were struggling to get good grades. For them, poor academic performance continued to be a threat to what they thought about themselves.

In explaining the results we have to look at both racial groups of youth in the broader context of their lives. The Black kids did not believe that school success was going to bring them the same rewards (status, a good job, money) that the White kids could expect. In other words, when confronted with systemic prejudice, some Black youth understood that playing the bad kid was more likely going to bring them a more powerful story to tell about themselves than trying to achieve good grades. The White kids were different. They were confident that if they did well at school they would be granted access to a higher social standing and the economic perks that come along with it.

The kids I work with – Black, White, Asian, and Aboriginal, poor, rich, urban, and rural – tell me that no matter what their skin colour or financial situation, if they feel like achieving at school is not going to bring them sufficient rewards, or that the best they can hope for is limited success at school, then excelling at street life and street smarts is a better way of feeling good about themselves.

Creating a positive identity takes three steps. Acquiring a label powerful enough to make one feel good about one's self is the first. After that there is the work of maintaining the label. But even that's not enough to ensure health. As most of the youth I meet learn early in their lives, their best defence is a strong offense. At-risk youth spend a great deal of time challenging the labels that others would have them wear but which they reject.

If we stop and really talk with teens they will explain all this, patiently, and with great sympathy for our limited capacity as adults to understand. We simply have to ask them the right questions. What we're likely to hear is that acquiring an identity is much like dancing in pairs when neither person knows who's leading.

Sex or Cuddling?

Jacintha, a 16-year-old whose family came to see me for many months at a community mental health centre, was definitely the one trying to lead, much to the dismay of her parents. In the process, they were stepping on each other's toes. No surprise, since the problem that was really the issue but which had remained hidden from the parents was Jacintha's awakening sexuality.

Jacintha had a boyfriend several years older than she. No one, not even her parents, knew this at first. Instead, they'd brought her in to see me because of the repeated blow-ups between Jacintha and her father, Jimmy. Jacintha's mother, Pamela, was in tears explaining her frustration with the two of them and their fighting. "It's got to stop, I can't take this any more" was what she said.

Jimmy is a janitor. He's a kindhearted, simple man who speaks deliberately. He always seemed mildly intimidated when coming to the centre. That wasn't a surprise. Inside the centre, he was in a world in which he didn't feel he belonged. He was older than me by a good decade. I'm sure my age, my office, the way I was dressed only served to make this whole "counselling thing" that much more uncomfortable for him. But despite his discomfort, he still spoke while Jacintha sat slumped in a chair, her legs spread, fingers thrust up to their knuckles in the pockets of her skin-tight designer jeans.

Several days before our first meeting Jimmy had slapped Jacintha when she swore at him, to which she had responded by flicking a lit cigarette into his face. My office at the time was not large, but even a classroom would not have been big enough to accommodate the tension which hung over the family. Jacintha just looked at the floor or appeared to admire the uninspiring artwork on my walls. One would never have known she actually wanted to be there.

My office was at the end of a long corridor and I can still remember the guard-like fashion in which Jacintha's parents brought the girl to see me. She'd come in sandwiched between them, Jimmy and Pamela flanking her as if expecting their daughter at any moment to bolt. They needn't have worried. Jacintha had no anxiety coming to see a "shrink," the term she used to describe me to her friends. Her agenda was to see to it that *her parents* got help, and the best way to do that was to play along and let them focus attention on her. It didn't take her too long to start talking, once she realized her parents were going to use up all the air time explaining what they thought the problem was.

When her parents paused to catch their breath, Jacintha launched her attack. "When my mom and dad and I get into a fight it might look like I'm what started the fight, but I'm not the real problem. I keep telling them this is between them two and not me at all."

"That's not really it," Pamela jumped in. "You're the one who's been mouthing off."

"You threw a lit cigarette at me," Jimmy added, staying calm, but obviously unsure where this all was going.

Jacintha turned to her father, her eyes moist, her voice angry but breaking. "I kind of felt I had to do it, to kind of justify myself, to say 'You were wrong and I was right.' I wasn't right by flicking the cigarette at you but you shouldn't have slapped me either."

I was confused. Who was the bad one here? Things had certainly gotten out of hand, but what was Jacintha's real story? In individual sessions with her later I came to understand much better what was going on for her at home and on the street. To hear her tell it, most of the conflict was between her mother and father. Her mother would endlessly try to tell Jimmy what to do and he would brood or yell at her in retaliation. It was Jacintha who was sick of the fighting. Jimmy had figured he should at least be able to tell his daughter what to do, if not his wife. He hadn't meant to be overly controlling and was in fact quite a gentle man.

"My dad can be really great, if he'd just let me grow up" was how Jacintha explained it. "And my mom, everyone loves my mom, they think she is so cool because she stays up with us and hangs out with us when I have a big sleep over. And my dad always takes us out and to places and to dances and stuff. So all my friends get along with them. And that's really important to me that my parents are like that and that my friends get along with them. Basically my friends come in and my parents say, 'There's the kitchen, get what you need.'"

So why the problems? Jacintha appeared at first glance to have mastered navigating her way back and forth between friends and family, liked her parents, could even talk with them, and had friends who were accepted when she brought them home. But finding out who she was and firming up an identity had become a complicated mess. There were her parent's problems, there was Jimmy's at times overly controlling behaviour, and there were friends who told her she was "nuts" to be pissed off at her parents. There was also sex.

Tired of her dad's controlling behaviour, Jacintha had gone out in search of a way to assert her identity beyond her father's control. She was also looking for a way that she could feel different from her friends, and more mature. To hear her tell it, she found all this when she met her boyfriend.

"With some kids I hang around with it's like if you're not having sex or have a boyfriend, then what's wrong with you? But the friends I'm mostly hanging around with now, it's like they think that's really stupid. We have sex or not but it's not 'cause all you're thinking of is the popularity you get if you're not a virgin."

"What did you decide to do? Which group did you want to belong to?" I asked.

"Halfway through grade ten I really changed. I changed schools too, to try and get with some different people. But my dad was like, 'I paid $500 for uniforms for you to go to the other school.' But I was like, 'I either go to my new school or else I'll drop out and enrol myself there. So you don't really have a choice.' I'm just not going to go to a school I don't wanna go to because he tells me to."

"But this just wasn't about a new school, was it?" I said.

"No. It was like I like myself and I kind of like who I am better when I'm at that school. I'm not pushed around as much. Like, I went through different phases with the kind of people I hang around with. And I like my attitude better when I'm around my boyfriend Jeff. He also goes to my new school."

"What's different there at the new one?"

"Like, I'm trying to lose my bitchy attitude around my friends. And like I don't want to be too loud or noticed, especially around adults. Like one of my friends, Jasmine, is so loud and obnoxious, and people don't like her for that. Like adults don't, and I don't wanna be like that. But I also wanna be sociable, you know, be able to talk to adults and stuff." She definitely had no trouble in that department, I thought to myself.

"So how does being with Jeff help you do all this? I'm not sure I understand."

"He's eighteen, and that's what's different. It's not like I have to be like all my other friends who giggle if a boy looks at them. I'm sort of past that. Last week was a year for us. We'd broken up for five months of that year but we got back together and have been going out ever since. I really like being with him."

"And what about sex?" I asked. "Your parents don't know about that part of your relationship?"

"A lot of my friends, when their parents found out, their dads were like really mad and started calling them sluts and everything and I was really scared of that. So I just do it and don't tell them. But I think that's what Dad thinks I'm doing and he's all worried and angry. So it's like he's thinking I'm a slut even though he's not sure."

It's at times like this that I get a sinking feeling, as if I'm on a roller coaster just cresting a big hill and starting to plummet downwards. It's hard not to feel almost overwhelmed by all the back and forth negotiating which is taking place between Jacintha, her parents and her peers. Jacintha is desperate for an identity as a powerful young woman in control of her life, her body, and her thoughts. And yet somehow, in trying to find that identity, she has created a great deal of stress in all her relationships, even with Jeff.

"I'd rather just be with him cuddling and like that, because it feels so warm and comfortable. I like that better than sex. Like compared to anything we do I like cuddling better and he told me he does too. I just think the sex made the relationship more serious. That's why I agreed. But it wasn't just his decision. I only did what I wanted to do. He respects me for that. Like, a lot of people say, 'You're too young to be in that kind of relationship,' but I honestly feel like I would spend the rest of my life with him. I just feel so loved and comfortable when I am with him. It's a feeling I've never had with anybody else or with nobody or anything."

Three things happened the more we both worked together. Two I intended, the third was just blind luck. First, Jacintha started talking to her parents about her sexuality. First her mom, then her dad. Doing so helped ease their fears and made Jacintha less stressed around the house. At least they knew what she was up to and, rather than imagining the worst, they could work towards accepting their daughter and her sexuality. They could also offer her advice, make sure she met with a doctor about birth control, and even get to know her partner. And they could let Jacintha know what they thought about the sexual identity she'd chosen so young. Like her parents, I would have preferred Jacintha waited, but the less we opposed her, the more likely we all were to get our wish. After all, Jacintha wasn't looking for a sexual relationship. Her search was for intimacy and an identity as an adult.

The second thing that happened was that Jimmy and Pamela began coming to see me to work on some of their issues. This opened up space at home for Jacintha to get on with her life. Her problems were hers, her parents' problems theirs. Jacintha felt pleased that she had been the one who played a large part in getting her parents to talk, and that too made her feel like an adult.

Perhaps that's why, in short order, the relationship with Jeff didn't seem so important to Jacintha anymore. Their breaking up was the third thing that happened. Without too much direction from her parents or me, Jacintha stopped seeing Jeff and drifted to a different group of kids where she felt mature, accepted and safe. Among that group, she decided she wouldn't be sexually active for a while.

The last time I met with Jacintha she told me, "The crowd of people I hang around with now don't drink, don't do drugs. It makes it a lot easier to be who I wanna be. Even at home, I don't have to hide what I do. Finally I just told my mom that there was drinking at a party I was at. I was drinking and I got really sick and I'm not going to do it any more. And she's like 'I'm glad you told me.' Instead I hang out mostly with these new kids. It's a whole lot easier now with my mom and dad. They're just not so stressed about what I'm up to."

Youth like Jacintha piece together an identity from a cornucopia of possibilities. While something like sex is a private event for many young women and men, it carries a powerful meaning in the broader social realm. Adults who convince themselves that their teens are just making themselves more sexually available for no good reason, or are using sex as a silly attempt to be rebellious, wind up mistaking sexual expression for loose morals or a lack of mental health. Serious studies that have engaged youth in dialogue have consistently found that their expressions of their sexuality are far more purposeful than adult rhetoric to the contrary would have us believe. Teenaged girls and boys are aware of the dangers of unprotected sex, of the value of relationships, of the emotional toll that even serial monogamy (one exclusive partner after another) takes on them over time. Yet they persist, just as we did in our time. But then, as feminists like Naomi Wolf have shown, sexuality and how it is expressed has everything to do with power. Strangely, don't we preach to our children to take control over their bodies, that their bodies should be respected? Isn't this exactly the kind of power we want young women and men to have? Isn't this power over their bodies a measure of their mental well-being? It strikes me the problem here is not whether a teen's sexuality is a sign of health or not, but who decides on the appropriate expression of that hormonal rush. Parents, or the teens themselves?

I admit that it saddens me that we have given some young women and men so few choices from which to nurture a healthy sense of self that sex becomes their most obvious choice. I meet many young people who became sexually active earlier in their lives and then have deep regrets later. A solution to a problem of identity at one point in life may not be the desired solution later. Sex, like a tattoo, has an unfortunate consequence of defining us for a lifetime. I've been pleased that recently more and more of the youth I meet clinically are choosing to experiment with their sexuality, but avoid intercourse. These are the same type of kids who tattoo themselves using the Indian technique of Mahindi which lasts only a few weeks, then fades. To my mind, both solutions are the right way to go. They allow children to experiment and acquire an identity without that identity becoming fixed in their lives.

Of course not all young people I meet have Jacintha's self-awareness and can avoid unhealthy patterns that bring more serious consequences. In some cases, acquiring an identity that brings them a sense of control and power can lead them down even more dangerous and self-destructive paths.

Burning Bridges (And Barns)

I met Andrew while he was in custody for burning down a barn. Fortunately no people or animals were hurt, though damage was estimated in the tens of thousands of dollars. I met him first while he waited to be admitted to a secure custody centre in which I sometimes worked as a consultant. He'd been strip searched, all his belongs taken away, had a shower and then been given grey sweats to wear while awaiting transfer to his living unit. He wasn't very talkative that day, or for many days to come. He was mostly a loner. His file painted a sad picture of a 17-year-old youth who had been previously diagnosed as suicidal and depressed, was on medication for Attention Deficit Disorder (ADD), and would be in custody for as much as a year, though half that time would be in a community based open custody facility.

Andrew had never broken the law before but had been headed that way for a long time, only nobody had really known. He had been a good student at school, though his marks had slipped dramatically in recent months. He wasn't known to any of the local social services. The only other rash act he had ever done before was writing a note saying he wanted to die, and then signed it, in his own blood, and attached it to a morbid essay he'd written for an English class. Extreme perhaps, but then Andrew was a voracious reader, and loved Stephen King novels and movies like the *Blair Witch Project*. The guidance personnel at his school took the incident very seriously, but a few visits with a child psychiatrist revealed nothing but an active imagination and normal teenage angst.

Though ADD, he had no trouble at school and in fact did very well when he took his medication and was motivated to do his work. "Where did this kid come from?" was what we were all asking ourselves when he arrived in custody. Neat, polite, smart, maybe a bit depressed, but to wake up one day and burn down a neighbour's barn just didn't seem to fit. That was until I talked to Andrew.

He reminds me of the boy next door in the movie *American Beauty*. The one ostracized from his peers for his eccentricities and abused emotionally and physically at home. People don't know if Andrew is creepy or just a freak. That was before he came to custody. Strange as it may sound, he'd decided that he'd try to figure out who he was by getting himself placed in jail.

"My parents don't know me at all, they know nothing about me" was just about the first full sentence I ever heard Andrew say to an adult, me or any other. I learned that at home he was the "stupid" kid who got picked on for everything. A middle child, he was seldom allowed the freedoms of his younger sister or the privileges of his older brother. Sandwiched, it seemed he was mostly ignored. He dressed like most kids, lived like most kids, was in fact the kind of invisible youth that even the school guidance counsellor admitted he'd never noticed. Dad was a building contractor, Mom mostly stayed home to work raising the children, and volunteered whenever she was needed in the community.

To hear Andrew tell it, the fire was a desperate attempt on his part to escape his anonymity. "I'm tired of it, nobody knowing what I'm about. So I trashed a barn. I knew I'd be caught. I left enough clues. Like they were going to figure it out." It was his father's gas can he had used and left at the crime scene. The owners of the barn and his family knew each other. His boot tracks were everywhere. It didn't take long for a tracking dog to lead police right to his doorstep.

"I didn't care what happened to me, I didn't care if I got caught. No matter. What's it matter if I'm here in jail or at home?"

"Your parents are pretty upset," I shared, knowing full well that this had been what he intended.

"Uh huh" was his reply.

It's difficult for most of us to imagine a world where arson is a solution and a year's incarceration the most effective way to acquire a powerful identity. Andrew's solution, however, is not unique from that of many of his peers who just want to shout at us adults to pay attention. Keeping kids like this safe, and diverting them from such desperate attempts to grab our attention, begins with understanding their worlds from their point of view.

Allison, the group home kid introduced in an earlier chapter, told me that when she was in placement, people in her community just assumed that all the youth where she lived were bad kids. That many of them were there because they had bad parents, or were coping with a mental illness, didn't seem to dissuade neighbours from seeing them all in the same way. Rather than fight, Allison and her peers played this bad situation for what it was worth: "We just picked up the label of delinquent and decided if they're going to call us that why not just show them." In some ways, Andrew's strategy was similar. If he was the stupid kid anyway, then why not exploit the role and become a *really* stupid kid in the eyes of his family and community?

"I'll show them!"

Of course, not every at-risk youth feels compelled to acquire a positive identity by acting out in ways that frighten their neighbours. Those who rise above adversity frequently join the melting pot of normal life, making the rest of us forget the harsh environments from which they come. They show us they can succeed, but we don't always understand the grandeur of their achievements.

The literature is replete with words to describe these youth: James Anthony calls them invulnerable; Robert Coleman thinks of them as survivors; Norman Garmezy tells us they are resilient; Sybil Wolin describes them as strong; while others have characterized them as thriving, hardy, invincible, or just plain good copers. These youth seldom appear in counselling to talk about their successes, much less about their secrets for coping. Why would they? As a society we tend to embrace them without hesitation, as if we expected them to show up in our world anyway. Arguably, these youth need our attention just as much as their peers who cope through problem behaviours. During my career, I have been fortunate to meet several such resilient youth and hear their secrets.

They are kids like Becky. She was the one who "rescued" Allison from her group home. Bright, attractive in a down-home sort of way, personable and committed, she evokes praise from just about everyone who knows her. I only met her because her mother, a sole parent, came to see me for therapy. Becky had come in to one of those sessions to offer her support. When I began a research project on kids who showed signs of resilience Becky came to mind. I asked to interview her and she obliged.

"I feel I've gone through a lot of problems but I think of myself as sort of mentally strong," she explained.

"How do other people see you?" I asked.

"'Becky, you love the world' is what they say." She laughed, as if the comment was true, but so inadequate to explain how she felt.

At sixteen, Becky had constructed for herself an identity as an environmental activist, a vegetarian and a member of a fundamentalist church. Meeting her, one could overlook her early history of abuse, poverty, and the years she lived in a violent home witnessing the severe physical and emotional abuse of her mother. Becky has found through her community involvements a way to grow beyond her past. There was something about her spunky and self-assured nature that hid what she'd been through. She was an expert at navigating the different expectations of her in each sphere of her life: friends, family, church and community. No matter where she was she never lost her sense of self.

I was oddly impressed that she chose to attend a conservative Mormon church but liked to dress in men's pants, a peaked cap, and a tie when she attended services. And she loved to spend time with her mother, not typically what we find many teenaged girls doing.

"I'm not embarrassed to walk downtown with my mom," she told me. One had to admire Becky's ability to collect for herself labels that felt right to her.

"I just like making friends. I have friends where my dad lives and here at my mom's, and where I used to live. It's easier that way. When you have friends to fall back on and you think, if you're down in the dumps, and you have someone to go see or you're walking down the street and someone's there and they go 'Hi,' and you talk to them, or you're having a bad day and there's a letter from a friend and they're saying they miss you so much, all that stuff makes me feel good."

"Is there one group you prefer? Does being a part of one group or another say something better about you?" I asked.

"No. I don't care really what anyone says about me. Well, no, that's not true. I care what my mom thinks and my close friends, but not everybody."

"Are you known in different ways to different people?" I asked her, trying hard to understand her life in its entirety.

Becky looked at me like I just wasn't getting it. She explained as if talking to a child, "When I work in my mom's restaurant, I see some of the other staff talk real vulgar, even to adults, and I used to think I'm glad I'm not like that. Ninety-nine percent of the customers were adults, so I had to act differently with them. You have to know how to act differently between teenagers and adults."

I think I was finally understanding. Becky was a traveller, able to pick up the labels which held the most power in each sphere of her life. Act like an adult when called upon to do so. Act like a teenager with your friends. Be a good friend. Go to church. Be socially active and valued by your community. But always, wherever you are, decide to be yourself as much as possible. Becky had done a good job of convincing just about everyone that the labels she had chosen for herself were fine. As I said, it's easier for us to accept the identity choices of teens when those labels fit with our social expectations of them.

Maintaining Identities

Acquired identities need maintenance. Peers and family play an important role in keeping the powerful and health-enhancing labels youth choose sparkling and alive. Sometimes we fail to understand this. Instead we encounter belligerent angry teens who appear to be messing up over and over again. We intervene trying to control them, substituting our identity choices for theirs. We worry about issues of safety. We throw new identities at them, forcing them into boot camps, schools, and treatment programs as if we, like Dr. Frankenstein, know best what form they should take. We mistakenly believe they are ours to create, put together as we choose.

Sometimes the kids who are out of control have the most to teach those of us who like to think we are in control. For good or bad, these children and their peers are social barometers, telling us just how well we are doing as a society. It's always been that way. Problem kids in Victorian times were abused, sold, shipped to the colonies, placed in work houses, or if less fortunate practically enslaved as chimney sweeps and miners to tame their simple desire to think for themselves and cope with the horrendous living conditions that typified their times. Today, street children who are throwaways and runaways found on the streets of cities around the globe are routinely murdered by paramilitaries in some countries, or forced into prostitution and crime in many more.

A Dangerous Survivor

To a teenager, maintaining an identity means forever building, redefining, and sharing whatever self-definition one has in an endless struggle to survive. Becky taught me this. Tommy, a dangerous and destructive 17-year-old, helped me understand how delinquent teens do the same things Becky does, relying on communities, peers and families to bolster an identity. A large strong boy, Tommy gets noticed wherever he goes, but for reasons very different than Becky's.

"I want people to think I'm tough," Tommy told me one day in a husky rapper-like tone that seemed to say, "Listen up, this is how it is."

"Like every time I'm walking down the street if people stare at me I'll go up and ask them what they're looking at. And ask them if they've got a problem or something. It gets me angry when people are staring at me when I'm just walking down the street. Makes you wonder why they're looking. But they always say they ain't got a problem and walk away."

Admittedly, if your goal is to be known as "one mean little f__er" then this is not a bad strategy to use to make sure people notice you. After all, Tommy did not have many other choices.

I met with Tommy several times in my office at the centre where I worked. He would be escorted there under guard from a local correctional facility. But it wasn't until we met at his home that I began to really understand his life and the choices he'd made. When I arrived one afternoon to talk, the townhouse was crowded with people, most of them relatives, some friends. Debbie, his mom, was sitting drinking tea. Some of the men were drinking beer. An old television was blaring the afternoon soaps but was being overpowered by the noise of three conversations all taking place at once. Tommy was his usually quiet and withdrawn self, using as few words as possible to express his thoughts.

"We can meet down in the basement, if you like." I had wondered where he and I would talk. I'd asked to come over to chat with him about his family and friends. He had said that would be fine, even showed some interest meeting outside my office. I felt a bit like a snoop, but we really can't, as professional helpers, understand people unless we also understand where they live.

Being at home was more the exception than the rule for Tommy. For the last four years he had not spent much time with his seven brothers and sisters, or his mother. He had been either in foster care, group homes or, as was more often the case, in detention for stealing cars. Debbie had moved the family around as her personal circumstances changed. She was just as much a survivor as her son. Five different men were the fathers of her children, and in some cases she wasn't quite certain who was really the father of which. Alcoholism, spousal abuse and child abuse characterized the history of the family. Of his siblings, Tommy most connected with his 18-year-old brother, Jason, who was in jail for one year on theft charges.

"No one messes with him," Tommy explained.

"Why's that?" I asked, not quite understanding.

"You haven't met him, but if you did you'd know why. People around here just know that it's not a good idea to mess with him. They treat him the same when he's in jail, that's all."

Tommy still sees his dad, Rob, on the odd occasion. But Rob hasn't been much help. Debbie keeps asking him to find his son an apprenticeship as an auto mechanic, but so far nothing has happened. Tommy got close to one of his stepfathers, Barry, though, like the others, Barry left the family abruptly. He literally went out for beer and never returned. Tommy's worst memories are of David, his mother's partner for five years when Tommy was little. David would make the boy kneel with screws taped to his knees while holding books out in front of him on outstretched arms. The only thing worse than the kneeling was the beatings he received when he dropped the books.

"Who do you count as your family?" I asked, trying to make sense of all this.

"Nobody here really except my mom. My friends are my brothers. And Jason."

"Are you part of one of the local gangs?"

"Like if more than five people are standing together then they call it a gang. Who really cares." He'd evaded my question and I didn't push, at least not during that meeting.

It's tough for Tommy to keep friendships with all the moves his family makes and his repeated incarcerations. He hopes his mom will stay put in one place but he knows that's unlikely. Debbie's current partner is a violent alcoholic and it doesn't look like she'll stay with him long. The family has only welfare coming in, which means there's no money for Tommy to join a hockey or football team. He attends school sporadically. He said he hopes one day to become a mechanic, though he has never taken an automotive class at school, even though they're offered.

"When I'm in jail I do okay at school, but not when I'm out. Being in is all right. I get to play hockey, train, all the things we can't afford when I'm here."

The more familiar I became with Tommy's world, the more it his need to be tough, strong and delinquent made sense. But being known by a handle like that demands vigilance, or else one's status quickly slips. Tommy fights back against anyone who he thinks is threatening him. Maybe to us that's not a sign of healthy functioning, but for Tommy his negative peer associations and street fights are a healthy adaptation that maintains for him an identity as a powerful kid.

What is it, then, about delinquent or non-delinquent behaviours that maintain "healthy" identities? From either type of experience, Tommy or Becky's, children tell me they derive a sense of personal competence. That's a powerful motivator. It's also sometimes difficult to see. Youth get very good at the most ridiculous talents. Sometimes it's as simple as them knowing how best to disrupt a peaceful family dinner. Other kids excel at break and enters. Fortunately, some find their talents expressed through school or the arts. Others are social butterflies who flitter from one group of friends to the next.

Whatever the skill, identities are maintained best when these skills are demonstrated in front of others. Our job as caregivers and parents is to look for the strengths in our youth. Skills handy in one context can be used in another. However, we forget to invite kids to bring along their strengths when we ask them to play by the rules. Shame. An adolescent like Tommy would make a wonderful hockey player. Big and tough, a real scrapper. I'm personally against violence in sports, but I seem to be in a minority amid the crowds that throng to my local rink on Saturday evenings. In an ideal world, Tommy would have had the opportunity to bring his street identity into the rink and perhaps have proven that he could fit in with kids we think of as healthy, if given half a chance.

Power plays a big part in which talents are valued and which ones are dismissed. Competence depends on context. It's an odd coincidence, but having a knack with guns and combat is a talent needed by both the militia and troubled youth who become thieves or join gangs. It used to be a clear-cut argument that one behaviour was definitely better than the other. As difficult as it is for us adults to accept, that's not always the way our kids see things. If you come from a community where you feel you fit in, then a talent using small arms is better expressed defending your country. But if you grow up feeling excluded, as many of the youth with whom I work tell me they do, then who is to say the war a child wages is not against the society which oppresses and excludes?

For youth like Tommy, acts of violence and theft have no relationship to morals. He does these things because he needs to. That's not an excuse for his behaviour, as much as a truthful acknowledgement of the way things really are for him. This is not entirely Machiavellian.

Most of these teens do not seek power over others, nor absolute power, but just enough power to feel healthy. Our modern use of the term power is tainted by the excessive use of force over the last hundred years that has left us reticent to share our power with anyone. In fact power can and should be shared. Another's empowerment, as social psychologist Isaac Prilleltensky explains, needn't diminish one's own power.

In the competition which teens are engaged in for control over their identities, the lucky kids are those who show competencies that are acceptable to society's power brokers: their teachers, the police, politicians, sometimes their parents. Unfortunately, amidst the chaos of his life, Tommy could only maintain his mental health by displaying talents that were valued by very few in his community. Those who tried to intervene in his life came to understand Tommy not as a bad kid, but as a youth with few options. Our goal became helping Tommy find places he could feel he belonged among people who might value what he had to offer. Unfortunately, for a youth like this, it can be tough to get any community to open its doors.

Depressed or Artistic?

In contrast, Margie, a talented but suicidal 13-year-old, showed an ability as an artist that had brought her recognition from those same power brokers, despite the mental health challenges she faced. She worked at her identity as the "artist" every bit as hard as Tommy worked at his as the "delinquent." Margie's solution, however, commanded wider respect.

At thirteen, Margie had already been hospitalized twice and carried the kinds of diagnoses that are hard to shake: depressed, disordered and disturbed were some of the descriptions I read in her two-inch-thick file. She had already made several suicide attempts following the break-up of her parents' marriage and the subsequent diagnosis of her mother's cancer. Her secure middle-class world had been thrown into disarray. Living with her mom, there was now the hassle of living on a small disability pension, the stress of adjusting to visits with her dad and his new wife, two homes to negotiate, and a myriad of other problems that would overwhelm any 13-year-old.

Margie told me candidly what she thinks of her health: "I have low self-esteem, I don't like myself very much even though there are people who like me. I don't know how to explain it but I'm just not in a very good mental state at this point in my life." She struggled to stay alive throughout the year and a half I worked with her. At times she'd become overwhelmed with the decisions confronting her. That's when suicide looked appealing.

"It's hard to decide who to live with. That's the worst. It's like if I move in with one parent the other will feel really bad. But neither one of them trusts me anymore. I don't have a lot of freedom to do what I want. It makes me feel horrible. It just feels like I have to do what I'm told no matter what."

This powerlessness prompted another suicide gesture the evening before one of our scheduled meetings. That seemed to have become her way of signalling when she was fed up and needing help.

"I tried to slit my wrists last night," she told me even before she had sat down in my office. "But my boyfriend Lance stopped me. I was really flipping out yesterday. I'm not as upset any more."

"It's a good thing you have someone like Lance in your life," I said.

"I'm actually happier now than I've been, ever. I don't hang around with the same people. And I'm still with Lance. They were all really worried about me. I had the knife right on my arm when he called."

I learned a great deal about Lance in the following weeks. He was sixteen and she was convinced he really loved her. All her friends liked him, but she was careful who she told about their having sex. "Being called a whore. Things like that. I beat up a lot of girls that said it to my face. When you're called things like that you get to believe it and don't feel good about yourself. You get called ugly. But lately, things have changed. People have really begun to like me and give me lots of compliments." Margie attributed this change to the new group of friends she'd found since her mom's illness. Her old friends hadn't been very supportive, so she moved on.

Her calling card in each group, the thing that caught everyone's attention, was not Margie the "suicidal" kid, but Margie the "artist." She is very talented and many of her friends have hung on their walls at home caricatures of themselves that she's drawn. For a time there was even one in my office. A large bespeckled head atop a much smaller body firmly planted in a swivelling office chair. She loves to show off her talent this way and is forever up to some project for her school or friends. She works mostly with pencils, but loves paints as well when she can afford them.

"I love being known as the artist," she told me several times.

Getting to know Margie was like watching a teeter-totter in motion: Margie's two competing identities each trying to save her, neither sufficiently heavy to tip the balance in its favour. But the fact that Margie has a choice between the two meant there was hope that she would find her way out of a cycle of self-destructive behaviour. Sadly, I lost contact with her after I moved away. I never did find out if her talent as an artist saved her from her other identity as a self-destructive youth.

Lift Off

There are as many different strategies used to maintain an identity during adolescence as there are youth to create them. Like Margie, some young people choose which parent to live with after a divorce, some decide how and when to become sexually active, like Melissa, and some decide which school to attend, or if to attend at all, like Tommy. They all choose their peer groups based on which fits best with who they want to be at a particular point in time. As we've seen, some join church groups, others Boys and Girls Clubs, still others street gangs, as ways of defining themselves which are accepted by whomever they define as important. Those that join street gangs, get into drugs, or put themselves in jail find a measure of acceptance similar to their popular peers, but accomplish this outside the communities from which they feel rejected.

Still other youth chose to work at jobs after school, or drop out of school altogether and find full-time employment. Some travel, some move to the street because they like who they are when they're there better than when they're at home. Each choice changes a child's trajectory through life, though many are forced to choose from a limited landscape of possibilities. Robert Sampson and John Laub have made a career studying what they call "turning points" that are responses by young people to the cumulative disadvantage that stymies their growth. Not every door, however, is open to every youth. Not every identity chosen can be maintained.

I sometimes draw on the flipchart I keep in my office an upwards arcing line in a bright bold colour. I talk with families about their child's path through life and how even a slight change in course early on can have a dramatic influence on what happens later. I learned that ofttimes, children, like their parents, have expectations that their lives will follow a predictable pattern. But the unanticipated forces of change can ruin the best laid plans. Sexual, physical, and emotional abuse, poverty, disability, illness, dislocations, and prejudice can demand of children adaptation that they may or may not have the resources with which to cope.

Knowing the critical times during a child's development when his or her life began spinning out of control can help a child and his or her family figure out how to bring that life back on course. If a child gets reacquainted with an old life story, he or she sometimes decides that an earlier path that was abandoned is worth a second look. That's of course assuming it's possible to marshal the resources, emotional, social and financial, necessary to travel that other path. Often it is the very people who most want youth to change who impede that change.

Parents ("You're nothing but a problem"), teachers ("You're not very bright, you'll never pass this grade"), human service providers such as social workers, psychiatrists, probation officers, psychologists and youth workers ("You're mentally ill, emotionally disturbed, troubled") constrain youth to self-definitions that have narrow social appeal. In those cases, it's not enough that youth acquire and maintain an identity that works for them. Equally important is the way they offer a challenge to these negative labels forced upon them.

Challenging

Allison knows about being looked at in ways she doesn't like. She left her group home and found her own place to live, but how does a teen like Allison without much power stand up and challenge the negative labels that others want to pin on her? Usually teens manage to do this through an awkward blend of words and deeds, both of which come out in crude and imperfect ways. Long before Allison looked after herself and changed what needed changing, she found ways to practise defining herself as powerful. Unfortunately, nobody realized her path to resilience was being charted right through the centre of the rocky shoals of delinquent behaviours.

When we first met, Allison was an angry and abrupt 15-year-old, suspicious of anyone trying to help her, but desperately seeking someone to reach out and show her how to express what she was feeling. Allison had witnessed her alcoholic father repeatedly beat her alcoholic mother before he died in a motorcycle accident when Allison was ten. Her older brother then continued the violence, beating both Allison and her mother, Nancy. Out of her own frustration, Nancy started beating Allison. Eventually, Allison, who at the time went by her first name, Katie, requested that Family and Children's Services remove her for her own safety. She went through five foster families and three group homes in just five years, becoming more and more a part of the group of kids who were the toughest and most difficult at school and in these homes. Her mother all but abandoned her to the social welfare system, deeply embarrassed to have had her daughter taken away and willing to accept little or no responsibility for the problems she had caused. "Katie" responded by making suicidal gestures when she wasn't playing at being a delinquent.

"Sometimes I'm very touchy," she told me when we'd first met after a referral from her social worker. "Sometimes I just feel 'Why am I here?' Like when I get off the phone with my mom I just go, '*Why am I here?*' Why do I do this to myself? Like when she says, 'I don't care what you do,' and I think it's not going to hurt me this time or it's not going to hurt ever. But inside you're tearing up. That's how it is every time."

She'd be crying by this point, sad sobs ruining the dark mascara which would run in streaks down her face.

"Are you still suicidal?" I asked later, after she'd calmed.

"Not any more, I used to be. Sometimes I just write things down on paper to get the feelings out. It makes me feel a little better. I believe everyone was put here for a purpose but I just haven't found one yet. We are all put here to do something whether it's good or bad and I just haven't figured why I was put here. Not yet."

It was a hopeful statement. Though she'd been referred to me for her problems, we wound up most sessions discussing her strengths and hidden resilience instead.

It was that strength which had made it possible for her to nurture a friendship with Becky, and Becky's mother, Cora. When Becky told Cora her friend needed help, Cora invited Allison to come live with them. For Allison, this was the first placement decision she'd made for herself in five years. Initially, Social Services refused to accept Allison's decision, though they eventually, with much arm twisting by Allison, certified Cora as an approved foster care provider.

It was a life-saving move. In the referral note from Social Services, I'd been told, "*Katie* has a great deal of rage which needs to be dealt with in order for her to finally be 'free' of her past." Having chosen a warm and loving environment in which to grow, Allison made great gains over the next year, changing dramatically the way she saw herself and was seen by others. The contrast between her newfound foster family and her family of origin could not have been more pronounced. That was when she changed her name, choosing instead to be known as Allison, her middle name, instead of Katie, which had been her mother's choice.

"At Cora's, I can act how I want to. I can act according to how I want to act, not how people want me to act," she told me one chilly February day. She'd arrived after school on time though dressed in the flimsiest of coats. I remember thinking to myself, God, she must be freezing. Doesn't she have enough money for a coat? Then it dawned on me how out of touch I could be. The jacket was black leather, quite expensive. She was dressed exactly how she wanted to be dressed, cold or no cold. I offered her a warm cup of tea instead.

"Cold day," I said. "Nice coat, though." She smiled, sipped her tea and after warming up a little, we continued talking about the changes in her life.

"Like before I had to like act this way, and with my mom I had to be on my best behaviour. And I felt people would stare at you. At Cora's I can say how I feel but on visits home I can't because my mom will PSSHWW! She'll explode. Like she'll freak on me for saying things. Like I never do right there, I never do right." She shook her head resolutely. Her black bangs swished in front of her eyes, making them hard to see. She took a deep breath, and then continued, this time less animated, at points almost mumbling her words. "I think she's jealous of me being at Cora's. And being happy. Really, I wish I could be back at home, but I know I can't because it wouldn't work."

It was from this shaky foundation that Allison had been putting her life back together. Even at age ten, when she asked to be removed from her home, she had shown an indominatable spirit to survive. Her choice of friends at that time had served her well as part of her escape plan. It has always annoyed her, though, that her friends are looked down upon by the rest of her community.

"They're just a bunch of kids trying to get through life," Allison explained. "You can't do it by yourself. We needed each other. If you're living with people who are putting you down all the time and don't give a crap about you, then it's going to be hard for you to keep yourself happy 'cause you won't feel good about yourself 'cause other people don't feel good about you. You can try, I know other people do, like they say, 'I like myself and I don't care what you think,' but inside I think they really do care."

"Were the kids who lived in the group homes your best choice of friends, or your only choice?" I asked.

"Before I was well 'I guess this is who I have to hang out with,' but then I felt better about myself and I thought, 'No, I don't have to take this any more. I don't have to be friends with just these people. I can grow and find someone new and still be friends with the others on the side.' If you don't feel good about yourself you're gonna be like 'They probably won't like me so why should I try.' I've come a long way! *I'm not just another group home kid. I'm Allison!*"

Allison is the archetype of the youth who challenges authority for the right to an identity of her own choosing. Not only had she forcibly maneuvred herself to a place where she could feel good about herself, she had managed to stay in touch with other groups of friends and get them to accept her identity as well. Far from being pressured to conform, her many different peer groups added to her sense of herself as a healthy young woman who could be anything she wanted. Her survival had depended on her peers, but she had used them for support each step of the way.

Part of the challenge before her now was getting her community to see her and her peers in positive ways.

"It bothers me 'cause not all teenagers are the same. They should see you as what you are, not because you're a teenager. They should look at how you act. I can act how I want to now, not how people want me to act. Like before I had to like act this way, and with my mom I had to be on my best behaviour. And I felt people would stare at me. But now I feel that I can tell a joke and don't have to worry about it. And with my friends I don't have to act a certain way to be accepted. Now if people don't like me for who I am, it's their loss, not mine. It feels good to not worry if they're going to accept me whether I dress like them or not, or if I have different hair than they do, or if I wear the right kind of makeup. It feels good, feels real good."

I was intrigued each time I talked with this "group home kid" who'd found herself. "How do you do that, keep feeling good?" I wanted to know. It was as if I was staring at a magic elixir but didn't yet know how to bottle it.

"I feel I have to have a lot of self-esteem and feel good about myself, good enough to stand up to people. Like even the social workers, or my mom, I got to tell them where I wanted to live, and there was no way they were going to stop me. I'd have just walked out of the group home. It makes me feel good that I can stick up for myself when I do.

"I stick up for my friends too. Adults, they look at you like you're just teenagers. Like a lot of people just look at you and say, 'That's why they do that, they're just teenagers. They're in that phase.' You know?" She had changed her tone, deepening her voice, imitating the voices of authority which had tried to keep her and her peers down.

"You hear that from adults all the time. I want to say back to them, 'Shut up!' It bothers me 'cause not all teenagers are the same. They should look at how you act and who you are, not just that you're a teenager."

"What do they see when they look at you?"

"Well, they judge you all the same." In that fake baritone she added, "Teenagers are all rotten; if they don't get their way, it's a big fuss." She smiled ever so slightly then let herself slip back to her normal voice. "Stuff like that. Adults get me so upset and mad 'cause they think well, 'I used to do this as a teenager,' but it's now and it's changed. I know what I used to do, but what I used to do isn't what you used to do," she said, pointing out the obvious. "Some teenagers are into alcohol and the car scene and a lot of adults think they all are. That's like a stereotype."

"What do you do? How do you get people to not see you like that?" I asked.

"If that's what everybody thinks then you become that way. I don't know if my friends and me ever got them to change it. We just picked up the label of delinquent and decided *if they're going to call us that why not just show them*." Allison and her group home friends had worked hard at living up to their community's negative expectations of them. I knew some of those friends of hers, knew that many carried with them the same problems she faced, and had found some of the same solutions. Only most of them remained stuck in those group homes and in the identity that came along with residence there. Sometimes the only challenge a teen will offer to an identity is to play it up for all its worth and further annoy those doing the labelling. Professionals call this resistance. I've learned to call it resilience.

Allison became an expert at taking an identity of her own choosing with her wherever she went, offering a challenge to those who would see her other than as she wanted to be seen. She's spent her time perfecting her skills, mounting an effective challenge to labels she rejects, effective in every sphere except when visiting her mother. For all the talent she has nurtured and shown in her peer groups, bringing it home has been difficult. There, the old stories persist.

"Sometimes it's difficult for me to challenge my mom, when she says stuff about me. I still find it hard to stand up for myself. You know? I think it's like a power, 'cause sometimes you feel like you don't have that power and sometimes you do. Like with my friends I'll stick up for myself, but with my mom, whew! No way.

"I feel more safe when people are around. If people are with me I can stick up for myself. But when I'm by myself I feel really alone. That's how it is at home with my mom. There's nobody there who knows me as Allison. I'm still Katie to her."

How different her experience is at Becky and Cora's. "There people care about me," Allison said. "We don't eat meat and our friends don't make fun of us because of that. Like before if you did something like that you'd be considered a nerd." Cora has had a big part to play in helping Allison find a new identity, picking up where Allison's peers left off. Strangely, we can forget just how important parents and other adults are in the lives of teenagers. It's not that they are the only important part of their teenagers' lives, but like any significant relationship a teen has, they are a piece of the puzzle which is needed to complete an identity.

"I used to be put down a lot at home. But Cora, she always tells me when I did a good job, and I think that gives me a lot more power, that there is someone to stick up for me. I'm so used to people saying this or that looks like crap. Like what I've done is nothing. And when people tell me I'm doing good, I feel so good inside."

The Violence of our Labels

Tommy, Margie, Peter and Becky, among others, show this same spirit of resistance, resilience and survival. Once I stopped focussing in my practice on what was wrong with the teenagers I work with, the more I have been able to see how effective their behaviours are challenging the negative labels that velcro to them. For me it's important that I question my participation in the emotional violence we do to the children in our care. We do violence to them when we inflict on them identities that limit their possibilities and narrowly define them. We make attractive the deviant lifestyles that bring with them self-esteem. This isn't to say we should let troubled adolescents run roughshod over our communities tolerating their misbehaviour. But fighting back by forcing equally oppressive identities upon them is not an effective solution. Too often, those labels say much more about us than about the teens to whom they are applied. We need to understand the role we play in constraining children's lives.

Thinking back to my conversations with Andrew and the way he could be so polite, one would hardly suspect this was the same child who scared his community with the randomness of his violence. Andrew has never seen himself as someone who "wants" to hurts others. And yet, in streaming him into a system designed for delinquents, we help to create an identity for him as a criminal. The risk is that in jail he will become guilty by association, known to his community as just another delinquent kid. What's more, as John Hagan and Bill McCarthy found in their studies of street youth, children who are exposed to more disturbed and criminally adept individuals are likely to develop criminal capital, the ways and means of sustaining their dangerous lifestyles. Given the peer group a child like Andrew encounters inside custody, or in other institutional settings, his further development as a delinquent shouldn't surprise us.

For other youth, time inside with their buddies and the handle of criminal is exactly what they want, the power and prestige that comes with being part of that group. For a surprising number of youth, jail offers them little or nothing except a time to decompress. There is a saying that if the only tool you have is a hammer, then every problem is a nail. Thankfully, our criminal justice system is beginning to understand that for many children, incarceration does not produce the changes in children we want. It even fails as a diversion to future crime once a youth has spent time inside and figures out how to survive while there. Unfortunately, however, as we expand diversion and other community based programs for young offenders, we continue to build more secure facilities which separate youth from the influence of the peers, families and communities from which they come. That's a mistake. In the melting pot of delinquency which kids find behind bars, they seldom discover the identities or resources they need to turn their lives around. Incarceration has to be a last alternative. A community of concern that provides opportunities for youth to display themselves in ways they say are healthy, and accepts that young people have unique solutions to their problems, is a far better use of our dollars and human resources.

If incarceration worked, then why, we might ask, do countries with the highest rates of incarceration, such as the United States, have the highest rates of crime? Furthermore, why has building more jails done nothing to decrease the number of people being placed inside them?

Maybe if we understood better how kids grow up feeling good about themselves we'd be more ready to halt the proliferation of kiddy prisons and put our social and economic capital where it can really help kids: back into their communities, opening up opportunities for youth to feel like they belong there as contributing members.

Chapter 4
Shop Around

Strategy Two: Shop around. Encourage youth to be part of different peer and community groups. These give them opportunities to explore new self-definitions while practicing the skills necessary to construct a healthy identity.

Julio had never lived away from home. His world was a few city blocks. It was an eye opener when he took a leap of faith and signed on with an international youth exchange. Suddenly seven blocks must have felt conspicuously small compared to seven continents. Julio left a tightly knit group of peers known throughout his community as mostly "good kids" who got into mischief now and again. His community was happy to excuse their youthful exuberance, as long as it didn't get out of hand. Thrown in with youth from across his country and from an exchange country half way around the world, Julio had to take all of what he'd learned at home about creating a group identity and put it to good practical use.

Youth exchanges have a profound and lasting effect on young lives. My experience working for them has taught me it's not just the travel, the cross-cultural exposure, and the informal development education that creates a lasting impression. It is as much the sudden shock of being uprooted and forced to adapt to a new peer group which brings an unusually eclectic array of talents and personalities together. It would take years of traveling to meet such varied groups of people, Westerners and Easterners alike. During an exchange the possibilities are immense for each individual participant to put together an identity story that suits him or her. Julio dreamed of being the traveler, of making something important out of his life. On the exchange he could try on the role of international ambassador, while also being one of the group's emotional spokes that others relied upon for support when times got tough.

Towards the end of the exchange, I remember vividly how impressed I was with Julio's way of calmly creating unity among his peers. He had a finely tuned sense of justice and achieved a moral standing in the group for his deeds, rather than his words. I still remember the day his uncle sent him from Germany a tiny piece of cement. There we were, in a rural village in Pakistan, a world away from Europe, and Julio walked around our living compound with this treasure on display in the palm of his hand. "It's a piece of the Berlin Wall. My uncle sent it to me. He was there when they tore it down last month."

What looked like cement became embodied with the luster of diamonds. Julio's treasure added to his moral legitimacy in the group. In his own way he had found an identity that had been difficult to cultivate in his neighbourhood back home. Though he'd been thirsty enough to leave and search for it, it would have been hard in his own community to find others who valued so much a piece of craggy cement, much less appreciated the one holding it for bringing it to their attention. Sometimes, I learned, it requires taking the ordinary out of the commonplace if one is to see what something really is.

When we accept that children have their own truths we take the first step towards helping them find a healthy identity. But like any skill, they need to practice the art of convincing others their truth is "good enough" for them. They need exposure to diverse groups of peers and adults if they are to find an identity story which travels well. Kids who are stuck with singular self-definitions seldom negotiate their way around more than one or two groups of peers. Youth who find acceptance for who they are, like Julio, grow into that position of power by learning how to participate in the collective conversations which label kids good, bad or otherwise. If we open up for discussion what constitutes the truth in our own homes, we take the first step towards equipping our children with what they will need to interact with peers, and move from being stuck with singular self-definitions to having others accept them for how they want to be known.

They need to practise these skills in more and more diverse situations. For those of us fortunate enough to have experienced living in different communities while growing up, the serendipity of our lives provided these opportunities. For those of us who enjoyed instead the stability of one home and one community during our childhood, we may lack the skills necessary to negotiate a widely accepted and healthy identity.

Parents should encourage their children to experience different peer groups. Often we mistakenly assume there is only one right group for our children to be in. In my experience, those peers are usually selected by parents who are themselves comfortable with one particular type of kid. We neglect to pay attention to the evolving capacity of our children to write their own personal narrative. Psychologist Dan McAdams talks eloquently of adolescence as a period when children become very adept at creating the myths that will guide their lives, seeing themselves in storied and historical terms. It's at this point that children seek affirmation for their personal ideology, the matrix of beliefs about how the world should be. Parents can participate in the construction of these beliefs, but the task of adolescence is for children to begin development of their personal myths in earnest. To overly control this process sets a dangerous precedent. Children should be the ones who have to sort the wheat from the chaff. Besides, we adults are often too far out of the loop to know which youth (and which identities) are healthy and which are not in the context of our children's lives.

Often I meet through my work young women who are in committed relationships with abusive partners whom they met in peer groups approved of by their parents. I meet children from lower class homes who are pushed into middle-class peer groups where they are constantly being put down for what they don't have and can't afford. These kids end up as cannon fodder for middle-class bullies who leave their disadvantaged peer's self-esteem in tatters. Instead, we need to leave the evaluation of different groups of peers to the teens themselves. Our job as caregivers is to encourage and facilitate contact with as many different groups as possible, laying out before our children a buffet of fine choices. It's up to the hungry child to do the job of choosing.

Recall, if you would, Tommy, the young man I described as stuck in the identity of a delinquent. One might think that given his life circumstances there would be few opportunities to find a diverse group of friends. Who is likely to accept him, much less tolerate his stubborn and violent approach to life, except other delinquents? But the same can be said of upper-class youth who inhabit the communal wastelands of wealthy suburbs with their homogenized television culture. In both places, there are opportunities for children to explore different peer groups, but we have to help them look. Thankfully, there are schools, sports facilities, cultural events, not to mention volunteer activities, youth clubs, and a community full of adults who can act as bridges between children and new opportunities to build powerful identities.

Those Other Kids

Sometimes, however, it is teenagers themselves who are the problem, not the world in which they live. We all know teens who don't want to do anything but hang out with one group to the exclusion of all others. There may not be much we can do except, like the cheering section for a losing team, continue to hold out hope. Sometimes it takes teenagers years to discover how they are different from their closest friends. It can take many more for them to find out how they are different from their parents.

A favourite book of mine is *Jonathan Livingston Seagull*, Richard Bach's tale of a young gull who dared to be different than the rest of his flock and spent his days perfecting the art of flight. "Why?" his mother asks him over and over again. Miserable, she wants to know what it is that stops him from becoming more like the other young gulls who happily spend their days looking for food, behaving as they should. The young gull tries to ease his mother's worry, explaining fervently that he seeks knowledge of what he can do, not the comfort of a life lived in orderly co-existence without challenge or excitement. So earnest is he in his quest that he wastes away to bone and feathers until, as would be expected, his father admonishes him that winter is near and food will be in short supply. Wisely, but without regard for the young gull's passion, his father encourages him to study how to get food and to leave aside his useless pursuit of the artistry of flight.

Like so many youth, Jonathan succumbs to social pressures to conform in order to find acceptance and takes on the identity of the other gulls, anxious to be the best he can be within the confines of the flock. It of course doesn't work, as one would expect. Strange, but Bach's book struck a chord with millions, and yet when it comes to recognizing and valuing this same spirit in the youth we caregivers have under our own wings, we are as hesitant as the adult gulls to allow space for such nonsensical experimentation.

Jonathan's stint of conformity doesn't last, as we would expect. Soon he is back to practicing his flying, only this time he abandons the flock to make his way on his own. Until teens find out how they are different from others, they may not be hungry for anything other than that which life has served them. Why should this characteristic surprise us when we watch children eat the same thing for lunch 210 days of each school year?

Fourteen-year-old Sophie, though, had this zest for life. She was different from her peers and in a quiet way nurtured an identity as unique. She loved variety and sought it out at every turn. Perhaps it was what we managed to offer her, or maybe it was something special inside her that drove her to look for different types of experiences with peers and adults. Probably it was both. Sophie grew up alongside her twin sister Patricia, neglected by an alcoholic mother, and forced to suffer through many dislocations and foster placements. However, unlike her more delinquent twin, she had a much greater interest in school and the people she found there. That interest made all the difference in others' perceptions of her choice for a healthy identity.

It was the contrast in the paths both Sophie and her twin sister traveled which was so interesting. Perhaps just to be different from her twin, Sophie had early on shown more interest in school and people outside her immediate circle of friends. Along the way, this spark of curiosity was noticed and a few people came forward to offer their help. There was a teacher who saw in Sophie some talent and reflected back to her some possibilities she'd never considered, like going to college or university. She was encouraged to join different sports teams, enticed into a public speaking contest, cajoled into being a class monitor. The result was that she began to find herself in the company of different kids, kids like herself who were moving out of their comfort zones.

But Sophie still had to live in the world her sister ruled. At home Sophie could rant and swear every bit as well as Patricia. She liked to hang in her sister's shadow when out on the street. There, she was known not just as Patricia's twin, but as the smarter, more athletic of the two. Her friends at home still accepted her because she still played by their rules. At least she did at first.

As Sophie grew she became more adept at staking out her individual identity with her peers. She was still limited by the peer groups she could find, so her first step was to tell them how she was different. She was well motivated in this regard. Take for example her decision not to abuse drugs or get into other serious trouble. "Like, to go out partying and get drunk or high and go do this and go do that and go somewhere where I'm not supposed to be and stay out past my curfew, I don't do that stuff," she told me. "I have standards for myself. Like, I won't do anything anybody else tells me."

"How did you decide all this?" I asked.

"Like, I see my mom and some other people who drink and I just know there's no way I'm gonna become like that. That's not gonna be my life. It might be my sister's, but not mine."

Mirroring

It would be her life if she didn't find something else to be. That's where the mirroring of others around her, both her peers and adults, help. When Sophie looks into their faces, she sees things about herself that make her stand out from the friends she grew up with. The more youth drift between peer groups, the more likely they are to find what talents lie hidden beneath the identities forced upon them.

I try to orchestrate these experiences. Case conferences are usually just an excuse for everyone at the table, parents included, to pitch in their two cents and add to a child's problem-saturated identity. Peer groups can do the reverse. They can offer a child a healthy identity story. Rather than put endless energy into having adults discuss kids, I prefer to talk with kids themselves about each other. I love to invite into my office the friends of the youth with whom I work. I usually get the kids I'm working with to extend an invitation on my behalf. Then we talk. We'll talk about their group, about what they like about their lives, about their parents, and what they find difficult or pleasant about those relationships.

A parent can do the same thing by making space for adolescents to bring home their friends. Get to know those kids, if they'll let you, and try to understand why they have made the choices they did. While they're in your home it's especially important to do two things. First, look at them closely and try to see the positive and powerful things that your teenager likes about his or her friends. Ask yourself, "What is it that draws my youngster to these kids?" That's a critical question, one you can ask your child directly after the friends are gone. What is it that they mirror back that your son or daughter likes? There has to be some good reason for the relationship, as practically every child has more than one choice.

Second, take a close look at how your child's friends are looking at your kid. What role does your child play for them?

In Sophie's case, I met some of her friends, more by chance than design, at her home during a visit to meet with her mother. There in the living room were three girls and two boys who had dropped around for a few minutes. Doing my best to not be bashful I sat down with them for a while and asked them about themselves.

"You're Sophie and Patricia's friends?" I said innocently and then introduced myself and why I was there. Sophie piped up, "He's our shrink," to which she got a chuckle and we were off and rolling.

"I've wanted to meet some of the girls' friends for some time. I hear you made quite the splash on the front page of the newspaper," I said, referring to a recent article about this group of kids in the community weekly. That article had portrayed Patricia as the good-for-nothing leader of a bunch of out-of-control youth. I had just paid them the highest compliment I could. Suddenly there were five Bonnie and Clydes anxious to tell me their stories. Starting with recognition of teenagers' strengths, no matter what those strengths are, is often the best enticement for them to speak.

"But you're telling me mostly about what Patricia does. I'm just as curious about Sophie. How is she different? What's special about her?" Shy giggles, hesitation, a few "Ahh, well . . ."s. Then Sophie's closest friend said, "She's just nice, that's all. You know. Like the rest of us get into lots of trouble, but she doesn't. Except with her mom." They laughed. "She does really well at school, and does sports. None of us are much into that stuff."

It wasn't anything I didn't know already, but it told me that Sophie had managed to drift successfully back and forth between this group and her peers at school. In the to-ing and fro-ing she'd managed to convince everyone of her talents, and be accepted for what she wanted to be. But she had only learned that talent for negotiating a healthy identity through the experience of moving back and forth between groups.

Later, speaking with Sophie alone, I asked her about these friends of hers. "They're all great people, just not like me – they get into trouble sometimes. I guess I'm a bit different."

"What about your life at school?" I asked, trying to help her compare the two, to see what she made of the differences between her peer groups.

"It's not just my friends at school, but the teachers too. Like, there's this one teacher, I don't know if I'm his favourite student but he really treats me very good. I think the other kids see that and so don't just think of me like my sister. Patricia could do what I'm doing, but she doesn't want to."

I'd have thought that keeping up with her neighbourhood friends would drag Sophie down, but this was never the case. That's just the old peer pressure myth disguised. It was while negotiating a new identity with her old friends that Sophie developed the skills she needed to write a new story for herself with kids very different from her whom she met at school.

Besides, in the event that children make mistakes in their choices, the solution is to help them cope with the problems which arise, not to restrict future choices. Our job as caregivers is not to solve our kids' problems as much as to hold our children's hands while they get on with the hard work of growing up and figuring out who they are. Real consequences are far better teachers in life than the fictions we can preach to our children. Most kids who mess up know they mess up and don't need to be reminded.

A year later, when Patricia and Sophie had a party while their mother was gone overnight, I heard their friends had trashed the home. Both girls knew afterwards that they had let things get out of hand. The problem was now to fix the place up, make amends and to think long and hard about the friends they keep. Sophie was much more distressed by what happened than Patricia, who had too much at stake to get haughty with her friends. No such chains on Sophie who let loose on some of the same kids I'd met. They forgave her for her rant and even admitted that it was pretty crappy what they'd done. A broken window on the rental unit was still the girls' responsibility to replace with birthday money, but there were no other long-term consequences.

I never want to live that type of crisis, but if I do, then I hope I can remember to keep my cool enough to help my kid learn from his or her mistake. If children are going to have friends like those then they are going to get painted with the same brush. That can be a healthy experience once in a while. If their friends are not like that, then the act of deciding they are different will immunize them against other more dangerous behaviours later in life. That's my wish for my children: that they have the wisdom to know who they are and the skills to share with others the stories they tell about themselves.

The best way to help our teens nurture a diverse group of friends is to help them find opportunities to display their talents. Ever been down at the local rink and seen a parent rooting for a child who looks as awkward on ice as a fish on a bicycle? At times like those I'm left wondering if maybe the child wouldn't rather be somewhere else. It's a fine balance, but in general, if a teen appears to have a talent, then the

"Try it three times, then you can quit" rule seems to get the best results. Certainly, some kids need to be pushed towards greatness. But if pushed into dangerous shark-infested waters, then the wary youngster is more likely to respond with anger, mistrust of his or her caregivers, and finally, a diminished sense of self-esteem. It's important that we give children opportunities to lead us to where they feel safe while also showing we believe in them and what they can become.

I remember taking Connor, a smooth talking 17-year-old, to see a career counselor at a local university to discuss if there was a way to interest her in attending. She was the type of kid who would surely make an excellent lawyer, and in fact had already defended herself on several charges. I can still recall the day she'd dressed the part of the barrister and eloquently told the judge to consider the facts as she'd presented them and release her. It hadn't worked, but she had impressed both her friends and the staff of the community facility where she continued to be housed. It just made sense that this kid find her way to a university even though no one in her family had made it past grade twelve. At the time, the only option she could see for herself was to pursue a trade. It's not that that was a bad idea, only I'm not sure Connor had ever been told that university was even an option.

We toured the campus, sat in on a class, met with a counselor, and had lunch. By the end of the day, Connor could at least see that becoming part of an institution of higher learning was an achievable goal. She looked the same as the other kids and she certainly understood what they were talking about in class. But these things alone would never be enough to draw a youth like Connor.

The Adventure Factor

What I've learned is that at-risk kids also need an adventure factor to be part of anything they do. Like the girl who can't go to the all-night drunk, it's not enough we offer kids sensible choices and expect them to be reasonable and take them. There has to be a hook, something that makes them feel a little on the edge, a little gritty, a little exposed. While there is nothing wrong with an orderly calm 9-to-5 existence, that world won't entice our children. I often chuckle when I think back to Connor's visit to campus. I thought the adventure of higher learning would be the draw of a challenging education. Not so. For her, the adventure factor was all the young men she saw while there and the hormonal rush she experienced. Needless to say, touring the sports facility had been an eye opener for her.

Sadly, none of it was enough to motivate her to go. Connor has yet to make it to university. She did go to college for half a semester, then dropped out. Last I heard she'd left home. I'm still hopeful, though, that she'll realize her potential some day. I can only speculate that Connor may have been afraid of what she would find at university. She'd certainly have been more emotionally vulnerable there. She would have had much more worthy opponents academically and socially. She never talked about this, but in the days following our visit, I remember a moodiness and reticence in her I hadn't seen before.

Leading our children to new peer groups needn't be as clever as this stunt I pulled with Connor. Most communities have numerous outlets for youth to express themselves. We needn't be shy about sharing with children in our care much of who we are. Our personal interests are often the best bridges to inclusion for at-risk teens. We need to ask ourselves what are we ourselves doing on a Saturday night? How do we find adventure in our lives? What is our lifestyle? Who are our friends? In the answers to these questions we may find clues to the places kids might want to drift as well.

There are no easy solutions to encouraging diversity in peer associations. It becomes even more difficult to help teens when they face social and financial barriers such as race, class and ethnicity, not to mention poor academic performance, mental illnesses, physical challenges, and histories of abuse and neglect. When these barriers are compounded, they can make the risks facing a child appear insurmountable. At such times, I encourage parents to seek help. Any assistance can be much appreciated. Aunts and uncles, grandparents, the corner shopkeeper, a teacher or other professional, the local church, recreation centre or sports club can all be a source of support to our teenagers. If we can't find a way to build bridges for our children from one group to another, then perhaps others can.

Chapter 5
"I'm Okay, You're Not"

Jacintha, the young woman who flicked a lit cigarette at her father after he slapped her, told me once with great enthusiasm, "Everyone likes to have friends and you feel important when you have lots of friends surrounding you all the time." She especially liked it when her friends came to her with their problems. It seemed to say to her that she was trustworthy and important. "I find it easier to solve other people's problems than my own," she told me, half laughing. It's a role she cherishes, and one which allows her to demonstrate the same talents other youth show in school or at music. Strange, but I often hear parents say they wish their children would stop being so available to help their friends and look after their own lives better. I've learned the two go hand in hand.

Helping others, teenagers develop the skills to help themselves, as well as a story about themselves as strong and competent. It's that story which is critical to their success. As Jacintha explained, "I have more knowledge than my friends, or so they think, and I'm the tough one in the group. I protect them if they get into any type of trouble like fights and I would be there to save them. . . . I've gotten so many letters from my friends saying 'It's so good that I can talk to you' and 'I trust you so much.' I love getting those letters. They make me feel so good that people look up to me."

It took some time, but eventually Jacintha's parents came to appreciate just as much as their daughter her special talent as a good friend. This, despite the risks they perceived when she hung out with youth who were already getting into serious trouble. It's difficult, but important, that we as parents and caregivers not jump to conclusions about our children's identities, conclusions which can inadvertently leave them having to defend themselves against put-downs they don't deserve. They frequently know better than us who is "okay" and who is not.

Sticks and Stones

"Sticks and stones may break my bones but names will *really* hurt me." Most youth I meet, good, bad or otherwise, tell me over and over again that if they are going to be healthy in mind, body and spirit, they need to know that others hold them in high regard. If they feel rejected in one sphere of their lives, they will go seeking acceptance in another.

Mark was one of the first to explain this simple truth to me. I remember the first time we met at the centre where I worked. I could hear Mark's measured foot steps even before his hulking form filled my doorway. We politely shook hands, mine up to the wrist disappearing inside his enormous mitt. Mark is a big fellow. At age fourteen he stood well over six feet, and well beyond 250 pounds. A giant compared to his peers, he would fit in well on a varsity football squad. Though he was a gentle giant by the time I met him, his parents tell tales of having trouble restraining his violent outbursts as early as age three. By grade one he was an 85-pound, 6-year-old who, when in the full throws of a temper tantrum, could be remarkably dangerous, both to himself and anyone nearby. It didn't surprise me that Mark had been stuck with labels over which he felt little or no control since a young age.

His parents had compensated for their son's size and temper by becoming extra vigilant to his moods. They had had to keep a constant eye on him. Despite the ever-present tension in their home, they had never abused him, and were deeply hurt that their son was fixated on killing himself. Starting when he was very young, they had been Mark's conscience, having to hold his impulsive outbursts in check. Roy, his father, recalled sitting with his son on the floor, his back against a wall, Mark between his legs which remained crossed over the boy, Roy's burly arms wrapped around Mark's chest, the boy's hands held down by his sides. Mark would struggle and plead to be freed but if let go would persist in flailing himself around, attacking anyone who came close. Those awful sessions in which Mark would have to be restrained could last thirty minutes or more until, exhausted, Mark would calm down. Thankfully, Mark's father was a big man himself.

Mark's parents said it felt like their six-year-old, at age fourteen, had stopped growing on the inside, but had woken up one day to find himself in a man's body. The implications were scaring everyone. It was like the entire family was on guard against Mark and what he could do to himself or others.

Roy worked as a computer programmer. Mark's mother, Alisha, was a retail associate with a local women's clothing store. They lived in a comfortable older home in an area of town being slowly gentrified, watching their neighbourhood transformed by wealthy well-educated people who were buying cheaper properties and calling them "heritage." Mark had watched his street change almost as much as his body. Now in the throes of adolescence and a hormonal onslaught, Mark knew others around him felt he had become even more of a danger to himself and others than when he was a little kid. Like his home, he himself seemed to be fitting in less and less with his surroundings.

When I met him, Mark was just back from six months on a closed psychiatric unit for teens. He'd been placed there after laying in a bathtub of warm water and carving his wrists until the water turned red. Thankfully, he'd sliced crosswise and survived. His parents had known something was up. Mark had been actually more compliant, better at sharing his stuff with his nine-year-old brother, and had fewer outburst prior to the incident. He'd come home from school and all but disappear, take long showers, tidy his room. Each change, in itself, seemed innocent enough.

By the time we met, Mark had successfully finished his in-patient treatment and needed some after-care in his community. That was when I became a part of his life, a connection that would last well over a year. All five of us met in my office, which tended to feel cramped or cozy, depending on your perspective, at the best of times. With Mark and his family present, it felt like I was in a land of giants.

When I'd meet Mark alone, which he preferred, he would tell me he always felt "tight" during family sessions. It was like he was that six-year-old again, being forcibly restrained from not just saying what he wanted, but being what he wanted. It was Mark who helped me understand the connection between feeling emotionally healthy and experiences of control and competence.

I asked him once what mental health meant to him. He thought about the question for just a moment, then shuffled his feet, sighed and sat erect. "Definitely being able to cope with life and my problems and to control my emotions," he told me with emphasis on the word control. "And not being so severe in cases when I get angry, not going into a rage. When I get depressed not sinking so low, you know? Just able to control it." He paused.

"Anything else?" I asked.

"Yeah, being in control of your mind. Thinking I'm an okay person. Being inside that hospital you have to be really mentally strong."

"It seems like you've been told that you're out of control a lot. If I'm hearing right, your parents are saying you have to change your behaviour, or maybe that you have problems," I said calmly. "If that's the case, then what's going to happen?"

Mark just smiled. "They know shit," was all he said and changed the topic.

An adolescent can't experience control over their mind, much less the labels which attach to them, unless they have experiences which convince them they are in control. This is where both peers and families play a role. Both are forums in which the adolescent can find these experiences which attest to his or her personhood. Even when these experiences are negative, they still offer the teen the hope they will have some say over their destiny. Each experience adds to an evolving story about what a young person is capable of doing. These stories, as they grow, offer an identity and names by which the child will be known. The turbulent times many families experience might be thought of as pitched battles to see whose labels are going to stick with the strongest glue. Names can be a dangerous weapon. Mark knew this, as did many of his peers. What teens need is to know it's okay to be themselves in all their complexity. Ofttimes what they hear are instructions telling them otherwise.

When we met weeks later, Mark and I talked more about what makes a youth mentally healthy. He took me on a guided tour.

"When I was younger I wasn't teased at school. It's like at that age it almost doesn't matter what you do unless you do something really horrible, people will like you. But even then I was picked on and teased by some people. And then in grade three and four, I definitely was."

"Must have been rough," I said, encouraging him to continue.

He paused, stared at the floor for just a minute, then came back to his story, as if he was really telling it to impress himself. "I think I left that school without a friend there. They just decided I was different and that was no good. They didn't like me because I was different. I'm different because I'm overweight. It's all it took. And then they tie in glasses with it just for the extra jab!" Marks fist shot out like a George Foreman punch, a big fleshy arm flashing by my face, his fist inches from my head. I gave a start, took a breath and nodded. He dropped his arm back down casually at his side, as if in defeat.

"I wanted to be like everyone else, to hang out with all the cool people, to at least have some friends, you know. I never really did fit with anyone until grade six. What I've noticed is that once you get older, people get more open-minded and accept people for who they are. And like in grade six it sort of started and got better and better. I was different but so is everyone else.

"I remember talking to this girl a couple of times and this guy just kept insisting that we were going out, which we weren't, only he was really rude about it. But what's ironic is that by the end of the year I was pretty much friends with everyone at the school, even him. It was great at school. I could talk to whoever I wanted."

"Sounds wonderful," I said.

"It was great, but it also wasn't that great sometimes because I was still insecure. And worrying. And like, I mean, I would be talking to a whole group of people and be wondering to myself what they really think of me. Were they using me, or did they really like me, or was it one of those things that they really hated me but couldn't tell me." Mark was looking at me, his eyes puffy, his gaze intent. He'd stopped slouching, his arms were up again waving in front of him, only this time not pretending to attack, but pushing aside unpleasant memories, wiping the slate clean of the moments of his life when he had no control.

"Like, I could never trust anyone in that way."

"What about at home?"

"And home was really bad! It was like I would leave home and put a mask on. My life was completely different at home and at school. I was two completely different people. At home I could be mad or depressed or anything. But at school, it could be the movies I like, the music I listen to, stuff like that, I could get teased about anything. So at school I did everything I could to be cool so these people wouldn't reject me. Like, I stopped talking about all the music I really liked or the movies."

"But at home you could fit in?"

"I didn't want to act at school the way I acted at home because I knew I would definitely be rejected. It was like a mask I put on. But it's like a mask to cover up the scar."

"What's the scar?"

"I wasn't really happy at school but I just *acted* like I did to fit in so people wouldn't know how I was really feeling. I hated myself . . . completely." Mark stopped speaking at this point. Our time was almost up, but we would go late and keep his mother waiting outside. He liked to do that sometimes. It struck me as odd that even when it might appear to us that kids are healing, fitting in, they tell me that at times they are just playing at being good. It's not that different from playing at being bad. They use the same skills.

Mark eventually did stop hating himself. Strangely, it was through his relationship with the other patients on the psychiatric ward that he found what he was looking for most. The doctors, he said, did nothing for him, but like Jack Nicholson in *One Flew Over The Cuckoo's Nest* or Winona Ryder in *Girl Interrupted*, the wisdom of those we label insane can sometimes be greater than that of their healers.

"In the hospital everyone knows what your problems are. And you don't get that feeling of rejection because they're in the hospital too," Mark said. He discovered that his being "crazy" was something that could give him a special status among his peers. He had made friends with other kids at school who felt as upset about life as he did. He had become a street-level therapist ferreting out other youth who might be contemplating suicide, a crusader who wanted to convince youngsters to throw their lives with all the gory details right in their parents' faces, rather than throwing their lives away silently.

Finding Normal

I've seen this pattern more and more frequently, now that I understand better what it is: teens in search of health. I watch them moving between parents and peers looking for the support and acceptance they need to author personal stories. Serendipity plays as much a part in this search as the efforts we make as caregivers to push children in this or that direction. While I never understand completely what the teens I meet are doing, I am certain they are on a quest for an environment where they can feel normal and healthy.

As an outsider it can be difficult to understand the meaning of what is being communicated across generations. It can feel like our youth speak in a different language. I remember being taught early in my professional training a valuable lesson about communication. As professionals we're taught to pay attention to people's body language as much as to what they say. The person sitting in front of us arms crossed, bent forward, breathing rapidly, perhaps shaking, may or may not be experiencing severe trauma. The office window may be open and a draft blowing down their back.

With kids it is much the same. We have tended to overly psychologize what we see them doing. Sometimes they are simply nurturing or maintaining their mental health. What we label as disordered behaviour may be nothing more than a survival strategy. The "illness" we see can sometimes have more to do with the politics of labelling than with mental health. Sometimes we just have to close a window, but instead we medicate, treat, and institutionalize. When we hand over some of our control over the definition of mental health to teens, we find them and their peer groups doing whatever they need to do to stay healthy.

Let me give an example. Fifteen-year-old Gaetan, whom I met some years ago while working with a Children's Aid Society, knew exactly what he needed to do to survive. Far from thinking of himself as an emotionally disturbed child, Gaetan fights an uphill battle to be declared a leader among his delinquent peers and a strong independent child by his community.

"Mental health to me is having lots of friends, going out, being liked, knowing that you're accepted, just knowing that you're really in with at least one person keeps you mentally stable."

"And who likes you?" I asked during one of our scheduled meetings at his home. His mother had left the room so it was just Gaetan and his younger sister, Stacey, who remained curled up on a chair in the living room where we were meeting.

"Well, my mom of course. And most of the kids I hang out with. We might not say it like that but I think they're really there for me." Stacey looked offended.

"What about me?"

Gaetan just laughed. "Oh yeah, like I'm going to say that in front of you." Gaetan waved a theatrical fist at his sister who pretended to spit back in Gaetan's face. It was about then that their mom returned and told them both to stop being rude.

A few weeks later, Gaetan and I had a chance to speak alone. He was excited when we met and pulled out of his pocket a much tattered school board notice which warned parents there was gang activity at their school and advised ways to prevent their kids from becoming involved. It seemed to Gaetan that he and his friends who hung around the school parking lot were being singled out as a problem. For a kid from the wrong side of the tracks, with two alcoholic parents, and little hope of ever finishing school, he must have figured to be at the centre of a controversy was his fifteen minutes of fame.

"They took a picture of us one day. We were all just sitting there outside the school. Some of the teachers called us slang and trash. They think we're no good. I don't know why they think that." He wasn't upset in the least, just defensive, with a kind of in-your-face rhetoric that begged me to understand, but also told me to just sit there and listen. I knew a few of his friends. A motley crew of boys and girls who smoked, and most weekends found some way to get into trouble. Gaetan felt he had been singled out, not by name but by description, as one of the principle troublemakers, a kid parents and teachers thought was always fighting and out to prove how tough he was.

Gaetan's mother was not happy about her son's notoriety, but then, when I talked with her later, she just shrugged. "What can I do?"

she said. "He won't do nothing I tell him. Last time he got pissed off he stole my car and smashed the bumper. I had him charged but his probation officer said nothing much was gonna happen even if he got back to court."

Gaetan on the other hand was pleased. Now he had his status. And now his whole group had their status. He was feeling great, like he finally counted for something. Who was I to argue?

It would be some time later that we managed to talk about this again, only this time I wondered aloud if any of the leadership skills he demonstrated with his peers got used in other parts of his life. Is he always the delinquent, the kid everyone is told to hate?

"I don't usually want to fight actually. When I was playing sports I never got into a fight. But people are always talking, like they go 'Gaetan, you're so tough' and they want to fight. Actually sometimes I stand up and tell my class to 'Shut up.' Like sometimes when everyone is fooling around and the teacher can't do anything, I say, 'Shut up or I'll beat you in the head.' It's great. This year I get along with all my teachers."

It was a start, I figured. We would go down this same path again. Only this next time I wanted to see if Gaetan had any other story to tell about himself.

"Do you know what other people think of you, besides the school administrators and your friends?"

He immediately thought of the court ordered assessment done on him to advise the judge in sentencing on charges related to some park vandalism. "Yeah, I read my predisposition report and it said how I assaulted a person before and all that. And I look at somebody else and think that person's cool but deep inside I know that person's a retard because they're just messing up their life. Like, I look down on myself for all this. Really. I know I shouldn't have done what I did, but nobody really understands either."

Despite sentiments to the contrary, Gaetan's behaviour is an ongoing spectacle meant to keep his attention diverted from the sad truth of how little power he has. On the street, with his peers he pushes aside some of his feelings of inadequacy, the stark knowledge of his poverty, his neglect by his parents, even his loneliness. He likes himself best when he can imagine himself in the fiction he and his friends create for their audience of adults.

The street saves him. But that salvation comes at a price. What Gaetan forgets is that his parents reject their son in part because of his behaviour. At school, though Gaetan has the potential to be a good student, he frustrates his teachers who do not understand what he's up to or why.

Drifting

Fight or flight, anger or depression, delinquency or community work? The possible pathways that youth can follow towards healthy coping are too numerous to imagine. Youth work with whatever they have been given or can find. A modern day parable might help make this clearer.

A Story of Drift

Once upon a time an adolescent found himself (or herself) adrift on a vast ocean. He couldn't quite remember how he had come to be there, only that as if out of a dream he had one day awoken to find himself alone and at sea. He had enough food and water to survive a long time in his small wooden craft, and over time easily mastered the skills he needed to survive the elements. He wasn't particularly afraid, feeling somehow in control of everything about him except the forces of nature: the wind and sea, the sun and the rain. He felt strangely safe there in his little boat. But something was still amiss. He was lonely and, therefore, not very happy.

What he longed for most were others who would be his friends. He missed his parents too, but somehow he knew he would see them again. Even here in the middle of an ocean, their presence was like the salt in the water which lapped against his boat – invisible, yet perceptible in the spray and mists that soaked into him. He would have to content himself with his solitude until he could reach landfall. While at first that had seemed a daunting task, navigating was becoming easier with each passing day.

His craft, though small and seaworthy, was easily buffeted by the winds of chance that blew from all directions. When he had first awoken and found himself with one hand on the tiller of his small boat and sail unfurled, any small gust would take him wherever it liked, leaving the boy at the mercy of nature's forces. Day by day, though, his experience as a helmsman grew, and he became better able to pilot his boat to distant islands that appeared like bright beacons in the intense noon-day sun. Winds that had once forced him farther out to sea were now tamed and by using rudder, sail, and on calm days, oars, he began to direct his craft wherever he wished. However, despite his new skills, he could not always reach those distant lands. Sometimes unexpected storms would cause him great concern and he and his boat would come perilously close to capsizing.

Then one day, through courage and good fortune, he found his way to an island nestled in an archipelago snaking across the sea like the stars in a constellation. The island had been the easiest to get to and he was pleased with himself and his growing skill as a sailor. He landed there and quickly realized he was not alone. The island's inhabitants had a unique culture, and they quickly accepted the boy as one of their own when he displayed the special talents and skills the islanders valued. When he first landed, the boy hadn't been sure what these people expected of him, but he soon found that with all the skills he had acquired through his adventures over the previous months, he was well equipped to impress them with at least some of the special things he could do. On that island the boy was pleased to be given the name ____ which let him and others know he belonged there. He quickly came to enjoy his new identity. By acting like the other islanders he found the friends he had been seeking. He also learned that by being one of these islanders he acquired the same status shared by everyone who lived there. These inhabitants were feared and respected by their neighbours.

Time passed and the boy grew. He discovered new talents now that he was older and living back on land. However, as the seasons changed he became tired of the pattern of life in his adopted homeland. He wanted the islanders to continue to accept him when he showed them the new skills he had been practising, but they refused. They only valued him for the skills and talents he had shown when he first came to them. When he showed them what else he could do, they didn't celebrate his accomplishments, but scorned and ridiculed him. For the boy's efforts to be different he was given another name, ____, only this one made him feel stupid and isolated him from others. Frustrated, angry and depressed, the boy returned to his boat and set himself adrift once again, anxious to find a place where he could share with people the person he had become.

The boy kept repeating these adventures and became very adept at fitting in wherever he found himself. He came to realize that the only thing worse than having to be someone different on each island was being alone at sea, where he felt he had no identity, and no recognition from anyone for how special he was. More time passed and he was beginning to notice a change in how he behaved on each island to which he travelled. On one of these islands he had finally been able to convince a few of the inhabitants that his way of doing things, learned through his now numerous travels, was just as good as theirs. Even if the islanders never changed and did things how he did them, they were willing to let the boy do as he pleased, as it harmed no one and they enjoyed seeing him happy.

Little by little the boy was learning many new skills necessary for his travel and was soon ready to set sail again. Only this time, rather than drifting aimlessly, he very purposefully navigated his way back to one of the islands he had landed on previously. There, he proved to himself that he was capable of convincing the local inhabitants he could be different than them, and still be a valued member of their island community. What's more, he was able to challenge some of them with his ideas and began to find others who liked his ways of doing things more than their own. While he never settled on that island, he began to understand that he could be accepted for who he was wherever he went. It was at that point that he realized he was very happy.

One might think of all youth as adrift on just such a vast ocean, across which snakes an archipelago of tropical islands, each populated by different people. High-risk teens, and indeed I suspect all teens, when fed up with simply acquiring, maintaining and challenging the identity constructions they find on one island sometimes have the choice to set sail again and take the chance that the winds and currents of life, combined with their strength and talent as a voyager, will allow them to drift to someplace else where they can be more the person they want to be. Of course, this adventure depends on whether the youth's boat is seaworthy, and the happenstance of what life brings. Details such as multiple family moves, incarcerations, hospitalizations and subsequent releases, will play a role in how teens drift between labels. At-risk teens just have fewer labels to find than kids who come from more privileged positions in life. The risk factors which challenge them limit their choices and are forever threatening the trajectory of their growth and development.

Navigating their way around negative labels can be done in one of two ways. Teens can stay where they are and fight to be seen differently, or go travelling. In the first case, the child shuffles the deck in the hope of being dealt a better hand. This works well for children who come from more stable homes and communities where their needs are being met. My neighbour's son recently gave up Band at school, preferring to put more time into sports. He'll still have time to play some music. Much to his parents' chagrin, he's part of a heavy metal group he formed out in the garage with a few friends. From what I've heard so far, I don't think I'll be buying an album of theirs too soon. But at least he had choices. As one door closed, another was sure to open.

Moving between social "islands" and the identity constructions that each offers is a much bigger challenge to the identities assigned high-risk youth by their families and communities. The older the child, the easier it is for him or her to move. Change like this is akin to the gambler who not only changes casinos, but also the game being played. If a gambler likes being a gambler, then there is no need to change that part of his or her story. But in some cases, gamblers get tired of being seen as gamblers. They might take that love of risk and chance and put that same talent to good use as a stock broker, circus performer, high steel construction worker or emergency room physician. So it is with high-risk youth and the negative identities that attach to them. Some adolescents manage to transform themselves into something of benefit to others, some simply find ways to express these same identities in less destructive, more acceptable ways. Good parenting, and good clinical work, starts with understanding the strengths hidden beneath troubling behaviours.

This is what I try to do with teens – extract the good from what they are doing and, hopefully, manage to find a new place for its expression. If I'm successful, and engaging, they leave their more destructive behaviours behind, opting instead for wider acceptance of the talents I help nurture into existence. Drifting between groups of peers is one way teens do this all on their own. Peer groups don't force identities on teens; youth use their groups to express aspects of personal identities that bring them the most power and acceptance. The drifting can either be purposeful or the result of chance. In either case change results.

This idea of drift has always had a dark and evil connotation. It has usually been thought of by researchers, such as David Matza, as a drift "down" into subcultures that challenge the status quo and put our children at even greater risk than what they experienced where they were previously. There is the sense that youth drifts aimlessly. And we continue to talk about our children "drifting" into drugs, or gangs, onto the streets, into prostitution, or into jail. What we have failed to see is how this drift, in whichever direction, allows youth to reach places where they feel valued, hold responsibility for themselves and others, feel competent, safe, and where the relationships they have bolster their mental health. Understood this way, a crack house can do much the same thing as a safe house, a night of under-aged drinking the same as midnight basketball in a local high school gym. The choice depends as much on what resources are available, and how much power each gives a teenager, as on the sense each makes and the consequences each brings. Just because we "build it" doesn't mean teens will come, unless we understand how participation affects the stories teens tell about themselves. I certainly don't want our children to need to drift into dangerous lifestyles, and while my work has focussed on helping youth drift elsewhere, I am more aware now than ever of the real reason kids drift into trouble. Counter-intuitively, they are on a search for health.

We would have needed a satellite to keep track of all the drifting around that William did. I worked with Will for many years, right up until his death shortly before his seventeenth birthday from a drug overdose. Will was a child full of wit, though his humour was dry and often pointed. It was difficult not to like him even when you found out all the crazy things he was up to. His parents had put up with him for years, intercepting the school and community who more than once had come knocking on their door for retribution or restitution for what Will had done. Broken windows, stolen motorbikes, swearing, assaults, petty vandalism – it seemed weekly there was something else Will had ruined which needed fixing. His parents are great people. Chuck, his father, is a golf pro, his mother Tina a dog groomer. His older sister is into track and field, and does well at school. Their home is a tidy bungalow in a small town, away from most of the problems we associate with big cities. How Will ever managed to create for himself a progressively more dangerous identity mystifies me to this day.

Shortly after he turned twelve, he found himself in hospital for the first time. He bounced from there back home, to a residential adolescent mental health treatment facility, back home, then into custody, to an aunt's home for a time, back to treatment, this time on a hospital pediatrics ward for suicidal and drug-addicted youth, and then into a drug rehabilitation centre. In between he found the time to associate with a group of kids who were equally adept at manipulating the system to do whatever they wanted it to do.

"When my friends heard I was inside again, some of them applauded me. Some of them said, 'Right on!' 'Good job!' 'I thought you had it in ya!' My other friends put their heads down and said, 'It wasn't worth it, Will, screwing up your life.'"

"What do you think about both opinions?" I asked.

"I think that the people who are saying that it's good are stupid. 'Cause it's not good and I can see that. The ones who are saying to me that my life's destroyed, I'm saying, 'I'm only fifteen, I should be out having fun.'" Will and I had this conversation during a forced hospitalized while he was on probation; the court was not willing to leave him on the street because of his escalating pattern of drug addiction, violence and property crimes. He and another friend had been high and needing some money for more drugs when they'd robbed a small convenience store of $85. Unfortunately, one of Will's friends had smashed a pop bottle over a clerk's head when he told them to get out of his store. All four were picked up shortly after while walking away from the store. Will understood the seriousness of what he had done, knew that he had screwed up. But he had by that time nothing else upon which to build an identity. His drift for years had been straight down and into a life of crime.

The team who worked with him, including his parents, were always at a loss to explain Will's behaviour. All we knew was that for Will opportunities had presented themselves and whereas most kids would have turned away from them, Will was intrigued by the fast-paced lifestyle of the problem kid, the money to be had dealing drugs and stealing, and the status it all brought him with his peers.

I asked Will once, "How did you meet those friends of yours, the ones who are all in trouble that you told me about? Most of them are older than you, aren't they?"

"When I was in need, all you people out there that are good people didn't give a shit, but the people you call 'scum' and that gave a shit. It wasn't just to see a young kid they could hook on drugs. It had nothing to do with that. Nobody put the drugs in my hand. Nobody said take them. But they offered me a warm place to stay and food to eat. Didn't even offer me drugs. They used them, right, and I asked them if I could have them and they were like, 'Sure, go for it.'"

Will had found his way to these people when he had run from home, though he already experimented with drugs and drinking long before he actually found a crowd where he felt he belonged.

"I had no place to stay and I was out on the street for three or four days," he told me. "I got a little bit of dope off one of them. Buddy said, 'I've seen you around a lot,' and I said, 'Yeah, I'm on the street for a while.' He just said, 'Not no longer.' Just like that. He didn't know me from a hole in the ground."

"Was there anything expected in return?" I wanted to know.

"Not a thing. I did things for return, but nobody asked anything of me. I'd make runs for them, deliver things. I'd have stayed with them, but the police kept picking me up, taking me back home or to the group home, now the hospital. I hate being in these places. It sucks. Everyone just thinks they can run my life."

Not unexpectedly, Will looked at that moment anything but like he could run his own life. In secure treatment, alone, he was still slightly shaken from how much he had messed up. He was really still just a kid, but in way over his head. As the months went by he would admit that he had screwed up pretty badly, would try to get back to his family and argue for them to take him home, would argue that he really understood what he had done. But right then, at that moment while we were talking, what he wanted to convince me was that he had his life under control, at least when he was on the street.

"When I'm on the outside I think I'm doing a good job and I hate people telling me what to do. I hate it. My friends have taught me how to handle myself and to not let people tell me what to do and try to push me around and take things from me. How to scam different things, how to get money. It all works."

Will had drifted out of a home where he had always felt different and into a world where, oddly, he felt he belonged. "I've always been different. I can't explain it. My family's supportive and all. They know I make bad decisions, though. I've always made bad decisions. There's a piece of cake over there, there's a piece of dope over here." He was sitting in front of me, his arms stretched to the sides. "And I know, I just know," he continued, "eating that cake over there would be better for me in the long run than smoking that, but I'd just always go for the thing that not's so great.

"My friends are like that too. It's pretty good with them, except they're all in jail now. There might be two, maybe three, that ain't."

"What kinds of things did they do to get in jail?" I asked.

"Assaults. One's up for murder, two's up for murder." Will told me this like I would tell my neighbour there's a special on hardwood flooring at the hardware store, matter-of-fact, and without any embarrassment. "That fellow they're accusing of rape of that little girl. Him too. I don't know, they're all in jail for different things, robberies and stuff."

"And what's it like being in their company?"

"Proud!" That was all he said; smiling and boastful, he just sat there, letting that word echo amongst the din of other residents whose voices could be heard beyond the room where we were talking on the ward that housed him.

"Do you have any friends that haven't been in jail?" I asked after a time.

"Yeah," Will shrugged. "They're boring 'cause they just don't ever want to do anything that's fun. Like get high, cause trouble. Right now, if you're gonna be my friend you've got to like to do drugs."

Will had found the excitement he was looking for. He had left behind the mediocrity he perceived at home and was enjoying his youth in a way that baffled most of us who knew him. But the closer I got to Will, the more his life story made sense. It wasn't a life I'd choose, nor did I want him stuck in this downward spiral, but on the streets Will found acceptance more readily than anywhere else in his life. At home competing with an older sister who was a star in everyone's mind, he'd have had to work much harder to get noticed.

Chance had brought him a peer group who took him in. After that he had searched for opportunities to be an even more dangerous person that had kept him drifting deeper into trouble. Many of his caregivers tried to erect roadblocks in his path. His parents pleaded with the courts, with group homes, with social service administrators for more chances for their son, more treatment, and more help. They would pay for him to join any recreational activity of his choice. Later they would pay for in-patient detox programs. Local youth organizations offered Will work, and the municipality gave him summer employment as part of a program to help at-risk kids. But everything would fail, because for Will, there was no problem. He had managed to maneuver himself to where he wanted to be. His parents followed behind, visiting him in one treatment facility after another.

They would eventually visit their son's body at the morgue after he overdosed. But by that point several of Will's friend had done the same. Somehow, it seemed to all of us who knew him that despite all our best efforts, he was still associating with people who he felt mirrored best his importance. By his actions he had elevated his reputation to that of one of the most reckless youth in the community. It frightened and frustrated his parents beyond measure.

Will's life taught me that not every child will be saved. But I have taken what I learned from him and used it to help other kids who are open to drifting in new directions. I find I am most successful in my work when I show that I understand the power and control that comes with living an oppositional life. For that lesson, I will forever be indebted to Will.

Hope

While drifting, there is always the chance that something new will present itself to help a high-risk youth change his or her course through life. Gaetan has a teacher who likes him, and a social worker who believes he can do better. Even then it still takes personal effort by children to make a move in the right direction, whichever direction that may be.

There is an old joke told about a man of great faith and little wisdom caught in a flood. An evacuation notice is issued and hand delivered to him by Emergency Measures personnel, but he insists on staying put, telling the authorities that his faith in God is absolute and that God will save him. The water rises and the man builds a wall of sandbags around his home. A boat comes by to take him to safety, but he tells those on board to go away. "God will save me," he assures them.

Finally the waters have risen so high he has to climb to the very peak of his roof. A helicopter hovers overhead offering a rope, but still the man insists he is waiting for the Lord, whom he is confident will not let him perish. Well, he of course drowns. When later he is face to face with God he asks the Lord why he wasn't saved. The Lord looks at him in disbelief.

"I sent you a letter, a boat and a helicopter. What more were you expecting?"

It's like that with youth. They drift through their childhoods in search of healthy identities. Sometimes chance opens doors before them, but it is still up to them to seize hold of these opportunities. We too, as caregivers of all stripes, can help provide what teens need but it is up to the teens to avail themselves of what is made accessible.

It's not easy for us to accept that high-risk youth will frequently act out in ways that frustrate our efforts to help them. Not every child, even with opportunities presented to them, will choose to drift to where they are at less risk. Time and again I meet drug addicted teens from middle- and upper-class homes that are fine safe places for children. I also meet wonderful and caring parents from economically vulnerable homes, or homes where there have been forced dislocations, job losses, immigration, or plain bad luck. In both cases, there is no discernible need for the youth in these families to fundamentally challenge the identities they have been offered. There is sufficient choice, love and acceptance to meet a child's need for power, control and competence, or at least that's what it looks like to us adults. But there is also the youth themselves to consider.

For some of them, like Will, there is the allure of other lifestyles. Youth find solutions to the normal developmental challenge of creating a healthy identity by exploring behaviours that cause their families and communities worry and grief. Parents will tend to blame themselves, or the child's peers. Neither strategy will help us understand the patterns of drift in the lives of at-risk youth. Instead, we need to see what these youth do as pathways to resilience, even if we disagree with the choices they have made from the few options they have available.

This needn't discourage us from trying to help. The hopeful side of this drift towards mental health is that clearly youth are actively engaged in a quest. When we accept their pattern of drift as a search for health, and a creative and powerful resistance to the oppressive forces in their lives, then we can join them in their search, better positioned to help rather than hinder their growth.

Chapter 6
Complex Stories for
Complex Lives

Strategy Three: Listen closely to the complex stories young people tell about themselves and their world.

Adolescent lives are more complex than we imagine. We like to think, for example, of someone like Anne Frank, whose story of her two year confinement while hiding from the Nazis during World War Two has become a legendary tale of resilience. And yet, Anne was not the dutiful child one might expect. She writes in her journal of her desperation to be seen as something other than a problem child by her family and the others hiding with them. Remarkable that this girl who could remain absolutely silent for long hours day after day in order to avoid detection could still be mislabeled as a rebellious and quarrelsome teen. "I'm boiling with rage," she wrote, "and yet I mustn't show it. I'd like to stamp my feet, scream, give Mummy a good shaking, cry, and I don't know what else, because of the horrible words, mocking looks, and accusations which are leveled at me repeatedly every day . . . I can't let them see the wounds which they have caused, I couldn't bear their sympathy and their kindhearted jokes, it would only make me want to scream all the more. If I talk, everyone thinks I'm showing off; when I'm silent they think I'm ridiculous; rude if I answer, sly if I get a good idea, lazy if I'm tired, selfish if I eat a mouthful more than I should, stupid, cowardly, crafty . . . ."

Today, the journals of youth who have been placed in care are every bit as poignant when read, their lives intricate tapestries of emotions and unexpressed pain. Our children's truths are embedded in the stories they tell about their lives. But even appreciating a child's own truth is only one step to a deeper understanding of the child and his or her relationships with friends and family. Understanding a teenager's life that one meets in a clinic reminds me of trying to understand a movie's plot when we come in late and have missed all the important opening scenes. In we walk, the plot moves on, relationships between the actors become more complicated and the action is well underway. We may enjoy what we are watching, but there is always that uneasy feeling we've missed out on what's motivating the characters. It gnaws at us because we aren't getting the big picture. Maybe that's why Hollywood keeps producing sequels. Audiences love to feel comfortable and familiar with their stars.

The lives of high-risk youth are no different. Even with our own children, we can feel like we've walked in on their lives because so much of their growth and development takes place among their peers. Judith Rich Harris in her ground-breaking book *The Nurture Assumption*, argues that parents exert a very small influence on their children, far less than expected. While I would agree that children's peers, siblings and cousins are of great importance to the maturing child, I think parents are, like all intimate relationships, just as likely as any other individual to play a large role in the story a child writes about him- or herself.

Just because we are a part of our child's story, however, we mustn't assume we understand the plot more than we really do. Too often, we adults act as if our story about what our children are doing is the story that best describes them. We have tended to think of our stories as the more powerful ones. So much so, that we have codified the stories we adults tell about kids into elaborate classification systems of disease and dysfunction, such as the American Psychiatric Association's *Diagnostic and Statistical Manual of Mental Disorders*, the *DSM-IV*, in order to explain our children's behaviours *to us*. Some children accept these outsiders' views of their world. Many do not. If we give kids half a chance, they may tell us where we've erred.

Take, for example, a child diagnosed with Attention Deficit Hyperactivity Disorder. ADHD has become a common diagnosis for youth having trouble in school or involved in delinquent behaviours. While there is much written to explain why more and more children are being diagnosed and medicated, we hear little from the children themselves about their experiences being labeled with ADHD. We know next to nothing about how the diagnosis affects youngsters' relationships with peers, or how the medications changes their behaviour when they're in unstructured activities.

There have been some pioneering therapists such as David Nylund, a social worker and well known author, who approach their work with these children with curiosity and have tried to open space for youth themselves to describe their experiences of being easily distracted, impulsive and risk-takers. These children tell a refreshingly different story about what it means to have this disorder. They talk about how schools don't suit them, how the thing inside them that others try to medicate away makes them more outgoing than their peers, more alert to what's beyond their classroom, more driven to push the limits of authority. Their story about themselves talks about their strengths and throws questions back at society about what we are expecting children to be.

I chuckle when I meet kids like this. True, they can't cope well with classroom routine, and they tend to be easily excitable, sometimes even annoying to their peers, but they have an energy all their own. I think sometimes that maybe this is just nature's little joke. If we were still hunters and gatherers, living with wild animals all around, these youngsters are the ones who'd excel. While studious folks like me were looking intently at our bellybuttons, we would become easy prey for every hungry foe. But not the kids with ADHD. They'd hear the every crack of twig, every paw's advancing step long before I did. Their scattered attention would save their skins while I'd be eaten for lunch. I think these youth challenge us to think again what it is we expect of our children.

Here's the problem.

I sat in on an interview recently between an adolescent girl, Candice, her parents and a colleague of mine, a family doctor who specializes in seeing children with this disorder.

"So you've been having trouble in school, eh?" she said.

"Uh huh," Candice nodded.

"The teachers think she's not learning, not because she can't but that there's something else wrong. They told us to ask you about ADHD," said Candice's mother.

"Yes, I have the reports from the teacher," the doctor continued. "Let me ask Candice a few questions. How do you do in class? Do you find it hard to sit still? Are you talkative? Anything like that?" she asked.

"Sometimes," said Candice.

"And at home, do you get into lots of arguments with your parents?"

"Sometimes." She was squirming lower and lower in her seat by this point.

"Do you ever find yourself checking things twice, like making sure a lid is on, or double checking a door, things like that?"

"Maybe, yeah, I guess."

"And when you eat, do you eat a little bit of meat, a little vegetable, a little potato, or do you eat all of one thing, then the next, and then the next?"

"No, I guess I would eat all one thing like the meat, then maybe the potatoes, maybe the vegetables at the end."

"If I read you out a list of numbers, can you try to remember them and repeat them back to me?"

"Sure," Candice answered, a spark of life returning to her otherwise melancholy voice. The doctor read the list, and Candice repeated it back perfectly. I admit I couldn't have done it. The doctor shook her head as if she'd expected this, obviously not pleased.

"I've always been great with numbers," Candice explained. "I can remember all my friends' phone numbers, even if I hear them just once. I can remember anything with numbers, like times tables, or amounts of stuff, really anything."

"It's almost like an obsessive thing then for you, this remembering?" the doctor asked her.

"Well, sort of, yeah," Candice replied, confused.

That was it, more or less. The doctor spoke for the next fifteen minutes about ADHD, about what the medications could do, and promised that the side effects would be minimal. Labeled and medicated, we left the office, Candice in tow.

She started taking the medications, but found they killed her appetite, made her stare at walls so much everyone but the druggies at school began to tease her about being stoned. She was, though, better able to concentrate on her school work. Her grades went up slightly. Soon, though, Candice started hiding her medication, preferring to sell it to other kids than use it herself. Her behaviour at home remained a problem. She and her parents still argued. She wound up back on my caseload.

By this point I knew a fair bit about Candice, but we hadn't talked about what had happened when she was diagnosed. Nobody had asked her what she thought her problem was, nor how she explained her behaviour in the context of her entire life history.

"Your parents tell me you've stopped taking your meds and that your marks are slipping. All that stuff. How about for you, what's really happening?" I asked.

"Not too much."

It wasn't a rollicking answer, but I didn't expect much more. Candice was probably expecting another labeling session.

"I've been curious to know what you thought of what happened in that session with the doctor." I continued, my voice perhaps betraying my own disbelief at what I had witnessed.

"She's an idiot. Like all that garbage about ADHD. And peas and carrots, and whatnot. Those meds made me so stoned, I could hardly do anything. By the time I got out of school it was all I could do to drag myself home and watch TV. It was weird."

"That's not the kind of kid you used to be, or are again now?"

"Nah, I'm the type to always be going, out doing stuff. That's what really bugs my folks, is that I'm never around when they are. They're like, 'You can't go here, you can't go there.' Always whining at me. You've seen them do it. You've met them. It's like I can't be myself, or be with my friends. So I didn't stick with the drugs. No point. I was doing a bit better in school but it was killing my time with my friends."

"You're the wild one in your group, then?"

"Yeah, I'm the crazy one who's always getting everyone to laugh, stuff like that."

"And how were you when you were given this ADHD label?"

"Hell, it's like I've been feeling like an f'ing loser lately. That's not me. And my boyfriend, he doesn't interest me in the same way. I don't know."

"What do you want to do now, about this?" I asked, fairly certain she was motivated to try something else.

"I just want my mom and dad off my case. But I'm not going back to Doctor Whatshername. I just want to be my old self."

Candice's problems never did alleviate themselves at home. She ended up in foster care when verbal battles turned physical and truancy turned into running away for days at a time. I'm not sure if she had ADHD or not. But what I do know is that the diagnosis and treatment caused her more grief than it cured. It changed her from the life of the party to a kid who preferred to be alone; it actually increased the likelihood of her becoming involved in drug-related activities by getting her to start using (albeit prescription medications); it made her feel her talents, such as her number mania, was something pathological, a sign of a disordered mind. It affected her sexuality, and her identity story.

Candice's story had many different threads; her academic performance and arguments at home are but two. If we'd spent more time understanding the complex warp and weave of all the relationships in her life, and the events which had formed her, we may have been better able to help her balance her need for help at school with her need to maintain her personal integrity at home and with her friends. The mistake was as much ours as hers.

I have a personal stake in Candice's story. Perhaps that's why her story stands out for me, from a career during which I've heard many similar stories. Raising my own children, I am disheartened to see them sitting dutifully in their desks focused on tasks that stunt their natural enthusiasm. My eldest child, now nine, has at times hated school, and felt like his behaviour was confined and the structure was a poor fit with who he is. The story he tells about himself is not one of failure just because he struggles to sit at his desk. He prefers to be known as the one who won the fifty-metre dash and the only third grader the grade five's let play noon-time soccer. My son does not have ADHD. He does not need medications. He is able to self-regulate. But he also knows that school doesn't fit him (as it doesn't fit for many other children like him). The trouble is that my son's story will not be heard over the din of institutional protocol and social expectations that demand obedient children. As Leo Rigsby, a resilience researcher from Temple University and educator explains, resilience has become a quintessentially American concept which has valued only one type of child and one set of behaviours, those characterized by individualism, mobility and financial success.

If kids have trouble relating to such homogeneous stories like these told about their lives at home by adults, they will be more inclined to turn to their peers for support. When I am privileged enough to hear the stories adolescents tell about their lives, I am told about youthful exuberance, striving towards goals, loyalty and support, experiences which, ironically, echo many of the values families hope their children will cultivate. But when we deny the expression of these stories, and we put children in contexts in which they are left with only problem-saturated identities given them by those at home and in their community, then is it any wonder they seek out a peer group which will value them for who they want to be? Too often, in these groups they find a place where they don't have to feel ashamed of who they are.

Gangs and Our Children's Stories

Nowhere is this more evident than in the case of gangs. While the general public and right wing think tanks push for more police on our streets as the way to combat gangs, their efforts have done nothing except take much needed municipal dollars and put them where they don't belong. We think we can frighten kids to go straight. This approach completely misses the point.

Youth tell us their gang affiliations are part of their identity and ofttimes a substitute for the negative labels thrust on them by either a family or community that rejects them. Joining a gang isn't something a child chooses to do outside the context of his or her life. It is part of a long quest for support and a sense of belonging that ends on the streets. We forget the power that comes from selling drugs, or stealing, or violence. These are seldom a child's first choices, but make sense when other doors are slammed in their face. We adults, lacking an appreciation for the road children travel, mistake for problems their dress, smoking or other behaviours that bring them feelings of social cohesion. Instead, we need to understand these behaviours for what they are, socially unacceptable and unfortunate solutions that fit with a particular point in time and place.

Besides, most of what we think of as gang activity isn't gang-related at all. Most of the serious research that has examined gang involvement by teens has shown that many youth who identify involvement with a delinquent group of friends form family street groups, or wannabe gangs, and that very few youth are actually involved in organized identifiable peer groups that have a distinct name and are consistently involved in organized crime. The image of belonging to a gang, of having colours, is often the most important aspect of gang involvement and what most youth want, rather than being caught up in a network of criminals. Estimates are that among delinquents, only 5 percent are committed delinquents who won't grow out of their problem behaviours. That is good news for parents and communities. Unfortunately, it's not a message politicians want to heed.

Instead we see much needed resources going to create gang suppression units that, according to one study by Carol Archibold and Michael Meyer, merely perpetuate the myth that the problem is more fact than fiction. In some rare instances, when there is social strife and inequality, gangs do grow to prominence. A colleague of mine working to prevent violence in Medellin, Colombia, tells me there are 127 authentic gangs operating in a city of three million people. More often, in Canadian and American cities, communities demand excessive force to deal with what are only unorganized peer groups populated with teens who have turned to each other as a substitute for family and community. Besides, in rare instances when gangs do exist, it is seldom teenagers who are in leading roles, and therefore, interventions to suppress gang involvement with teens must necessarily do more than criminalize their behaviours: we must find ways to offer teens the same plot elements to the rich stories they author among delinquent and dangerous peers, but in ways that maintain their safety and a strong identity.

165

If deterrence doesn't work to direct youth away from gangs, then what exactly does? If we think of time with the gang as a chapter in a child's life story, rather than the whole book, then there is always the hope that we as parents and other caregivers can co-author new plot lines.

Authoring a Group Identity

That's what a colleague and I did when we brought together ten youths in a custody setting where I worked for a time. These were youth whose lives were going nowhere – repeat offenders on a direct path to an adult institution. We met twice a week, the point being to start the youth on the path towards some new stories about themselves. Of course, that's not quite how we sold it to the kids. What we offered them was a space to talk about themselves, to be openly critical about their time in custody, and an opportunity to share time with youths not on their living units. It was an oasis offering some positive experiences of control in an environment where all their negative expressions of power were taken away. These were youths who had been written off by their communities and exasperated their parents to the point that they were glad their son or daughter was placed in jail. Our time together was to be different than other experiences in their lives. It was. The sessions were unlike anything I'd done before in my professional or personal life.

First there were the rules. As much as possible we tried to forget where we were. My co-worker and I encouraged participants to take a positive leadership role. We still had all the power and authority (and a panic button), but they had a great deal of say over what went on during group time. We did what we could to flatten the hierarchy, exerting our influence as members of the group, rather than imposing our rules. After all, we reasoned, where in these youths' lives are they seeing people negotiate for power? Their worlds were full of people who either told them what to do, or who they overpowered. So when it came to me asking the group not to use profanity, it was because I was asking them to consider my feelings as one of the group members, not because I had the power to make them stop. We reached a compromise. We all agreed not to swear (a rule on the living units as well) except when using profanity was a reasonable way of expressing strong feelings. That got rid of their tendency to put the "f" word in every sentence, but left them the freedom to make a strong point in their own street language.

As each group member joined, he or she was asked to tell the group the story of his or her life. Other kids listened and with the new member's permission, could poke and prod. Together, we tried to make sense of what had happened to land the youth in custody. We struggled to understand how and why custody made sense. We created a safe space where the expectation was that we'd support each other. We loved it, youth and staff alike. It took several months but eventually we created a different tone in the group than the kids experienced on the living units. Besides the openness to really talk about ourselves, the other two biggest changes which occurred were that these offenders learned what confidentiality meant and they learned how to play like children again.

Generally high-risk kids don't know how to play. They know how to get stoned, thrill seek, piss others off, compete, fight, disturb and create mayhem. But play, as in child's play, eludes them. Their guard is always up. So we shook ourselves a bit. We wrote poetry! And we laughed. Then we finger painted and ended up with more paint on us than on the paper. We watched films that spoke to the youths, like *Basketball Diaries*, not the sanitized Disney stuff which is usually allowed inside the facility. And we did some theatre. We actually staged the Christmas play ourselves one year. Except that the kids wrote the script out of their own experiences. This was no *Miracle on 34th Street*. This was a raw depiction of unfulfilled expectations, drunk parents and violence beneath Christmas trees. It was their old stories finally being given the voice they deserved.

Each of the things we did together gave participants a chance to be whoever they wanted to be. It offered them a place to start something new. It helped them look back over their lives and project a different future. Therapists at the Dulwich Centre in Adelaide, Australia, a group of clinicians known for their work which focuses on the narratives people construct throughout their lives, talk about authoring new old stories, and remembering the past. Both techniques encourage a different account of lives which have been plagued by problems: accounts that seek to richly describe people's strengths and the numerous but often forgotten exceptions to the troubled pasts which typify individuals labeled with psychiatric disorders. Similarly, the group offered the youths who attended a place they could connect with each other, and challenge what others thought about them, all the while authoring new *old*, and new *future* stories.

To achieve the vulnerability necessary to accomplish this work, we had to ensure confidentiality. The youth themselves decided to have a chair that would be placed in the middle of the meeting circle. On it would sit whoever broke the group's confidence. The accused individual would have to answer to all his or her peers (and us adults) for the misdeed. Believe it or not, kids actually kept what went on in the group private. One of the few times someone said something about what had happened in the group, the offender was actually placed on the chair at the next meeting and had to account for his actions. There were tears, and anger, and some threats, but mostly talk about how hurt people felt. These big mean kids were holding each other accountable in a way no one, including themselves, would have thought possible. Under the influence of their old stories, they would have solved this problem by "pounding the kid." But new stories about ourselves, based on experiences with newfound competencies, can take root if given half a chance to grow.

Even we group facilitators were bound by the same confidentiality, except when it conflicted with our professional responsibilities to keep kids from harming themselves or others, or being harmed. This drove some of our colleagues outside the group crazy. All of a sudden there was a place inside the institution they didn't control. Group members were able to gripe about their care with impunity. But the group culture made certain that if members of the group complained about things, then they also had to work with their peers to figure out a solution.

It was hard to put a finger on why this treatment formula worked so well, but it felt like the emotional tone on all the living units changed when this group was operating. The youths told us they felt some power in their lives in a healthy and positive way. They were being heard, opening up and experiencing themselves and their peers differently. That's the magic of authoring new stories. A small change can snowball into something big.

While we had the structure of the jail to help connect with these youths, most families have their own unique ways of spending time with their kids. If those moments provide children a space to tell their story on an equal footing with the stories told about them, they are much more likely to open up and start talking. Our job as parents and caregivers is to pay attention and really hear what we are being told. As much as we think we know better, or think we have advice to give, it's best to remember we are very unlikely to have much to contribute until we understand our children's accounts of their lives. Their choices won't make sense unless we grasp the complexity of their drift towards solutions, their random and purposeful selection of options for growth.

This is a hard sell for parents worried over a child's safety. Ironically, though, the more we restrain ourselves, the more we show caring through our actions (not words and mini-lectures), the more likely we are to nurture the kinds of reflective and worldly children we hope to raise.

Chapter 7
The Healthy Deviant

We use the term mental health and assume we are all talking about the same thing. I've found instead it is useful to think of mental health in two different ways. The first aspect of health is determined by the presence or absence of an organic disorder. By this I mean, is there any biologically based impairment which is threatening an individual's well-being?

There are many mental illnesses that fall in this category, or at least are at this point believed to be biologically based. Take for example schizophrenia, attention deficit disorder, depression, and sometimes alcohol and drug addictions. The cause of these disorders is said to be largely the result of one's physical makeup. The environment in which someone lives may "trigger" an episode of illness. The thing that most distinguishes organic disorders is that they are already inside us. While this can explain some mental illnesses, not many of us actually have these disorders. For most mental illnesses the cure is never as simple as "Take two Ritalin and see your doctor in the morning."

The second way of looking at mental health and mental illness is to look at the different individual, family and other social factors that either contribute to, or threaten, a person's well-being. An example will help to show the difference between these two aspects of health. My friend has a son who was diagnosed early in elementary school with Attention Deficit Hyperactivity Disorder. Unlike many kids who are given this diagnosis because they can't sit still (like Candice in the last chapter), Josh's symptoms clearly show that there is some organic root to his problem. He is easily distracted and has found doing his work in a noisy classroom extremely challenging. He fidgets, can't sit for long, and thinks through problems in ways which are different from other boys his own age. He has been taking Ritalin, a commonly prescribed medication for this condition, since grade two. However, you would likely know none of this if you met Josh. You'd be unlikely to suspect he has a mental illness, an organically based brain dysfunction.

Instead, you are more likely to meet a young man who is an active member of his high school community. He plays on two sports teams, is part of the school band, has a part-time job at a local Wendy's, and loves to read. When you meet Josh you would likely be most impressed by his self-confidence, his ability to communicate, his enthusiasm and abundant energy. He is a tall beanpole of a boy who moves around with a frenetic energy. The medications, he says, help him focus, but he keeps the dosage to a minimum as the drugs have many unfortunate side effects. These side effects can actually impair Josh's ability to do things which support his mental health. They can make him lethargic, glassy-eyed, lose his appetite, and even, as I mentioned in the last chapter, affect how he feels sexually. But on the whole, Josh's mental health is excellent.

He feels good about who he is, can quickly rhyme off a list of things he does well, is accepted in his community for how he wants to be known, and has many close friends. The absence or presence of a mental illness in his life tells us very little about Josh's experience of mental health. Josh does not let his illness affect his well-being any

171

more than an otherwise healthy and happy child who breaks his leg would say that his mental health is destroyed by being in a cast. Josh has great mental health *despite* his mental illness.

Of course this could change. If Josh was unable to control the symptoms of the illness, his overall well-being could be threatened. For example, if he could not succeed in school because he couldn't concentrate or sit still, he would likely feel less self-confident, perhaps become embarrassed by his academic limitations. He might begin to act out in ways that showed others how he felt about himself. A delinquent peer group would then be one possible solution to cope with how he felt and his lack of participation in school. When controlled, however, mental illness remains distinct from mental health and does not predict how a child will behave.

This point is too often missed in the assessments I read of vulnerable children. In these reports, the child's disorders are always given prominence over aspects of the child's health. We have developed a whole mental *health* industry which is concerned with mental *illness*. Professional helpers suffer from a "hardening of the categories." While we exude confidence in our ability to assess illness, we are reluctant to see the ways children survive. Josh makes it easy for everyone to see how healthy he is. It is far more difficult to perceive well-being when we meet children who achieve some measure of health in ways that are not socially acceptable. In such cases, the diagnostic labels we give children and which caregivers accept as true contribute to the problems these kids face. In such circumstances, youth literally run from their caregivers to peers where they feel their health is appreciated and where their illness is less debilitating.

I work with many institutionalized youth who have long histories of drug abuse. Rather than assuming they are unhealthy because of this behaviour, I prefer to ask them a very simple question when conducting an assessment: "What does doing drugs mean to you?"

Parents can ask the same question of their children. I have stopped asking, "Why do you do drugs?" as the question always implies that I have the right answer, and they the wrong one. Instead of putting kids on the defensive, I try to understand what the experience of doing drugs means to the individual child and his or her peers as well. Time and again, I am sad to report, I am told that abusing drugs is more "fun" than anything else these delinquents do. My experience is not unique. A number of international studies from South Africa, Hungary, Colombia, the United States, Australia, and Canada have demonstrated that many youth find recreational opportunities are expanded through drug use and other problem behaviours including weapons carrying, running away, and early sexual activity.

Therefore, rather than thinking a youth's answer too simplistic when he or she says drug use is fun, as many of my colleagues do, I am instead profoundly interested in exploring what this means. It is not as implausible as it may sound. Perhaps doing drugs for fun is really an accurate account of kids' experiences. If I was to ask many of my own friends why they drink at parties the answer would likely be the same: because it adds to the festive mood; it makes the party more enjoyable (especially in socially uncomfortable settings); it loosens them up; and it tastes good. Should it surprise us that teens approach substance use and abuse the same way? For the high-risk youth I work with, this elusive commodity, fun, is in short supply. Even when there are lots of opportunities to have fun in other ways, many youth still drift into drug-related activities because it is the easiest and most readily available way for them to enjoy themselves.

Coincidently, delinquent peer groups who place a lot of value on abusing drugs or drinking heavily are also the groups which are easiest for kids to join. Most of the addicted kids I meet are not very picky about who is in their group as long as each member supports the group culture. Being a delinquent, I've been told, is easy. Just pitch a rock through a window, steal something, or abuse drugs, and you're in. Finding mental health by excelling at sports, school, or negotiating a wider acceptance in one's community is not a path open to all our youth. For many children who come from the wrong side of the tracks society tells them they need not apply for acceptance even if they can find the resources they need to fit in. For other youth who have undergone severe trauma, abuse or neglect, delinquent behaviours offer them easy access to a powerful identity. And they're fun.

Mitch, who had just turned fifteen the last time I worked with him, had grown up in the suburbs with his middle-class parents. The family was typical of many in the community. They had some problems, but on the whole were doing fine. Dad had steady work, Mom had stayed home with the three children until they all went to school, then found a part-time clerical job with a local dentist. There were no alcohol or drug problems in the family. Mom attended church. Dad went hunting in the fall of each year. The family went camping together once a summer. Despite his stable home life, Mitch had been in and out of trouble through most of his teens. He had also been abused sexually when he was eight years old by a priest who had the trust of Mitch's parents. The last time we worked together Mitch was on his third custodial disposition, doing six months for the small part he played in an armed robbery of an elderly couple who were in their apartment when Mitch and his friends broke in. Mitch had been referred to me for treatment at a specialized facility because of his bizarre behaviour.

His parents had told me, "Mitch is a bright young fellow. But he's so tall and lanky for his age. We can't figure how he ever survives on the street without getting beat up. He hangs out with all the kids who always seem to be in trouble. It's a wonder to us he manages to stay alive." They had all but given up hope of rescuing their child from the street. Short of chaining him to his bed, they couldn't seem to keep him away from other problem kids.

Mitch is, in fact, a slightly built boy who stands over six feet tall, but weighs less than 125 pounds, with a quiet manner when in the presence of adults. When he's with his peers on the outside, he is just like them, outgoing, obnoxious, immature. In custody and during hospitalization, his behaviour was positively odd. While it's not strange to see institutionalized people behave in ways that might appear very different, Mitch's tenacity at playing the role of the "crazy" kid while insttutionalized surprised everyone, including myself. He had figured out that if he acted crazy enough people would allow him time to himself and he would be able to retreat to the safety of his room.

Within the institution, many of the simple survival strategies kids use on the street are taken away from them in the narrowly defined and regimented world of the institution. There are limited opportunities inside for these children to author an identity of their own choosing. Mitch didn't want anyone to know the secret of his abuse, and he didn't want to be vulnerable to any further abuse by those looking after him. His slight stature also made him a potential target for other boys. He had reasoned that going "crazy" was one way to cope. He became an expert at it. Periodically, he would do bizarre things like spend days in a fetal position curled up on the floor of his room, eating and drinking very little, rocking back and forth or banging his head into the cement brick wall. Needless to say, he got much attention this way, being so convincing in his role that the staff of the facility felt compelled to respond.

Mitch was given the label depressed, watched carefully, and referred to me for help. As the youth workers who looked after him and I slowly pieced together Mitch's history through conversations with his family and friends, it became more and more obvious that Mitch was not depressed, and in fact had successfully found a way to cope with how threatened he felt. He had manipulated the mental health system to his advantage. How he was behaving was perfectly reasonable at the time in the context of his placement. When we and his parents began to think about the world from Mitch's point of view, we began to have some success working with him on his own terms. Mitch's depression disappeared. He began to associate with other kids on the living units. He started talking on the phone to some of his old buddies, the ones who were getting their act together.

One of the ways we helped Mitch was by getting staff who we thought he might trust to enter his room and talk with him while he was curled up. Only they didn't badger him with questions. Instead, they just sat there for hours and talked off the cuff about anything they chose. Mitch had the choice to either keep up the crazy person act or respond to this barrage of caring and conversation. We knew he wasn't crazy, so the goal became letting him get to know us as his caregivers. We didn't insist he leave his room or do anything else to threaten him. It took three weeks until Mitch finally began to respond. I can recall one day when it was my turn to go in and talk, and as I rambled on about my life, the weather, just about anything, I could see a wry smile pass across Mitch's face. He and I both knew the jig was up.

With time Mitch stopped these bizarre but intelligible behaviours and found other ways to stay safe. He even began to talk about his past abuse as he came to trust those around him more. For Mitch, mental health and mental illness were not easy to distinguish from each other. The labels we had given him served little or no purpose until we understood Mitch's life the way he experienced it.

Feeling Good Means Feeling Powerful

Mental health is not something we "do" on our own. It depends on who is around us and what they offer us by way of sustenance and acceptance. Kids have told me that a large part of what they need to feel healthy is the support for the powerful self-definitions they construct for themselves.

Mikhail Bahktin, a Russian philosopher, once wrote: "Words belong to nobody." In my work I found that the labels kids give themselves are treated by adults as if we own them. We conveniently forget that we all create meaning for the words we use through our participation in public exchanges. What is taken for normal and a sign of good behaviour today can become antiquated and stodgy, or morally wrong and harmful to the public good, years later. There was a time, for example when we didn't even debate whether children should work alongside their parents as labourers. Now we use the disparaging term "child labour" to describe this same activity, even though the debate over what is and is not appropriate work for a child continues. We used to think of corporal punishment in our schools as evidence of good institutional discipline. As the victims of residential schools line up with the accounts of the violence they experienced, we are witnessing a redefinition of the term "discipline" from what was once thought to be a healthy and necessary way to instruct children. We now rightly see such behaviour as abusive acts by big people on those who are smaller and weaker.

Mitch was not "crazy"; he was a "survivor." We can help those who are put down by the language we use reclaim some power over the labels that get stuck to them. Squeegee kids on the streets of our major cities have done this and more when they argue for recognition as "young entrepreneurs" rather than "delinquent street youth."

But it takes more than one person to create these new meanings, just like it takes a whole community to raise a child. The youth I meet who are fighting to maintain their mental health struggle against tremendous odds. Under such conditions, it makes sense to me that they group together to find a common voice: "Birds of a feather flock together." At least together, they know what they are and are less vulnerable to attack. For many of these youth, that's how they feel, at war and under attack. Ultimately, their mental health rests on their feeling empowered.

There has always been the empty promise that if children would just agree with how we adults organize their world that they would be accepted by a community waiting to embrace them. I see little evidence of this. Even if these excluded youth conform they will still be poor, or the wrong colour, or from the wrong family, or appear somehow different in ways that disadvantage them. That they choose instead "deviant" lifestyles in which they have some control over their lives and manage to find what they need to sustain their mental health makes a lot more sense especially when you talk with kids themselves. At least amongst their peers, the pressure is off to be just like everyone else. When we try to help these youngsters without understanding this we merely exacerbate their already problem saturated lives.

Lorraine was like that. She knew what she needed to do to stay healthy, even if others thought otherwise. Lorraine was fifteen when I met her. Like Jacintha, the young woman who I introduced in an earlier chapter who was marched into my office with her two parents on either flank, Lorraine too was dragged in to see me. Like Jacintha, Lorraine definitely had things on her mind but unlike her peer, she didn't want to talk. Jackie, her mother, a sole parent, wanted to discuss her daughter's belligerent attitude, and get her to "mind" the house rules. Lorraine wanted to do whatever she liked and was not shy about telling her mother what she could do with her rules. Where Jackie talked incessantly, her daughter sat like a block of ice, keeping her distance from everyone. With a firm promise from me that I would not side just with her mother, and reassurances that I really did want to hear her side of the story, Lorraine agreed to meet with me individually.

I found that as long as I opened space for Lorraine to be heard, she would willingly talk about her life, her friends and her relationship with Jackie. The danger in this approach is that the one doing the listening has to be prepared to bring more than a professional detachment to his or her work; as helpers and caregivers, we have to be willing to accept the young person's version of events as authentic. I don't necessarily know if what I'm being told is the Truth, but I do know that what I hear reflects what an adolescent like Lorraine is experiencing and is therefore true for her.

Once we got going, we wound up discussing *both Jackie and Lorraine's* irresponsible and violent behaviour. With both mother and daughter back in my office some weeks later, my job became keeping the conversation flowing as these two women tried to find some common ground upon which to base a truce. They were literally competing with each other to see who would be defined as the healthier one. Both blamed the frequent flare-ups at home on the other. Eventually, they came to understand that their relationship shouldn't be a contest. They were both doing what they needed to do to feel whole.

Lorraine felt her peers understood her better than her mother. She was probably right. Jackie needed to offer Lorraine the same kind of opportunity to be heard that Lorraine found among her friends. A helper of any stripe can unknot these complicated situations, but parents can also do it themselves. Rather than disparaging the peer groups our children participate in, I prefer to learn what it is that works for teens in these groups, then try to recreate that for them in some small measure at home.

What Lorraine experienced at home was a turbulent and emotionally charged environment. Jackie had just enrolled in university at the age of thirty-eight. The family had moved to a new neighbourhood with less crime, but far from the children's friends. There were new schools to adjust to and last but not least, Mom's new boyfriend was around more. This was a particular sore point with Lorraine.

Four years earlier Lorraine had been sexually abused by one of Jackie's boyfriends. The man was never charged for lack of evidence, and though Jackie eventually left him, she never really believed her daughter. Jackie's ex-husband and father of both Lorraine and Lorraine's 17-year-old sister had been charged and found guilty of sexually abusing his oldest daughter when she was eight. Jackie just couldn't believe she had made, as she put it, "the same mistake twice." She was confident her newest partner was a "nice" fellow and that her daughters were safe. But she couldn't convince Lorraine.

It was unfortunate that two people who wanted so much to be with each other just couldn't find a way to connect. To cope, Lorraine had found other relationships where she said she would be both believed and feel safe.

"I don't bring my friends home. I don't know why, I just don't," Lorraine told me. I wasn't that surprised. At home she struggled to take back some control for her life from her mother by telling her mom what to do, whom to sleep with, and whether or not to return to school. To hear Lorraine talk, her mother needed all the advice Lorraine could give her, while Jackie felt it was Lorraine who was the irresponsible and dangerous one. Lorraine was open to taking advice, but had a strong independent streak and was always hyper-vigilant to any threat that might compromise her control over her life.

As she explained, "It's not that you solve problems by yourself. But if you decide to do something you decide it by yourself. Like, nobody tells me to do something that I don't want to do. It's my life and my body."

"What about with your mom? Who tells who what to do?" I asked.

"I give my mom lots of advice. She can really use it, but she doesn't much listen to me. She just keeps screwing up."

"And what's it like with your friends?"

"With my friends it's definitely not like that. We tell each other what to do but don't do it unless we want. But a lot of them think what I tell them is great."

Lorraine didn't mean to be bossy or get into punching matches with her mother; she just saw it as her way of surviving the chaos around her. Her older sister had already left home to live with her boyfriend, leaving Lorraine and Jackie to battle things out.

While it would have been easy to agree with Jackie that her daughter was just plain out of control and still dealing with "unresolved issues" related to the "alleged" sexual abuse, I chose instead to look at the situation from both the mother and daughter's perspectives. I didn't want to fall into the trap of thinking Lorraine "ill" even though she fit the criteria for a variety of disorders. Here was a teen who had taken on too much power and was acting more like a parent than most parents. In most circumstances such children come to be known as "parental children," a term coined by family therapist Salvador Minuchin to distinguish youth who invert the normal hierarchy with their parents and develop the responsibility, competence and autonomy usually thought in Western cultures to be beyond the child's years. And yet, given her history, Lorraine's precociousness impressed me as it provided her with the solution she needed to put her life in order. She was frankly fed up with being a passive pawn in her mother's life. I didn't think that was a sign of mental illness. In fact her anger looked reasonable.

I asked her once what it was like when her mother didn't leave the boyfriend who had abused Lorraine right away, after she disclosed the abuse. Lorraine practically spit her words back at me. "I was really angry," she said. "I don't know how she could have kept seeing him. It's disgusting."

As Lorraine told me and her mother more about her life, Jackie began to see the chaos her daughter had experienced. The more Jackie understood of Lorraine's challenges growing up, and accepted that Lorraine needed to feel in control, the closer Jackie felt to her daughter. In time, Lorraine came to appreciate a little more why her mother was finding it so difficult to let her daughter make her own decisions, and how awful Jackie had felt when for the second time she had inadvertently let one of her daughters be abused.

Our tendency is to look at a young person's peer group and think them no good. As Lorraine's story shows, her peers were possibly the only people whom she could turn to for emotional support. Outside her home, Lorraine acted very maturely. Though she had placed herself in some risky situations, she was the one in her peer group others turned to for help, even mothering. Lorraine knew about protecting others, and about surviving. Rather than being seen as a confused disordered child, amongst her peers she was seen as a responsible young woman who coped better than most.

During counselling, when "Lorraine the responsible teen" was introduced to Jackie, she was at first surprised, but later appreciative of her daughter's capacity to nurture others. It was a tough sell at first. Jackie was certain her daughter was just getting into trouble in the community. She was certain Lorraine would become either pregnant, abused, or go to jail if she continued hanging out with kids who appeared so needy and so desperate for someone to care for them. Jackie was doing what she could to raise herself out of poverty. It pained her to see her daughter the leader among peers who were sinking further into a life without hope.

But Lorraine was bright enough to know that in some ways her mother was right about her friends. Jackie's return to school offered Lorraine a role model, even though Jackie doubted her daughter had any respect at all for the efforts she had made. Lorraine saw her friends clearly for who they were. It's just that nobody had taken the time to ask what she thought. She was so often on the defensive about these special others in her life that she never had the chance to tell anyone how *different* she was from her peers, nor about her dreams for a life separate from theirs. Not surprising to me, I learned that the life she desired would include getting a good education early, so that she would not have to return to school like her mother.

From Negative to Positive

I meet many youth who must challenge the labels of dangerous, deviant, delinquent, and disordered that get stamped on them because of the way they react to what they experience. Acts of private misconduct become publicly debated among their caregivers as signs of psychopathology. Take for example Tammy, who was fifteen when we met. She had not only been sexually assaulted by a group of boys in her neighbourhood, but had come to be known as a "victim of abuse" or "survivor" to many around her, including the kids at school. With a bitterness that left no doubt how upset she was with being labelled, she told me: "That label survivor really pisses me off!" The suicidal behaviour which had started after the incident, scarring herself with razors and knives drawn across her forearms, had put her life in serious danger. Or so we adults in her life thought. But as Tammy explained, the greater threat to her well-being was the way one incident had come to define her whole person.

Ironically, the more people tried to help, the more the negative labels that repulsed her seemed to stick. When Tammy's father relocated the family for his work, I became yet another therapist in her life who she was certain would just carry on this old story told about her. In my work, I've noticed that it is not just the plot to these young lives which thickens. The files that capture their stories thicken as well, each new entry giving these youth more and more professionally determined identities. No wonder peer groups, especially problem peer groups, look so good. They are a way teens can fight back, tell us adults we don't have control over the abused children in our care. At least there Tammy was on an equal footing. She could change groups, or turn a negative label into a positive.

Fed up with trying to resist everyone's definition of her as the sick kid with the awful past, Tammy decided she would embellish the label thrust on her and become a peer support for other young women who had been victimized. Tammy became the expert on being a "survivor." For her, that was one way she could challenge the label she had in the community, redefining it as an identity associated with power and prestige.

But with professionals, it was another case altogether. With us she wanted to find a new story about herself, one unencumbered by this past episode in her life. We worked together doing just this. We talked about all the other things in her life that were not abuse related. We didn't avoid the abuse issue, we just shelved it for a time until it made sense to bring it out. There were boyfriend, family, and school issues to talk about. There was no end to issues unrelated to the abuse which we could explore.

The abuse was like ink in water, though. It tended to colour everything in Tammy's life and she and I both knew it. She said as much. But Tammy needed to be a teenager as well, a plain old sexually inexperienced teen. Perhaps that is what she found through our conversations, a resurrected story about being normal. There was plenty of time later for us to talk about her abuse and the effect it had had on her life. But first she needed to arm herself with a different story than that of the disempowered victim. Family therapists like Janet Adams-Westcott and Cheryl Dobbins have had great success locating stories in children's lives that contradict the "abuse-dominated story." Simple conversations, play therapy, art therapy, and drama can all be tools in this search for internal qualities that abused children value about themselves, but that may be hidden beneath the personae of the victim.

Tammy's self-destructive behaviours had been her first try at healing herself. They had helped her express herself, but not put the abuse behind her. Her role as a helper to other abused girls had been a clever coping strategy as well, but it too had left her stuck with a singular identity. Our work together was about helping her expand her options for narrating her life.

For most youth who are saddled with problem identities, their solutions are often complex negotiations with those around them for whatever health bolstering resources they can find. Frequently their solutions bring with them terrible consequences, for the child and those he or she frightens or hurts. But stopping problem behaviours is difficult if we first don't understand the power they hold for young people whose lives are experienced as emotional and physical wastelands.

The Power to Say Who We Are

A short while ago, I went to interview a young fellow who has had so many problems that it seemed a foregone conclusion that he would spend the rest of his life drifting from one institution to the next. Unlike the other people who had crossed his path, however, I didn't come to see him to talk about all the things wrong in his life. I came because I was sure he had something to teach me about staying healthy when living without meaning or hope of things ever getting better. His mother was surprised when I shared with her the purpose of my visit. I'd shown up on their doorstep as promised one sunny winter's day, a bag of donuts in one hand, my notebook and tape recorder in the other.

"You want to interview my son about his *mental health*?" she said, absolutely dumbfounded. "Now that will be different!" she laughed out loud, shaking her head in complete disbelief.

When I talk to parents about helping teens experience *more* power over the way they want to be known, I often encounter sceptical looks and wry smiles, as if people are questioning *my* sanity. Like the parent who couldn't imagine her son as healthy, we are fearful to turn over more power to youth who are likely already out of control. That is where the misunderstanding begins. I don't want parents to hand over their power over curfews, or no-drugs-in-my-house policies, or their you-have-to-be-in-early-on-a-school-night kind of power. I want them to give their children the right to say back to them and others, "This is who I am" and "This is what I need" while also understanding that what children are doing when they act out is a strategy to win the battle for control over their identities.

What we have failed to understand is that, first, if we don't give children a say over who they are, then they'll take control anyway. But they'll have to shout louder, more violently, and do things that annoy us even more in order to convince us we are powerless to tell them what they can and cannot be. Second, we must understand that no matter how odd their choice of identity, it is always a necessary expression of health-seeking behaviour. Like guided missiles, these kids navigate where they need to go to convince themselves they are accepted and find meaning in their lives.

Glazed looks of hopeless resignation or piercing anger and frustration usually appear on the faces of parents of deeply troubled kids who are told they must now understand the healthy aspects of their kids' problems behaviours. It doesn't help when I share with them words of wisdom from children like their own who advise us adults to surrender the battle over how our children are going to go about creating an identity. The sad truth is, the battle was lost long before we as parents ever noticed the problem.

I'm becoming more and more confident, however, that we can still win the war for healthy and safe kids, but we need to drop the metaphors of aggression and conflict, and start understanding that without opposition, our children don't have to fight as hard, or become as dangerous, in order to succeed at staking a territory for themselves.

I'm reminded of what a friend of mine, an instructor of Aikido, once showed me. We can use our opponents' own energy to defend ourselves. The person lunging at us is already off balance, unstable, easier to bring down if we don't oppose them, but instead amplify their energy, and *pull* them towards us, tilting them further off balance. Our tendency is to block our children, or fight back with forceful control that we are powerless to enforce. I prefer to see their outlandish behaviour as a communication. If they seek excitement, or a sense of belonging, or money, purpose, or even aggression, I am going to work with them to find all these same things in combinations that suit them. I am going to understand their behaviour as *purposeful* and work with this understanding in mind to change their behaviour in ways that keep them and others safe. Efforts to change young lives succeed best when they start from insight into the intelligibility of lives lived chaotically.

But still I hear parents say, "What, give my kid more power?" In fact, what I reassure parents is that I have found in my clinical work, with literally hundreds of families and teens, that when youth experience real power to influence how they are seen by others close to them, they become much more tolerant and respectful of the rights of others. In other words, as they become empowered, they are quite happy to share their power with others. This may not fit with many parents' experiences living with their youth. In truth, those who think they have given their child a say over their lives usually have missed the first step in the process. If one recalls Chapter 2, we must first make the effort to understand our children's truths. We need before anything else, and despite the great sense of loss we experience as parents when we do this, to acknowledge that our children's problems are sadly their solutions.

I believe the hesitancy and confusion I encounter when I ask people to give youth more power over how they are known stems from a misunderstanding of the term empowerment. Empowerment has become a buzz word of our times that has been misappropriated by the business world. It is not about "empowering employees for greater profit" as I once read on a workshop flyer. And it is not, as Nietzsche wrote, about the will to exercise power over others. Nor does empowerment mean giving power to anyone. The only person we can empower is ourselves. What we can do is knock down the barriers others, like our children, encounter in their search for personal power. We can make sure our children have the resources they need to experience themselves as healthy and in control of their lives: resources to learn, to play, to eat, to live safe, to feel proud of themselves, and shine in front of others. We as more powerful members of our communities can give children these types of opportunities. It is then up to them. Of all the things we provide, however, it is caring relationships that are the most important. It is by relating to others that teenagers discover who they are. We are all their audience.

Empowered kids are kids who are open to accepting differences in others because they do not need to take power from others to feel good about themselves. There was a little fellow named Justin, ten years old, down the street from where I once lived. He was a small child, only a few inches taller than my eight-year-old. He always had to have some child on the street to bully. Of course he couldn't attack kids his own age, so he tormented smaller children, easily outsmarting them, using language to insult them that they barely understood (thank God!). For that little fellow, the world was not a place full of opportunity but a place where he felt threatened and insecure. The only way he could convince himself he was worth something was by putting others down every chance he got. Desperate to feel good about himself, he barters with other for power but does so believing that there can only be one leader.

He's wrong. The most powerful kids I meet are the ones who understand that they can all be leaders. My power doesn't have to come at the expense of another's. That's what empowerment means. It's power based on sharing and caring.

Ten-year-old bullies grow up to be 16-year-old bullies. Tommy, who I introduced in an earlier chapter, spends much of his time standing on the shoulders of those he intimidates. But it is the adolescent sex offenders with whom I work who are the most adept at taking power away from others to bolster their own strange sense of well-being.

Not every sex offender has been themselves a victim of past abuse. But many have. Kyle, with whom I worked for two years, had been abused on at least two occasions. When he was four, he'd been forced by the 13-year-old son of his babysitter to "kiss and pull on" the boy's penis. This had gone on for many months before another child told his parents what was happening. The abuse had occurred each time the sitter left her son in charge of the children who came to her home. Then, when Kyle was ten, he was dropped off for an overnight visit with an uncle who had offered to take him fishing. Kyle was made to sleep in the man's bed and forcibly raped. As Kyle, by this time sixteen, told me, "I had no idea what he was doing. I didn't know anything about sex. I didn't know he could do that to me." Kyle never said anything about either incident to anyone until in jail for abusing kids himself, he finally began to talk about what had happened.

Kyle is one of those invisible kids. Slight in stature, homely looking, a kind of gentle passive energy about him. He was always the type in his apartment building who could be seen playing with the younger kids. He was a bit of a loner, not very good at school, some thought him a bit slow. His parents are easygoing working-class people who drive a battered Chevy truck, and have a big-screen television. Both work, though Mom is always home when the kids come back from school. Kyle's older brother has dropped out of school, doesn't work, and stays out most nights. If ever there was a kid who had gotten lost in our world, it was Kyle.

That was until a 3-year-old girl told her mother what Kyle had done to her. She'd talked about how he promised her she could watch the big television in his apartment, if she let him lie on top of her with her dress up. Afterwards, he'd told her not to tell anyone as she'd get in trouble for coming in to his apartment when Kyle's parents weren't there. She wasn't the only child he'd assaulted. There was an 8-year-old boy who he'd lured in to his home and paid to stroke his penis.

When the authorities began interviewing children throughout the apartment building, they found a number of other stories of Kyle's abusive or inappropriate sexual behaviour. None of the children said he'd acted threatening or mean. They had mostly been confused, some upset, some felt awkward. They weren't sure if what had happened was wrong.

Kyle was arrested and jailed for a year, forced into treatment, and taunted by his peers. His family was deeply embarrassed. They moved, denying that their son had done what he was accused of doing, certain the kids had made it all up. They knew Kyle wasn't much liked by other children. They believed it was their way of harassing their son even more.

When I started working with Kyle, both individually and in a group, it astounded me how he'd ever gotten to be sixteen and have so few of the social skills necessary to relate to his peers. He didn't have a clue how to be with kids his own age, and they were just as happy to ignore him altogether.

It's tough working with sex offenders, especially when one has children themselves. Kyle was easy enough to like, but he refused to take responsibility for what he had done. It took six months just to get him to begin to admit to some of the abuse. It took another six to get him to talk about his own victimization. "Nothing like that ever happened to me," he had insisted, even though we knew that in all likelihood he had been abused. Kyle was sharp enough to know that for many young men, being a victim of sexual abuse was a sign of weakness.

There are many different theories which explain why kids like Kyle abuse other children. What Kyle and other youth like him show me, however, is what happens when a child is without opportunities to develop a powerful identity. The only place Kyle could negotiate for himself a place was with little children. He'd already experienced what it was like to have someone use sex as a way of exploiting him. It was a simple matter of finding a way to use that same power to his own advantage. To him, sex with children made sense.

The problem with a child like Kyle is that treatment has to help him find an identity and teach him the skills he needs to be with same age peers, while all the while we know he is going to be rejected or worse by other teenagers.

"I don't have any friends. I don't know anybody at the new place we live," he told me. It wasn't going to be a situation that would change much either. "I don't see why I can't play with the younger kids as long as I don't do anything sexual with them. It's not like they won't tell. And their parents can be around. Seems kind of stupid. I never hurt them."

I'm not sure that Kyle ever really understood that he had in fact hurt those children. He knew he'd felt like they were his friends. I know he felt like he belonged with them. And I know he felt much more successful sexually with them than he would likely feel with his peers for a very long time. Kids like Kyle solve the problem of finding an identity but their solution comes at the expense of the rights and well-being of others. That's not the type of power that comes with acceptance or empowerment.

Missed Opportunities

It's a shame when children go unnoticed. Or their sparkling talents are left like bottles of pop after a party, opened, but forgotten, their bubbly quality wasted. Leo Buscaglia, who used to teach university courses on love, in his book *Living, Loving and Learning,* tells a wonderful story of a child and an art teacher. Buscaglia begins his tale by first reminding us that as individuals we mustn't become satisfied with being like everyone else. He then goes on to describe the harried art teacher many of us experienced in elementary school. In she, or occasionally he, would rush with art supplies that held out to us the promise of self-expression. But that's where it ended. The teacher would tell us all to draw trees, not meaning trees as we knew them, but instead the lollipop green things the teacher imagined trees to be. As Buscaglia so capably points out, she doesn't really tell us to draw a tree; what she tells us to draw is *her* tree.

Of course, the magic of the story is that such lessons seldom end with every student dutifully following directions. There has to be one child in every class, and indeed, many of the youth with whom I work are such children, who resist this pressure to conform. Labelled as conduct disordered, or just plain bad, they ooze their fingers into the paint, splash colour everywhere, insist on drawing pictures which are eyed suspiciously and then sent to the school guidance counsellor for assessment because they are either too violent or too full of exuberance. The little lad in Buscaglia's story who knows trees better than any teacher sprays his canvas with colour, only to be told he is likely brain damaged and will fit better in a class for children with special needs. It's so important we give children the opportunities they need to shine and to belong. Kyle's life is an extreme example of the child denied these opportunities.

That is the attraction of peer groups that sometimes, unfortunately, are of the delinquent kind. Peer groups are not unhealthy places for kids to grow. For kids growing up in toxic environments, peer groups offer a place they find safe to express themselves. For kids growing up in unhealthy environments, peers offer a place to add to their talents while learning how to deal with other people. Youth without a peer group are in more danger than those with a dysfunctional group.

The more we as parents and caregivers understand the power and health in the poor choices many problem youth make, the more we are likely to know how best to reach out and help. In most cases, for example, kids experience their peer groups as a place to feel empowered. If they don't feel that way, they move on to other relationships if and when the opportunity arises. Our homes can be every bit as empowering. We just need to understand what it is that happens in peer groups that makes our kids feel so special.

Chapter 8
Acceptance

Strategy Four: Accept the Unusual: Acknowledge the identity a youth chooses. Find the positive aspects of that identity and show whatever acceptance one can.

While it's important to help our children ferret out new stories to tell about their lives, the goal is to help them discover a new sense of self, a new identity. By the time we've helped them shout their truths, celebrated differences, recounted new stories and explored many and varied identities, teens are often closer to finding an identity story that they can like and which is more appropriate to life inside and outside our homes. It's then up to us to accept these unusual stories, or at least some of their more positive aspects. The child's peers will, in spite of what we as parents and caregivers choose to do. We should earnestly follow their lead.

Think back to when you were young. Several years ago I attended a museum exhibition which brought to life the dress and customs of teenagers over the past hundred years. It was a remarkable experience, looking back through time at what each generation thought cool, trendy and fashionable. The clothing was just as outrageous as today's, the music every bit as shocking, sexual mores always controversial, and attitudes as saucy and "in your face" as anything found on MuchMusic. It was humbling to think that children today are the same as we were then, searching for a unique and powerful identity that they can bring home. The marketing machine that helps push these changing images may have changed and become more sophisticated through the power of the Internet, music videos and a 500-channel universe, but the desire of youth to establish a unique culture persists. Apparently, the reticence of parents to allow their children to be different persists as well. I recall being impressed by what the media had to say throughout those one hundred years of youthful history. The same attitude on the part of the adult establishment was echoed over and over. Each successive generation was, and still is, told to not break *too* much with tradition, completely forgetting that when they were children, those doing the admonishing today did exactly the same as the youth they hope to control.

When I'm with children of any age, I try to remember the awesome imbalance of power between us. I can't make this inequality disappear, but I can pay attention to how it squashes the health-enhancing identities of vulnerable youth. I want their time spent with me to be an opportunity for these kids to explore their own identity stories in a safe environment free of criticism. That doesn't mean I remain "neutral" or pretend to be supportive of lifestyle choices I think are dangerous. Being genuine is rule number one when sharing time with youth. Like we were at their age, young people hate hypocrisy and manipulation. Instead of playing it neutral, I prefer to express my own opinions.

That is the difference between a conversation and a mini-lecture. In a conversation I only talk about my own experiences. A mini-lecture tries to impose what I've learned on those younger than me. Unless there is a real threat of danger, I avoid saying, "You shouldn't do that." As we all know, that's like waving a red cape in front of a bull. "Oh yeah, just watch me" is the likely reply. A slight improvement might be to say, "I don't like it when you do that," or even "I don't want you to do that, it worries me, I'm afraid you'll get into trouble." Then at least the caregiver is speaking from his or her experience, being less directive, though still saying to the young person, "I think I know better." If the same caregiver wants to show an appreciation for the child's skill at solving his or her own problems, and wants to share some guiding wisdom, I suggest a different approach altogether to the conversation.

Power Struggles

The first thing I have to do to have an honest and open conversation is clear up the sticky issue of power. In my experience, children seldom hear what adults have to say when it feels to them like who they are is being criticized by someone with more power than them. Instead of being critical, I work at getting us speaking together as equal participants in the conversation we're having. It's not as difficult or as dangerous as it sounds. I can share a great deal of power and still have plenty in reserve. In my experience, many parents fight battle after battle afraid to lose any of their hold on a child's life. To my mind, the parent who ends the day with a strong relationship and a safe and secure child, regardless of which battles were won or lost, is the parent who has won the war for a safe and healthy kid.

In a previous chapter I talked about a group for delinquent kids and how we gave them a great deal of autonomy in the group. While other staff worried we were giving away our all important power over these youth, we knew, and more importantly, the youth knew, that no matter how much we gave away, we were still in charge. After all, these kids were in jail. We could give them a great deal of leeway. Parents, in my experience, frequently have a great deal more power than they recognize. I have seen parents whose children steal their Interac cards and withdraw hundreds of dollars from their bank accounts *not* call the police. I have seen parents who can't get their kid to school still play taxi and drive them to the movies.

On the other hand, I have also seen parents who tell their child if he or she doesn't help around the house, then the family car is not going to be available for taxiing them to their friends. And I have seen parents refuse to be prisoners in their own homes, arranging for a bed at a relative's when their stoned child arrives home to a locked door after curfew. The power we have as caregivers is frequently there for us to experience, even as we share a great deal of our power allowing youth to exercise a say over how they behave and the identities that attach to them.

Encouraging these identities (without compromising one's own sense of self) means parents saying to their child, "I'm different than you" or "I don't think I could do what you're doing" or "What you've done is hard for me to understand." These are all ways of actually getting a conversation going that says we as adults appreciate the uniqueness of our children's identity but that we don't necessarily agree with the choices he or she is making. When a child's behaviour is life threatening or morally threatening, and I honestly believe I have the power to prevent the child from coming to harm, I add to what I just said, "And I'm going to have to insist you stop. I can't let you do what you're doing because I'm certain you're going to get hurt. I love you and I take seriously my responsibility to protect you." These are heavy sticks to wield and, as much as possible, I avoid using them unless absolutely necessary. Some examples might help to make this distinction clearer. As the saying goes, we can love the sinner, but not the sin.

Richard and Kim, parents of a 17-year-old named Jeremy, were at their wits' end to know how to get their son to be more responsible at home and quit drinking so much when out with his friends. They'd both done a good job raising their son or so it seemed to me. Even Jeremy credited his parents with having given him a good home to grow up in. "I know I've had it good compared to some of my friends," he said. But now, as Jeremy went his own way more and more, it felt to

Richard and Kim like they were losing their influence in their son's life. They were worried about what he was doing and frustrated by the endless arguments over chores and other expectations they had for their son at home. "We have no control over him anymore and he's going to get himself into trouble. We're 100 percent sure of that," Richard told me.

I certainly wasn't there to argue the point. Jeremy was going out and drinking heavily most weekends. He was stretching his curfews until they became almost meaningless. He did little or nothing at home by way of chores, and seldom even managed to eat with his parents. There was always the microwave and leftovers at the ready.

But that wasn't all of Jeremy's story. I learned that he worked at a local autoparts factory as a part-time cleaner, an after school and weekend job he'd found himself. One or the other of his parents had to drive him there as it was in an industrial mall outside the city. They did this happily at first, pleased to see their son working. More recently they were climbing into their car grudgingly, feeling like Jeremy seldom appreciated the efforts they made. He was, however, making excellent money for his age and was a good worker, according to the boy's supervisor. They would sigh, and make the drive.

Though Jeremy's parents loved him dearly, they admitted they didn't understand their son. It had become almost intolerable living with him. Tension followed him into the house like a cold north wind. He'd walk in and his parents' emotional thermostats would trigger, slowly warming them for the next argument. They felt powerless, scared and worst of all, abandoned.

I remember asking Richard and Kim what it was like talking with their son.

"It's pretty much always the same thing. He doesn't want to talk," Kim said.

"What about when he's going to work? Is he more cooperative then?"

"Oh that's better," Richard said. "Then he'll get ready, get in the car, we drive out there, it's a ways you know, but we don't talk much about anything on the way. Feels like we're a taxi most times."

"But he goes to this job steadily? Does well at it?"

"Oh yeah," they both chimed. Richard carried on, "He does real well there. I know that. But at home he does nothing, not a thing we ask him. It's harder on Kim, I think, than me. I just ignore it most times, but the two of them get into battles." Kim nodded.

"And what happens when you talk to him about all this, and about his drinking?" I asked after a moment.

"Well, we try to tell him not to drink so much. And I'm not going to give up on him keeping his room clean and helping around the house. For God's sake, he does more than that at work. He could mow the lawn or put the garbage out, or do some dishes, at least the ones he messes. That would be nice once in a while. And the drinking, when we talk to him he just shuts us out. 'Yeah, yeah, yeah,' like that. I keep telling him he's going to end up like his grandfather, a drunk. It runs in the family. I might as well be talking to that plant over there as waste my words." Kim sat exasperated, anxious for me to wave a magic wand and make Jeremy see the folly of his ways.

It took a couple of weeks, but together we came up with a plan that we thought might recognize the power Jeremy's parents still had over his life, and find a way to guide the boy, build the parent-child relationship, share some good advice, all the while still respecting Jeremy's growing identity as a kid with his own friends, own work, own future, and own schedule. It was quickly becoming apparent that Kim and Richard were living with a young adult now. They had to find a way to still be part of his life as both responsible parents and older, perhaps wiser, guides. When we met they told me what had happened and were pleased with the changes they'd seen.

"We took some of your suggestions, not all, but some," Richard said at our third meeting. "So if he's going to be an adult, we told him, then that's fine, in fact that's what we've wanted all along. I told him I was proud of him. He actually liked that. Mind you, it took a while to get the right moment to tell him all this. But I figured that since I had him captive in the car that was a good time. So I laid it out. Adults have some responsibilities. Either he starts doing the chores Kim asks or I would charge him like a taxi to take him to work. It's a 90-minute bus ride with all the transfers, so I thought, twenty bucks a day was fair. At first he didn't believe me, but I was serious.

"So the next day he hands me a twenty. Said, 'Fine with me.' And then sits there like I'm a taxi. But that was okay with me. I took the twenty dollars and went to the movies with Kim. The next day the same thing. But I think by that point he thought I was going to hand it back. I didn't. Anyways, he didn't have near as much for the weekend party. Then his next shift, he says he'll do his dishes and the garbage if he doesn't have to pay. And I said, money first, then we'll see. He wouldn't pay me and ended up getting to work an hour late by bus. I wouldn't drive him, but the next day, he did the dishes, and the garbage before he left for work. But we weren't rude or holding it over him. Right, Kim? You just said thanks." Kim smiled and agreed. Richard continued, "And since then it's been okay. He talks a bit more in the car with me. It's like some of the tension is gone. Maybe he feels more adult, I don't know.

"Next we're going to talk to him about the drinking. I know, I know, that we can't really do much about that. I just want to tell him about how much it worries us, and what we've seen it do to people. Maybe tell him a bit about his grandfather. Not like we expect him to turn out like that, but just to make him understand that's what Kim lived with and we're worried about him. But I don't think he's really heard the story of his grandfather. Kim thought she'd tell him, show him some pictures he might not have seen. Maybe get his grandmother to talk a bit about it. We've been telling him it's okay if he's out with his buddy, he can drink. That doesn't bother us. Just not like he does when he can't even get up the next day. Do you think that will work?"

"Sounds like a good plan to me," I said. "Let me know what happens."

I heard a month later by phone that Jeremy was acting much more like an adult and had told them he was easing up on the drinking, but not stopping. He'd told Richard he knew it was getting out of hand even before his parents started talking about what it had been like for his mother when she was growing up. Besides, Jeremy wanted to get his license and buy a car so he wouldn't need his parents to be his taxi. He didn't have the money to blow on booze anymore. I was pretty certain that now that Jeremy was closer to being an adult, not only in his own mind but also that of his parents, he'd make better decisions for himself. Best of all, Kim and Richard were pleased to have their son back in their lives.

The Challenge of Substance Abuse

What about when accepting our child's identity pushes us into unfamiliar territory? Or even means that we as caregivers must somehow tolerate behaviours we consider dangerous? What then? The challenge is to maneuver our way around our child's problem behaviour in such a way that we keep our relationship with our kids and show acceptance for those parts of their identity we do like, while still guiding them away from those that can harm them. This delicate balancing act is made easier if we approach children with an attitude reflecting the lessons learned from teens themselves. Respect their truth, honour their differences, understand their stories, and see their choice of identity as a voyage towards health.

Perhaps one of the most challenging areas of disagreement between adults and children is over the use and abuse of drugs. While we adults consume alcohol without social sanction, many of our children have turned to using softer drugs in the same way. To my mind, I have to make a distinction between using pot, hash, natural hallucinogens like mushrooms, even cigarettes, and abusing other more debilitating drugs such as crack, heroine, prescription drugs, or sniffing gas. In these latter cases, the evidence is clear: there is a risk of extreme harm and therefore, in my opinion, caregivers are justified in taking much more drastic and controlling action to save their kids. Few addicts who come down from such serious addictions turn to their caregivers and are angry at them for saving them. An identity is one thing, but perching one's self precariously close to permanent harm is another.

That is not always the case when a child uses softer drugs recreationally. Ofttimes adults come down hard on them, making them out to be addicts when, to the adolescent's way of thinking, they are no better or worse than their parents with their 12-pack of beer on Saturday night. It's at times like this that we have to think tolerance if our goal is to have a positive influence in the lives of our maturing teens. If we don't show them this respect and listen closely to their stories, then their peers will. Even if we vehemently disagree with our children's behaviours, it is still incumbent upon us to be there for them in ways that will be seen as helpful by them. This issue gets quite convoluted when one actually talks about softer drug use with kids and the identities that go along with being a user. Unfortunately, many youth see using cannabis as a reasonable alternative to alcohol because it does not have the same debilitating effects. What are we to make of this as adults? How do we reconcile the risk we perceive and the experiences of our youth which flout our wisdom? Even more, how do we argue with teens to avoid drugs when either we used when we were their age or "use" alcohol now?

Understanding the power drug use brings and the identity that goes along with it is the first step towards helping teens build healthy identities that are drug-free. Keep an open relationship, and talk from your own experience. Avoid the mini-lecture. That was how a colleague and I approached a group of teens and parents I met at a clinic where I worked. The more parents showed acceptance for what the teens were saying (even if personally they disagreed or worried for their safety), the more their teenagers revealed themselves honestly.

During one of our earlier sessions, Joan, a 50-year-old parent of two teenaged girls, turned our conversation to a burning question she had for the seven youth who regularly attended the group.

"I don't understand this whole drug thing," she said. "Why the drugs?"

"Why not? You drink, we do drugs. Big deal," said her 14-year-old daughter, Chelsea. The 16-year-old, Rebecca, sat mute, more hesitant to become engaged. With her eyes staring at the ceiling, she seemed to be saying, "You wouldn't understand if I told you. Why bother."

"Maybe I can help," I offered. "I'm curious too. What's the attraction about the drug scene with your friends. What's the draw, what makes using, or abusing, good?" I avoided the "Why" question like the plague. Like us, kids always feel attacked when they hear it.

This time Rebecca accepted the invitation. "Some teenagers are into alcohol, or drugs, and the car scene and a lot of adults think they all are. That's not the way it is. That's like a stereotype. Not all teenagers go out and abuse drugs. I don't want to get myself in too much trouble with the law. Like, I've gotten into trouble before but never too much trouble."

"But how do you know you won't get into trouble when you know they're illegal?" interrupted Cam, a forty-ish businessman, attending the group with his wife Jean and son Shane.

"How do you make the decision as to how far to go? How much to use?" Joan added.

"I guess it's all how much you feel like you can handle," Shane told us.

"Exactly," jumped in Rebecca. The other teens nodded their agreement.

"I don't do drugs or nothing like that," said Paula, an outspoken and, according to her mother, evil-tongued 15-year-old. "I know you think I do, Mom," she said, directing her comments to her mother across from her. Stephanie stared back. "It's like if you're out with your friends and they want to get into something like that, like booze or drugs, I've never done anything like that. It's all a question of how I feel. If I don't want to do it I won't. I make decisions for myself pretty much. Like, I have a lot of my friends who are addicted to drugs, but I don't do any of that stuff. Sure, I'll have a cigarette. But that's it. Like, as far as my friends come to making decisions for me, sometimes they'll have an influence on my overall decision, but not all the time. Sometimes I'll just do what I want to do."

Looking at these kids one would never have guessed how different they are one from the other, much less how they distinguish themselves from the street youth they spend time with. Each had a different relationship to drugs. The nuances of those relationships became evident as they spoke.

"I've never been too sure if I believe you," answered Stephanie, with an honesty that surprised us all.

"Well, believe it," said a defiant Paula. I did and knew from many other conversations that she was telling the truth.

"So like help us out," said her mother. "Sure, I smoked a little when I was your age, but it just feels like today everything is more dangerous. I hear the stuff you kids get is all full of chemicals. And then there's all this stuff about gangs. And the police. I don't know."

"If someone asks me 'Hey Shane, we have two grams of hash, do you want to come over and get high?' well, I'll sit there and look at them for a second and then maybe I'll go or maybe not. I think it through. It's just our way of having some fun. It's not always got to be some big dangerous thing we do." Shane was trying to help his father and the rest of us understand.

I decided to jump in as well. "I think, Shane, what the problem is here is that you and your friends see using drugs differently from your parents. It does feel like it's around more than ever. I think I'm hearing everyone say they are concerned and afraid for what's going to happen to you."

That stirred the pot a little. This time it was James, a quieter 16-year-old who had had some trouble with the law. "If I see my friends doing heavy stuff, I say to them, 'Why are you guys doing this? You're just wrecking your lives.' Makes me kind of angry that someone would do that kind of stuff. But I don't care, if someone wants to go out and be stupid like that then I don't care. I'll talk with them about it but if they still want to go out and do it, then fine. At least they'll know not to ask me again to do it with them."

"And the harder stuff is different from the softer stuff?" asked Joan. "Is that what you're trying to say?"

"Of course."

"Yes."

"Like, duh!" chorused several youth at once.

"And are you worried about losing acceptance if you don't do the drugs?"

Rebecca took the lead this time. "I don't care. I feel accepted. I have friends who are real dopeheads but I can decide for myself what I do. It's just a group of kids, not some evil cult."

"It's my life and my body," said Paula, voicing what many of her peers were trying to say.

This caught the attention of many of the parents. All of sudden it was becoming clearer that here were teenagers who had been listening all along, who had heard the encouragement over the years to take pride in their bodies, to value themselves, to stand up to the pressures from others to be anything but what they wanted to be. In that room, an honest exchange was taking place across the generations, in large part because the parents were listening and trying to understand the world of their teens. What they were being treated to was a glimpse at the power teens look for when designing an identity among their peers.

"I don't know, but to be a teenager today you have to dress a certain way, be a certain way," said Chelsea. "You have to do drugs and drink just to fit in with certain groups. But if you don't care about being accepted then no problem. I don't know about it all 'cause I'm not like that personally. I might light up a joint and my friends would be like 'Wow! You smoke this all the time?' and be like this, blah, blah, blah trying to be cool to make everyone believe they know all about it. But that's just stupid. I don't do it to show off. I do it because I want to have fun. It's a lot different than before 'cause there wasn't as much peer pressure back then. You probably can't understand."

I had to chuckle to myself. Even as we adults leave behind the myth of peer pressure, our kids keep it alive. Even as we try to listen to what they have to say, they like to throw back at us what they believe our experience was as youth. "I'm not sure that's how it was for me," I said. "I'm glad to see you're thinking for yourself, though." The other parents smiled. "How do you cope with the peer pressure?" I asked, preferring for the moment to use the language Chelsea had used.

"Well, I've been to lots of parties where there's lots of drinking and lots of drugs. Don't get me wrong. I've drank and done drugs a couple of times. But if I don't want something I just say no. Like I've had someone cram a beer down my throat and say 'Come on, come on, have a drink,' and I just said, 'No, I don't want to.' Same with drugs. It's like if you get a name, there's two types of names, a follower and a leader. For me to say that I'm a leader, everybody knows that so you can be cool and say no. That's just as much cool as saying yes."

"Well, that's reassuring to hear, but does there always have to be drugs around? Can't you kids get together without someone always bringing it along?" This time it was Shane's mother, Jean, who wondered aloud what for many of us was still the issue.

"It doesn't have to be. But they're there," said James.

"I used to drink all the time. As soon as I got money that's where it went." It was Collette this time, a 16-year-old who had come to the group steadily, but spoke less than most of her peers. "Alcohol and cigarettes. I was 13, 14 and 15 and did lots. I quit smoking, cigarettes that is, since I started coming here. But to be with my group they all either drink or smoke and I thought to be in with them you had to do the same. Sometimes it made it worse. Sometimes it made my feelings inside even worse. Like sad. And I thought it was maybe an easy way out, but it just makes it worse. Makes you feel even more of what you feel inside. It makes it go deeper."

"Has it stopped hurting as much since you stopped drinking? Stopped smoking?" I asked.

"Yes and no. I still smoke dope sometimes. But the rest of it, no. A little high now and then keeps me level. It's really just like once a month, not much more."

Conventional wisdom says that drug use can cloud one's ability to cope with problems and may worsen situations for teenagers. But that wasn't always the case for these teens. Sometimes by participating partially in a peer group that does drugs, a teen finds a strategy to gain acceptance along with a self-definition he or she likes. While it may be a poor choice, it may be the least harmful of the choices a teen could make.

"I do the same," said Rebecca. "Sometimes a toke is better than getting all screwed up and thinking about killing yourself, or anything like that."

"I don't know if I'm convinced, but I hear what you're saying," said Cam.

"I wish you'd both stop, but I can't tie you up, keep you from your friends," added Joan.

"What I'm hearing the teens say is that they are doing better than we expected. At least now we know what they're thinking and that they're trying to figure this out. It sounds like all of them are doing much fewer drugs than we thought," I said. The parents nodded. The kids sat there smugly.

A conversation like this didn't set out to change anything. I've never in my career managed to change the drug use habits of a teen by myself or through any one conversation. But I have seen conversations like this one snowball into a series of steps taken by parents and children that help parents accept their children's lives while making children more open to hearing both their parents' concerns and advice.

From communication there comes the possibility for more time to be shared together. There's far less anxiety among parents when they at least know truthfully what their kid is up to when outside their homes. And there is also the added bonus that when mistakes happen and kids mess up, maybe, just maybe, they'll go to their parents for help. That kind of relationship doesn't just appear during a crisis. The goodwill that makes that happen builds over time, when children feel understood and their identity constructions are seen as the solutions they are.

Chapter 9
Rough Seas

The oceans teens navigate are not full of endless possibilities. That might be a comforting thought for those who want us to believe that *every* child can one day become a national leader. Some children beat the incredible odds against them, but as is more often the case, many do not. When I talk with adults about how children live powerful but harmful lives, I'm often asked, "But then why don't kids choose other ways of behaving – ways that are acceptable to us?" Unfortunately, the question assumes that all children have equal opportunities. Without intending to, it blames the victims for their victimization. Different environments and different life circumstances exert varying degrees of control over individuals. Our life choices are circumscribed by the limited number of choices available to us. What we bring to life and what life dishes out largely decide our fate.

I think of these barriers to a healthy identity in three concentric circles. At the very middle of the three is a small circle that holds all of a child's personal characteristics like their emotional or intellectual intelligence, physical attributes, including gender and race, and any mental or emotional problems that may originate deep inside them. In the second circle are all the family issues. Has the family been dealing with violence, separations, or the death of one of its members? How much stress is the family under? For every child I've introduced up to this point, these familial factors are just as important as personal characteristics to understanding why a child chooses one "solution" over another.

The third concentric circle contains all of the community and cultural barriers we experience, all of which interact with these personal and family characteristics. It's not just that one is a girl or a boy, or that one's family is separated or divorced; it's what our culture tells us girls or boys from "broken" homes should be and do that creates problems for kids.

In this outermost circle are also the real life barriers kids experience such as neighbourhood crime, family poverty, the sameness and uninspired uniformity of the suburbs. Understanding kids means looking critically at the availability of whatever it is they need to sustain mental health and feel both competent and in control of their lives. Recreational opportunities, good schools, and safe neighbourhoods are just some of the things kids need if they are to be healthy. In stable, middle-class communities, these things can be in abundance, and yet still kids feel an oppressive pressure to conform, to fit in, to look the same and act the same. The result are kids who feel like strangers in a strange land, even though from the outside they look like they fit in.

The Child in Focus

It's been my experience that families often want to start by telling me about their children in terms of what they are, as much as what they do. We like to attribute the problems children experience to some flaw in them personally. I hear phrases like: "He doesn't learn very quickly," "He has always acted impulsively," "She has her mother's temper," "All the Tremblays are like that," "It's a girl thing." We too quickly want to simplify problems to one cause and one effect.

Strangely, what can be a weakness to a parent can become a strength when a teen finds the right place to express him- or herself. If you're "dumb" according to Dad, then hang with drop-outs and prove you don't need school to be successful. If you have a different body shape, hang out with others who help you feel that your shape is just fine. Have a physical challenge and feel you're never going to make it at sports, then turn to a group of kids where the physical impairment doesn't matter and learn to survive and thrive despite it. It's not that high-risk kids ignore their limitations, but that they just get around them and the stigma that attaches to them.

Over the years I've worked with many youth coping with physical and mental challenges. They demonstrate, like their emotionally im- paired peers, a remarkable ability to find friends who help them feel every bit as powerful and accepted as others. Jason, who was sixteen when I knew him, was born with a birth defect. Though it appeared he simply walked with a limp, he in fact wore a prosthesis on his right leg below the knee.

Jason had been getting into trouble for years. He was not good at school, he couldn't do many sports, or so he said, and he didn't make friends easily. His mother was a single parent raising him and his younger sister on little money in a much deteriorated public housing unit. Jason's world was full of real barriers to a positive self-definition. Many in his community saw him as "crippled," "stupid," and "white trash." Yet despite all the problems in Jason's life not associated with his leg, Jason's emerging pattern of delinquency, his disregard for the property of others, his frequently assaultive behaviour, his risk taking and drug abuse were all blamed on his never having adequately adjust- ed to being physically challenged.

Jason didn't think that was his problem at all. In fact, he found his life as a delinquent a way to cope with the craziness he saw all around him. Besides, with his friends he was seldom thought of as "crippled" and instead was considered by them as one "mean little shit" who loved to vandalize his neighbourhood with impunity, his behaviour being excused in part because of his disability. Jason's peer group offered him ways to feel powerful while at the same time hide his "problem." Such things as skater clothes, with their long, loose-fitting bell-bottomed shapes, helped him disguise his artificial leg. The fact that the fashion was in vogue summer and winter made it even more attractive, as Jason avoided the issue of wearing shorts.

"I just try to hide my leg as much as possible. People have only just now found out at school. I cope with it by just doing whatever anyone else does. To me it's just my leg. I was born that way. I can walk just as far, I can run fast. Like, everyone can run faster than someone else. I can swim. It's not really a disability," he shrugged. "It's just different."

Though Jason was pretty certain his leg was no big problem, other things in his life were.

Poverty, a lack of academic success, boredom, and the disadvantages of being from the neighbourhood where he lived had left him with few choices for success, with or without two legs. His peers and their lifestyle was a great fit for someone in his situation. Among them he had pieced together an identity of the rebellious, racist, anti-establishment type of kid. His opinions tended to put everyone off but his like-minded peers.

I can recall asking him once about his neighbourhood, who he got along with and who he didn't. He told me about the different groups on the streets where he lived but he wanted to be sure I saw him as an individual. That was when he started talking about the neo-Nazis.

"I'm not a Nazi," Jason said. "At least by their rules. I like black people. I don't find anything wrong with black people. I just don't like Arabs. I like Chinese people, though I wish there weren't so many of them here. It's after all our country. Like, the black people and us and the Indians were here first. I don't hate Jews. I don't even care about religion. I just don't like the way black people have all these organizations and want all these rights. Or feminists, I don't like feminists. It seems to me they don't want equal, they want more rights than we have. Like my uncle says if you're a citizen of this country you should just be a citizen when you're getting a job. Not a black man or a woman or a white man."

Though I find comments like this very hard to listen to, I don't find it surprising to hear it any more when I work with kids who are going nowhere in their lives. It's a way of thinking that fits with a world where they are scared and feeling threatened. I always eventually confront kids on their racist, sexist beliefs, but first I get a relationship with them. I need to understand what it is about the power of these beliefs that is so attractive. What is it about hate that draws them into relations with others who only want to feel powerful at another's expense?

Jason's disability might play a small role in his choice of peer group and identity. But to think of it, as some did, as the only reason he had gone down that path gets us no closer to understanding Jason or helping him. After all, if he didn't associate himself with the ideas of neo-Nazis, then where else was he going to find some power? In school he'd all but been written off by his teachers. He blamed them for his lack of commitment and academic success.

"I'm not dumb," he insisted. "I don't think teachers should be able to boss me around. It's not their life, it's mine."

"I didn't know you were being bossed around," I said, trying to help.

He let out a low nasal snort, as if dismissing me and my ignorance as so obviously below him that it was hardly worth the effort to set me straight.

"My teachers, my mom, adults, they think they can boss me around. It's always like that in school. Teachers think they can boss you around. Sometimes I just don't listen, and they'll try to give me a detention, and I won't go. What are they going to do? Give me detentions, or suspensions? But they don't do anything. It's not really that bad being suspended."

"I know your mom's pretty concerned about the suspensions and your skipping. Is there any way you can do things your way but still get your school year finished?"

"It's pretty dumb my skipping off so much. Thing is I skipped off so much that I realized I could fail, so I started going every day for two months. Figured that way I could get the year. Then I found my marks went down. I don't know how it could happen. So after that I didn't go much. I started skipping again. Like, what was the point. I failed English because I didn't hand in one stupid assignment. I did all the other work and got perfect on tests and everything, but my teacher still failed me."

"Who do you blame for that?" I asked in a tone that hopefully showed I really wanted to know, that I wasn't assuming I had the "right" answer to my question. Too often kids know we just want them to say "I blame myself" and though they oblige us, they seldom mean it. Jason took my invitation and told me what he really thought.

"Well, it's pretty well the school. They fail you because it's their rules that you have to pass in every assignment. And I failed a course because I didn't pass in a thirty-mark assignment. And in music we had a new teacher. And, like, I was just learning to play and doing pretty good. And then when I started straightening out we got this new teacher and she didn't know how much I skipped before and just thought I didn't know how to play as well so she failed me there. Actually, I was keeping up with the people in the class and playing just as well. But I had to keep going to the hospital for my leg and it was weird the way every time I went there was a test."

And there were a lot of visits to the hospital. It would have seemed to Jason that indeed the more he tried, the less it made a difference. Things at home or in his neighbourhood certainly weren't going to get any better even if he went to school. Being a drop-out, a mean racist street kid, and a delinquent all seemed to make sense. The personal barriers he faced, his leg, his lack of academic skill, were just a part of a life full of barriers to his well-being.

Expectations

It's important that we understand how expectations by others, peers and adults alike, surround kids like Jason. Teenagers experience these as immutable scripts that tell them how their lives will be lived. Teens who say they have always been seen as "losers" by their families and never expected to amount to much are already at a great disadvantage to do likewise. While many of the personal barriers children like Jason face are characteristics they cannot change, the expectations which people have of children like him say more about the people doing the labelling than the one being labelled. Professionals and non-professionals cast their bias like nets over those whom they meet, trapping kids into patterns of behaviour. Just try and get a kid who's been a problem child at school to change and one will see how the child's teachers and parents become suspicious, wondering if the child is really just out to trick them. A child who tries to oppose what others expect of them is likely to find his or her voice silenced by the loud and unified chorus of caregivers who say they know better.

Gender is one particularly powerful barrier to a child's choice of identity. Years ago, I employed on a summer grant a young woman of Chinese descent named Lisa. She had a gift for thinking critically about her world. She also had a love for the antiquities and wanted to become an archeologist. At age sixteen, she had tried to introduce this idea to her parents who had decided that the only appropriate training for their child, especially a female child, was an education in Business or Law. I do not profess to understand why these two professions were legitimate occupations for a girl, while the life of Indiana Jones was not, but that was the rule and, for Lisa, she didn't have it in her to disobey. The consequence, she was told, would be the loss of her parent's love, support and approval.

Those kind of ultimatums make children vulnerable to being taken advantage of by anyone who orders them around. Rather than learning how to negotiate an identity, kids like Lisa must either give up who they are or run straight for the door and out into the street. There they find peers they can turn to for support with a force and commitment which would have been unnecessary in other circumstances. By choosing the right peer group, the cast off child not only finds a new family but also confronts his or her real family with its failings. Finding a group of powerful peers solves primal needs for both fight and flight at the same time. It needn't be like this.

The Family

Families are buffeted by the same winds of change and circumstance as their children. Crises that the whole family experiences can't help but have an impact. If we recall Jacintha's parents and their conflicts, or the mistrust Lorraine has of her mother and her boyfriend, or the extreme abuse and neglect Tommy experienced, or the emotional violence Alex put up with, then it becomes self-evident that stressed parents with their own problems contribute to stressed kids. Similarly, families who survive in the emotional wastelands of orderly boredom, in which it is more important to look like the Cleavers than to celebrate the eccentricities of the Simpsons, restrict their children with expectations of "sameness."

Kids who feel disadvantaged by their family's situation, whether that disadvantage is real or imagined, will go looking for friends and opportunities to give them what their family can't or won't. Sometimes they find those door openers on the street among peers, or even in jail. Sometimes, as with Lorraine, Alexander and Mark, they find these peers in recreation centres, treatment programs or at school. Where the solutions come from depends on the way the barriers a child faces interact one with the other. Barriers connect like pieces of a puzzle. We can never get the whole picture of a child's life by simply looking at individual or family problems. We need to understand the child's community and culture as well.

Culture

If we look beyond the child and his or her family, we find other barriers that affect which identities at-risk youth choose. Our culture, especially pop culture, can and does limit the identity choices available to our children.

After all, children are no different from adults. How we should act, dress and run our relationships are all dictated as much by the magazines at the grocery store checkout as by our parents and friends. Our culture acts like a huge fun house mirror that reflects back to us a distorted image of what we can be. But while we are looking at the mirror from the outside, we should never forget that we are also participants and authors of the very culture which oppresses us. Each time we participate, or choose not to participate, in society and its rules, we either add to those rules or offer a legitimate challenge to them. Unlike the expectations I discussed above which are put on us clearly by those closest to us, these cultural expectations are much harder to discern, more ubiquitous, and sometimes in their own sneaky ways, much more aggressive. Our culture circumscribes our choices. We still maintain the personal power to pick from the smorgasbord of life whatever behaviours we so choose. The problem is that the availability of options is limited by the constraints of the culture in which we are embedded.

Culture does not announce itself to us like the parent who admonishes us to choose this career or that one. Culture seeps into us through stories and images passed to us a little bit at a time. Though there are few truths in our culture that are chiselled in stone, we often forget that how we think things are is just a reflection of how we want them to be. How we dress, what we eat, when we sleep, what we do with our day, our relationship with money, expectations placed on us to be consumers, who we associate with, how we express (or hide) our sexuality – all these aspects of our lives are influenced by our culture with hardly a thought given to the impermanence of these supposedly commonsense rules.

One bright young woman, Meaghan, whom I met while she was in custody, struggled to find a way to fit in with the culture around her. While I quietly admired her determination, I couldn't help but think that it always sounded to me like she was going to have to kill her soul if she was ever going to fit in. I wondered to myself if it was really worth the price. According to authors like Mary Pipher, who works with and writes about adolescent girls, Meaghan's not alone in her dilemma.

Meaghan had, like many others, come from a violent home where her parents had fought for years, resulting in numerous visits to women's shelters when the danger to Meaghan's mother, Trish, and her three children became too great. The situation would calm and Trish would return home again, trapped by few options and the belief that the kids needed their father. She coped by becoming cross-addicted to alcohol and prescription medications. As a girl, alone and drifting quickly to the street, it didn't take Meaghan long before she found older boys to look after her and mentor her into a life much like her mother's. As she explained calmly, and with great insight, "I guess I'm in custody a lot because of my friends, well, my acquaintances, really. It was easy to do things like they did. I saw people do all sorts of crime. I know it was wrong what I did. But I didn't have what it takes to get what I want the right way." Getting what she wanted had meant becoming very adapt at jacking cars and armed assaults.

She didn't have many people other than other delinquents to help her. Through her association with them, she found a way to help herself.

"My friends take care of me. It started really when I was thirteen. That's when I first moved to town. I was just so young but I matured early. Do you know what I mean?" I nodded, guessing I understood. I was fairly certain she wasn't just talking about her appearance. She carried herself with an uncanny presence and demonstrated a wisdom that seemed well beyond her years.

"Nobody knew my age. I wouldn't tell them because I was so insecure. But once they got to know me and stuff, they took care of me, just like I was a little kid."

"And you liked that?"

"Sure, it was great. But when I found my boyfriend, Doug, then I really didn't need them. They were there to party with and have fun with. But, Doug, he took care of me. He washed my clothes for me and he fed me and stuff. And he protected me. And I went off with him and then everybody else that I knew, I just left them. I didn't need them anymore. Does that make sense?"

It did. It was sad to watch this spirited young woman with so many talents slipping without resistance into the role of the dependent female. But there was more to the story than just the one plot line.

Try as she might Meaghan could never stay in that one-down position. She could out-think and out-perform many of the guys she met, including Doug. It didn't surprise me to learn she was the one who convinced one of her female friends to steal a car and go for the joy ride that ended tragically when Meaghan hit and injured a 10-year-old boy during a brief high-speed run from police. The car eventually careened off the road and rolled several times. Her co-accused was paralysed. Remarkably, Meaghan walked away all but unharmed, at least on the outside. To hear Meaghan talk about it all, Thelma and Louise would have been proud. Only problem was that now in jail, Meaghan was having second thoughts about her behaviour. Ironically, I'm not sure that what she was experiencing, this withdrawal from all that had let her survive, was as healthy for her as it might have seemed. In confronting her behaviour, Meaghan was left with an emptiness that came from finding herself in a culture which made her invisible as a young woman. "People look at me now like I'm kind of useless."

"What's going to happen when you get out?" I asked.

"I don't know," she said. "A lot of people say that I have the talent and stuff to make something of myself, but it doesn't mean anything to me. I just want to be able to have a job that interests me a bit, like a cook in a big restaurant or something. You know? Go to school for that and learn. Do you know what I mean? I'd just be happy to have a job that supports me and keeps me alive, *rather than making something of myself*, something like that."

"That really sounds like two different things. One sounds like just a job, the other, an occupation, something to get much more caught up in," I said.

"Well, I guess an occupation isn't really that important, but a job. I don't think of myself as a hardworking citizen. Because of what I did. I don't think that I deserve it."

"So what will life be like?"

"I won't cause problems. I'll just wake up and go to work and live." I wasn't sure if as a system of care and rehabilitation we could call our interventions with Meaghan a "success." Surprisingly, she wasn't depressed. She was just, well, nothing. Flat. She was drifting from a place in life where she could excel into a dead zone.

Fortunately, and not so fortunately, Meaghan's life didn't quite unfold as she predicted. When the choice came down to the mediocrity Meaghan just described or the allure of a life of crime and drugs, the latter won out easily. Not long after her release she was back where she had started. For her the culture my colleagues and I represented held little attraction, even though our world was hers for the asking. What we had failed to do was help her find a way of being a part of our world, while still resisting its assumptions about how a young woman is supposed to act. We had failed, not individually, but as a culture, to entice Meaghan because we hadn't shown her clearly how she could live a spirited life within the confines of her community's rules.

Knowing that culture is "make believe" does not necessarily set us free from its oppressive force. But a concerted effort by a group of people who put forth a different idea of what culture is can sometimes offer up a formidable challenge to the forces of conformity. Meaghan's peers offered her something besides what she perceived as a bland middle-class existence. Teens need peers with whom to flock if they are to challenge the culture we hand them. Without peers, the individual child is just a lone voice crying for help. But a whole group of like-minded peers can do more. They can yell. They can mount an effective resistance to how things are supposed to be. Think of the Sixties. Though each generation finds it difficult to accept the wisdom of the next, I am certainly ready to admit defeat and let youth help to shape a better, more tolerant, environmentally sustainable and socially benign world that values the diversity of a global village infused with novelty.

Not that all delinquents are going about their criminal activities thinking they are building a better tomorrow. Quite the contrary. Often they are taking pot shots at the institutions that do not understand them and have ignored what it is they need. There is a point in every conversation I have with troubled teens when I feel we are not just talking about what they did, but about what society expects them to do. I feel like I become the reluctant mouthpiece for my generation which wants kids to behave and conform. At such times I have to remember that sometimes what I appear to be asking them to do is ludicrous. Why am I trying to convince them to finish a general level education, when these high school "credits for dummies" (as some like to call them) won't even get them into college vocational programs? Who am I to say that dropping out and selling drugs is not a better choice, given the circumstances? I wish it weren't, but sadly, there are moments when I am working with youth and it becomes all too clear that they may have a better plan than any I can offer them. My job then becomes much more challenging. I have to stop looking at the individual child and start thinking about what needs to change structurally in our society so that kids don't need to become delinquents or deviants to find ways to express themselves as non-conformists.

The Real World

The social barriers that challenge high-risk youth as they search for healthy identities are embedded in the very real life circumstances in which they live. Poverty, communities in the process of decay, violence, either in their homes or on the street, the availability of drugs, the lack of access to education, health care, or counselling, overworked staff at social services departments, a lack of recreation facilities, and a government that just doesn't care enough, these are real barriers that affect the choices some children have for healthy living. Child poverty threatens healthy identities as surely as an abusive parent. In the absence of options, teenagers turn to the only resource they have, the street and the powerful ways one can carve out an identity there. When I see youth hanging out late at night downtown, I know that some are on those street corners entirely by choice, having other places to be. But I also know that for others, that is the only place that makes any sense for them to be.

Through relationships with peers, teens can maneuver around these social, political and economic barriers. Peer groups have an uncanny knack for finding fun that doesn't cost very much. So many of the kids I meet who lack financial means find creative, if not destructive, ways to feel good about themselves in a consumer society that says wealth equals happiness. We should marvel at the way marginalized youth pull off this trick of creating a powerful and healthy identity, while many other youth, privileged and with abundant opportunities, struggle to do the same.

Christian was one of those kids from the wrong community who started with next to nothing and was likely to go nowhere. He was from a community where if you said you were from there, people tended to look at you a certain way, as if they knew you more than you knew yourself. Christian didn't tend to disappoint. A hard-drinking, car-thieving kid, he ran with an older crowd who spent most of their evenings in front of the liquor store trying to get someone to buy them some booze. Usually they didn't wait long. Then it was party till you drop, or fight till you drop, and sometimes both. It was a world I only glimpsed now and again when I visited, but one which I could never really understand.

"There's not too many around my place that care much for getting a job, or school, or the police," he told me with his characteristic candour. We'd met while he attended a drug rehab program, having agreed to attend instead of going to jail. "Maybe now that I've been sober for a time it will be different when I go home, I don't know," he said. He now and again thought he might even go back to school, though wasn't sure it would work. "It's just there's so many young fellows around and you can't really concentrate anyways. There's just too much excitement going on when we are all together I don't get time to get to school."

Most of Christian's family survived on public assistance of one sort or another, or worked part of the year in seasonal jobs. The ones who were doing better tended not to want to have much to do with kids like Christian, and tried to keep their own kids away from him and his group of friends. Personal and family barriers, chronic poverty, almost no professional supports, and few if any diversions for the kids, meant he was growing up with limited options except to become another generation living the same life as his parents and grandparents.

Sadly, a generation or two ago prospects may have been a bit brighter for Christian and kids like him. There would have been farming and fishing jobs that demanded young people feel responsible and grown up. Expectations would have been different too. Thirty or forty years ago people had far less, but seldom felt poor. Today, Christian and his friends are rural youth trying to live like their urban peers. Except they have far less cash, hardly anywhere to go and even less to do. Getting into trouble offers the most amusement.

The kinds of risk factors that Christian confronts on a daily basis grow in power exponentially as their number increases. Having to confront one risk may be manageable; having to take on two is like experiencing four, and having three is like being crushed by eight. The more challenges we face in life, the more we can become burdened and the greater our need for help coping. Ironically, often the only help available to an overwhelmed child is a peer group full of youth with the same heavy loads in life.

When I work with youth, or work with their parents and caregivers, it's important I address all the barriers they face, personal, family, and cultural. Only then can I understand what forces are conspiring to drive children to create the identities they do. In today's world where the expectation by both therapists and those who come to see them is for individually focussed psychotherapy, it can be a difficult sell getting people to see the way children's identities are constructed out of the social fabrics of their lives. We want to psychologize problems and keep them neatly housed inside individuals. We don't want to go down that slippery road of seeing how we all contribute to the very real social conditions which make our children seek out "problem" behaviours.

Marni taught me this as much as anyone else. Here was a 14-year-old girl very adept at negotiating with her family and community a new set of rules to replace those that others assumed were written in stone. Marni came to counselling with her mother Libby, her father Bob, her older sister Kirsten, and her younger brother Patrick. Our goal at first was to help Marni cope with her father's mental illness. I was told everyone in the home had adjusted just fine. Bob was diagnosed with manic-depression after spending thousands of dollars on a cross border shopping bonanza and then becoming violent during a confrontation with border guards while returning home. Libby has had to work long hours to get the family out of debt while Bob has spent his time laying on the couch arguing with the children.

Although Bob is now on medication, and his behaviour is under control, Libby is still very anxious and worried. Neither parent has had much time for Marni in the last two years. She's been expected to replace her mother around the home and act responsibly, keeping the household running. Marni said she was fed up being told what to do.

Her parents say Marni used to be a "good girl," always helping around the home, never getting into arguments, pleasant to be around. At the time the family began counselling, however, I was told a very different story about her. Marni was suicidal, skipping school, sexually active, smoking, spending money "frivolously" and refusing to go to church, a big part of the family's Sunday routine. When I met her, Marni had just come back from running away for two days during which time she had tried to harm herself by slashing her wrists with a pocketknife. Marni explained that she felt like she was expected to be the "mother" while at home, and that she did not feel ready or able to do the job.

"I want things to be back how they were before my dad got sick," she told me when we had a chance to talk without her parents in the room. It was a simple enough wish, but one I had no power to make happen. Whether Marni liked it or not, things would now always be different in her home; however, we decided, they could work better for her than they did now.

I got some clues how Marni and I might make things change by asking her about her life out among her peers. With them, Marni is a different child altogether, an outgoing and assertive individual. She has a boyfriend with whom she is not sexually active, a decision more hers than his. Her parents, of course, don't believe her. She also likes to break with the gender norms of her peers and is very proud of her success in an automotive course at school. Unfortunately, her mother can't see the sense in Marni studying auto mechanics. Needless to say, Marni has had to spend more and more time away from home with her friends to keep a lid on her anger which threatens to overwhelm her at home.

"I usually see myself as somebody who gets along with practically anyone. I don't put down people for how they look or what they wear, especially 'cause most people have control to decide those things for themselves. I have that control. I make all my own choices. Like being

224

with a guy or not, and who my friends are, and if I smoke or if I don't smoke and stuff like that."

We spent much of our time together talking about each of these choices. It was a helpful way to find the good among all that her family saw as bad. But one part of our conversation more than any other stands out for me.

"I've been put down a lot lately this year for taking a bunch of automotive classes," she told me one day in late June just as school was wrapping up for the year. "But it's just a bunch of guys high on themselves who think no girl can do as good as them. Everyone before pictured me as this person doing this very girl-like thing and never getting into stuff like that. And now all my friends are like 'Ooooh! How can you do something like that?' But I like it. Now my friends think it's really neat that I'm into that kind of stuff even though they're not that kind of people . . . I don't really try to be like my friends 'cause I think that's really stupid, but it's neat being different. Makes me feel great that way."

Marni's biggest "problem" wasn't her behaviour outside the home; it was her failed attempts to carry a positive self-definition as a teenager from her community back into her home. With her peers, she was accepted both as a member of their group and as a unique individual. She'd carved out that niche for herself. There at least she could gently challenge the expectations others placed on her. With time, they'd come to accept her as different.

But for Marni's parents, their daughter challenged what they held as sacred and normal. At the time, it was too much for them to handle on top of everything else. They came to counselling with the expectation that I would fix their daughter. Instead, Marni fixed herself once her parents unpacked some of their baggage regarding how their daughter, and young women in general, should behave. Though I was hesitant to say it, I couldn't help but think that Marni's peers had a better handle on what a teenaged girl needed for support than her parents. I was sure Libby and Bob had Marni's best interests at heart, and loved her deeply, but they had sacrificed their relationship with their daughter in their battle for control.

It was sad to watch the family interact because Marni still wanted her parents to have a say in her life. Because this was the case, in time we managed to get the parents back into a parenting role, and Marni back to being a kid. Only this time, Marni wasn't the same dutiful child she'd once been. As Buddhism teaches, we can never wade into the same river twice. In the new story about herself that Marni brought home, she was respected for what was unique about her while she picked from among her family's strengths what she needed to stay healthy. Together, as a team, she and her family were quite adept at keeping everyone safe and rebuilding their lives. It wasn't the fantasied world of Marni's early childhood. It was better.

Chapter 10
When the Blaming Stops

Strategy Five: Stop blaming peers. See youth as an equal participant in the construction of their group's identity.

When we blame our children's peer group for our children's behaviour we forget the most important thing about group culture and values: we all play a role in creating them. When we try to distinguish our child from other "troubled" kids, we become distracted from what should be our real purpose, that being to look at how our adolescent participates, either positively or negatively, in the decisions his or her peer group makes. It's more comfortable to imagine that "delinquent" peers have control over our child's behaviour, and that our child is innocent of blame. The myth of peer pressure helps shelter us from the truth. A child in a group is a participant in that group, even if in the role of follower he or she does little more than play the audience for others. There is no neutral position when it comes to the construction of a group identity.

Perhaps that's why peer groups have so much potential to help in the healing process. As a society we are making it too easy for children to become stuck with singular self-definitions. From the time our children are young, many parents become taxi drivers for their children, ferrying them from one self-improvement program to the next. While our efforts are to be lauded, sometimes we have become the ones doing all the work negotiating our children's place and identity with those around them.

In most suburban neighbourhoods there are no longer the swarming masses of children roaming in search of the next pick-up game of hockey, or creating elaborate tea parties out behind their homes on back porches. Once public spaces for children which were under their control have become structured forums in which fun and skills are combined to teach our children what we adults feel they need to learn. It is certainly safer this way. But does it meet our children's needs for an unstructured world of peer interaction in which they can self-direct their explorations for a powerful identity? In organized activities can they find the same opportunities to experiment with ways of being and expressing themselves? The problem with the over-programmed child is we as adults are doing all the discovering, while the child is given the message "We know best who you should be." Of course, there aren't that many alternatives left for parents who would prefer to put their kids outside with the simple instruction to "Go play." "With who?" will be the most likely response from most children residing in our bedroom communities.

At figure skating I am a "skater." At baseball, I am a "pitcher." I don't find out much else about myself in either role. And I certainly don't have much latitude to express how I am different from others on my team. Too much conformity and structured interaction constrains any hope of exploration and self-definition. Sure, a little structure is necessary and helpful. But programmed days which follow one upon the other are just as likely to burn out children as lead them to a healthy sense of self. It's a gamble most parents now take.

The result is I am seeing more and more youngsters like Jill, who at age eleven, came to see me because of depression. Twelve months earlier Jill had been a talented gymnast who had won her city finals only to place eleventh the following month at the regional championships. Not bad, I thought, but as it turned out, not good enough. Jill had her hopes set on the national team, and even at age ten, an eleventh place finish was not enough to attract the level of coaching necessary for her training. All of a sudden she realized that she was not the best, and that she would likely never make it to the Olympics. To her mind, she had become washed-up at the age when most kids are just beginning to think about anything beyond tomorrow.

When Jill came to see me she slouched down in a chair, her hair a dishevelled mess of tangled brown wisps. At her mother's prompting I asked Jill about her life as a gymnast. She mumbled back to me that she had "retired." It was the use of the word retired which so astonished me. I didn't think an 11-year-old could "retire" from anything, much less that at that age any door could be closed. But that was simply not true for a gymnast in Jill's world. Her entire self-image, from body to friends, to social activities, to diet, to play interests, had all been shaped by the rigours of practice and competition. It took me some time to put aside all my preconceived notions of how unburdened childhood should be. It was difficult at first to tune in to where Jill was coming from and begin to engage in conversations about her life and the singular definition with which had she become stuck.

She'd had no other life to speak of since she was three. After school she had trained for hours. When she wasn't training there was fundraising to be done for the gymnastics club. Even summers were not totally without their routine as stretching and strengthening was a year-round necessity. Her parents loved her dearly and, to be fair, it had been Jill pushing them to let her train so much. They had been the ones cautioning her to relax, to find more friends, to play other sports. But Jill had one script in her mind. She obsessed on being the best, and for a moment appeared to have achieved her goal. But she was only a local hero, when she wanted national fame.

By the time we'd met she had lost interest in all sports. She had practically no friends because she stopped hanging out with the only girls she knew who had continued to practice at the gymnastics club. Her marks at school had sunk to an abysmal low. She was talking about suicide. She hardly ever washed. But she was, thankfully, willing to talk.

We worked together for a time, and Jill did find her way to some new interests. What she taught me, though, has stayed with me. Jill needed a number of different peer groups. Instead she had just one. All through her childhood when her circle of peers should have been expanding, growing outwards, she had actually choked off contact with others, all except those who shared one particular lifestyle.

Jill's doing much better now. She shows no more signs of depression than most children her age. We didn't have to meet very long. At first there was a lot of mourning to be done about lost dreams, and huge gaps to fill in Jill's life now that she had decided to stop training. She was encouraged to return to gymnastics and help younger children train. But the problem that still remained was how to get Jill connected with other peer groups. In searching for an answer, Jill, her parents and I thought about what it was that had so excited Jill about her sport. Her parents, to their credit, had never forced her to compete. It was Jill who had been driven to succeed. She loved the recognition from family and friends, the team uniforms, the travel, the girls she met along the way, all of whom convinced her she was part of a special and elite group of kids. Unfortunately, it was all a house of cards that too quickly collapsed.

While her peers at school were widening their range of experiences and broadening their choice of self-definitions during their years in upper elementary school, Jill had been on a singular course through life. Now with that gone, it was not going to be easy finding another activity for Jill to do that would help her feel as good about herself.

Though she had nurtured a very positive identity, she was every bit as stuck as any delinquent in an inflexible role. She needed, most of all, to develop some skills to negotiate a more complex identity for herself. That's where peers came in. They could offer her a way back to health.

Ironically, we discovered that Jill needed a peer group that was *less* dedicated, responsible, disciplined, and driven: a group of kids who knew how to chill out, play, fail, screw-up and walk away. It was difficult to think where exactly we'd find these kids, or how to link Jill to them. Then serendipity stepped in. The solution was as simple as the family vacation Jill's parents had planned. It sounds absurd, but it's true. No psychiatric intervention, no elaborate behavioural plan, no intensive psychotherapy. Just a vacation. Travelling around with a pop-up trailer from campground to campground gave Jill a chance to meet lots of other children. Jill, of course, did not go willingly. At first she pouted and stormed about a "stupid trip" and how she'd be bored, and told everyone that camping "sucked." But once out there meeting new peers with whom she had no history, and to whom she could show off her monkey bar tricks, she slowly found a way to negotiate a new identity for herself that built on who she had been.

Dangerous Peers?

In Jill's case, she was young enough and malleable enough to quickly adapt to new surroundings. The peers she found offered her acceptance that brought with it a certain status because of who they were and who Jill was. But when the status peers offer a teen is perceived as either lower than parents expect or downright dangerous, then our tendency is to turn on our children's peers, blaming them for everything our child is becoming.

"My parents blame my friends for everything I do. That's pure crap. I do what I want to do when I feel like it. My friends don't make me do anything." I remember 14-year-old Clayton telling me this. He was speaking as much for himself as a whole generation of kids whose free agent status has been threatened by overly cautious parents.

I'd met Clayton and his twin brother Jake while an outreach worker for street kids. Neither boy had to be on the street. It was a strange community where they lived: on one side of an urban green space a community of half-million dollar homes, on the other, a blue-collar neighbourhood in decline. The youth themselves largely ignored the differences, meeting on the common ground of park benches and basketball courts that were forever in need of repair. As the kids huddled, women in designer track suits strolled by pushing prams while street alcoholics collected old newspapers to make their beds for the night. It was a landscape of contrasts, offering a wayward teen endless possibilities for both trouble and creative self-expression.

Clayton and Jake stood out when they drifted into peer groups made up mostly of kids from the lower-class neighbourhood. They lived in the "good" homes. Their parents both had full-time careers, one in law, the other in real estate. A nanny looked after them most days after school, but mostly they looked after each other. They were bright in that mischievous way of brainy kids who have no discipline. They were masters at building smoke bombs that went off with a regular frequency at school. They could steal cars and pick locks. They delighted in magic tricks and outsmarting the police. Needless to say, they drove their parents crazy and delighted their friends.

I remember meeting their folks on two occasions. Both times the boys had gotten themselves into trouble of one sort or another and their parents had to come down to the park to hunt them up. It was difficult not to feel sorry for them. They looked so out of place in their children's world. If I was there at the same time, we'd chat. They seemed to appreciate my services as a "cultural interpreter."

What they could never understand was why their kids had chosen this scene when the boys had unlimited access to any place, any activity they wanted. There appeared to be few barriers in front of them. In the minds of Clayton and Jake's parents, their children's behaviour had to be blamed on their peers. It was obvious that these other kids were leading the twins astray.

They were in some ways right. Those kids in the park offered the boys a path to find whatever it was they were searching for. If those kids hadn't been there, Clayton and Jake would surely have looked elsewhere. But with a peer group at the ready and just a short walk from home, the boys had an easy time of it bringing their search to a satisfactory conclusion.

I never fully understood either what the boys wanted, except that the chaos of the street attracted them like moths to a flame. That self-destruction was assured mattered little. Several days after Jake had been charged with public mischief for setting a smoke bomb off at school, he and his brother were back out among their friends laughing about his latest prank. "Our dad's a lawyer" was what they told everyone. "He'll take care of it." It occurred to me then that this was all a game for them. While for many of the other youth in the park this was survival, for Clayton and Jake this was adventure.

That evening around 8:00 p.m. the boys' father came to the park to find his sons. A curfew had been set and he meant to see that at least Jake obeyed it. We chatted for a few minutes, him chain-smoking, me listening attentively. We both watched the kids a little way off, a strange mix of skinheads and more fashionably dressed youth in designer labels. It was cold that evening, so mostly everyone was standing around, shoulders hunched, feet tapping to a collective beat that no one else could hear. I still remember the forlorn look Jake's dad had on his face. Utter disbelief that this was happening, that he was there in the park looking at his kid. I don't remember what I said, but I do remember him going on about "those damn little shits" and not meaning his two boys.

What leads two kids with just about everything into this kind of trouble? What was so attractive about clever displays of delinquency? The twins found support for what they wanted to do from their friends but they weren't being led by them. Of that I was fairly certain. For one thing, though the boys hung out with skinheads, they never wanted to look like them. While their friends were into street brawls, Clayton and Jake knew enough to stay away from these more dangerous pastimes. I had to admit I found the way they kept themselves safe intriguing.

The more I came to know the two brothers and watched them relate with their peers, the more I saw how they contributed a playfulness to their peer group culture. Their love of science and games loosened the group up, made them much more interested in playing practical jokes on others than seriously hurting them. In some ways, the twins' presence moderated the tendency of the group to be more delinquent and dangerous.

The boys also made it easier for the kids from the blue-collar side of the park to venture into the upper-class neighbourhoods from which they were otherwise excluded. Clayton and Jake had no hesitations about bringing their friends up to their place when their nanny was there. With their parents, it was another thing altogether, but with only the nanny to worry about, the boys were quite happy to share what they had with their friends. The boys were also much more comfortable at places like the YMCA and in other public buildings like the library. There, they didn't feel like outsiders, and in fact encouraged their friends to take up offers from street workers like myself to come in out of the weather and use the gym and weight room at the local Y. It wasn't that the Y was particularly aligned with one community or the other. It was just that any structure at all seemed to scare away Clayton and Jake's skinhead peers. Perhaps, I mused, the parents of these other kids should be thanking the two boys for their positive influence on their children. I don't think the twins' parents would have believed me if I'd told them the good things their sons were doing for these other youth.

In return Clayton and Jake found kids willing to take the risks they loved to take. These were not young people afraid of a little trouble. It pleased Clayton and Jake to no end to have their pranks appreciated and their praises sung by delinquents with rougher edges than their own. Among these peers they had found the type of expressive mirrors they sought. They just didn't seem to want what their parents had to offer. Maybe they were upset with being left alone so much, maybe they had some other problems. It wasn't really my job to find out. And they weren't talking much about that stuff, either. The only problem they had, to hear them talk, was getting caught for their pranks.

A child who is helped to understand that he or she can contribute as an equal participant to how a peer group behaves is being equipped with the skills necessary to build a healthy identity. Too often we convince kids they are being led around by their peers, ignoring any significant contribution, good or bad, that they might be making to how their friends think and act. I have seen parents of substance-abusing youth in total denial of their own child's role supplying other kids with drugs. I have seen these children be excused for their behaviour and the blame placed on other youth, who in the parents' minds were mistaken for the bad influence. I have seen children who were thinking up the crimes be told they are "good kids" (which they can be), except when they hang around with "you know who."

The danger is twofold when parents blame peers. First, a child's personal responsibility for what he or she does is taken away. And second, the child does not experience recognition for the one identity which is uniquely his or hers, that of delinquent. In the case of the youth who want to be master criminals, or who want the tainted prestige of drug dealers, they are left having to try even harder to be even greater trouble makers. How else will they convince others they are free agents?

Becoming a Free Agent

Parents who don't blame their children's peers for their kids' problems are free then to ask children to help them understand why they behave the way they do. I encourage parents to ask kids what their role is in their peer group; to ask them what it is like hanging out with friends; find out what it means to them to do drugs or be delinquent; What are the benefits? What are some of the bad things that happen? Who in the group is best at it? What's special, unique, or different about their child?

If a conversation like this gets rolling, and it will when we approach kids with a belief that their truth is worth knowing, we can then go the next step and help kids learn how to contribute to group culture. What happens when the teen suggests the group do something different, or more of the same? By finding out what happens when children speak out among peers, we find out about their status in their groups. We also learn if there are things about the peer group they either like or dislike. Knowing that can help us design a world beyond our children's peers which offers them the same stimulation, challenge and support.

I ask most of these questions in a tone that is uncritical. I want to be inquisitive, not judgmental. I want teens to feel like they are educating me, imparting wisdom where there is only a dark void of ignorance. The more they despair for me, the more motivated I find they are to educate me. But there is nothing false about this. I genuinely know I do not understand. I want and need to learn about their worlds in order to help them find a way to be healthy inside and outside their homes.

Our homes can be a forum in which children learn how to express themselves while experiencing a respect for their opinions which inoculates them against poor choices outside our homes. How often do we consult with our children about what to do on a Saturday afternoon? About what to buy? About anything to do with *their* home, or *their* lives? Another much more serious example of this occurs with children who have experienced the divorce or separation of their parents. It is still unusual to meet children who were asked for their opinions about what living arrangements they would prefer after their parents split. Sometimes young people are consulted, more often their opinions are ignored in favour of the practicalities that impinge on the lives of adults.

We simply do not teach our children well at home how to have a say in the construction of values and norms. Little wonder they are ill-prepared to do so with their peers. In the absence of the skills they need, they substitute passivity for compromise and bullying for negotiation.

Instead of blaming peers for our children's problems, a healthier, more empowering approach is to offer our children the experiences of power from which they can learn to exercise a say over their peer group's culture. Successful relationships with caregivers create fertile ground in which teens sow the self-confidence necessary to celebrate their unique identity outside the home. We adults have a role in helping children function well in their peer groups. But that role is limited to the part we play in writing the stories which are our teenagers' lives. Our task, should we choose to accept it, is to help our children author a story of resilience while teaching them in our own homes the skills they need to promote it. Blaming peers instead of doing our job will get us nowhere and drive our children into more and more desperate straits.

Chapter 11
Breaking Down Walls

It's 7:00 on a weekday evening, three weeks before municipal elections take place. There's a knock at the door and one of the contenders for a seat on our local council is there on my porch, pamphlet in hand, smiling, eager for an election win. Tonight it's an older man, a fellow newly retired who used to work for the same municipality he now wants to run. "We need some fresh ideas in there," he tells me. "I've watched it from the inside for thirty years. The backroom deals, the waste, the way people are treated unfairly. That's why I'm running. I think things can be different."

Turns out that for five of those years of service this same fellow ran the local sportsplex, an outdoor pool and arena in our area which is always in use. We chat about his time there, about how things are changing. There's a plan afoot to finally invest five million dollars and build a large aquatics centre, but the expense and upkeep have scared away every previous municipal council. No matter that other much smaller communities an hour's drive from us have such facilities. The men, and a few women, who have held sway in council haven't wanted to be the ones who would have to raise taxes, or redistribute funds away from sidewalk repair, or worse, the extra policing they always seem to need to deal with the bored teenagers who swarm the tourists who flock each summer to where I live. I begin slyly working the fellow around to seeing things my way.

"Times have changed and things can be different," I agree. "Take playing hockey. It's just too expensive for most families to afford to have their kids in it anymore. But we keep building more ice surfaces," I said to him. Then, before he can defend his love of the game or his reluctance to build a pool, I ask him, "What was it like when you were a boy?"

I think he knows where I'm going with this. "I hear you," he says. "When I was a kid it cost two dollars to register a boy for the season."

"Now it costs four hundred, and girls and boys can both play." He nods. "But what with the equipment, skates, road trips and everything else, most families are spending two or three thousand a season, per kid. You know, for most of the families I work with, whose kids are on the street and getting into trouble, they just are never going to come up with that kind of money."

"Yeah, it's a problem, I agree," he says.

"Makes swimming and the price of a bathing suit a pretty cheap alternative," I say, smiling. "Kids can swim evenings and on weekends for a few bucks. Have a place to be. Both the boys and girls like it because they can sort of show off in front of each other. I know of a community the same size as ours with an aquaplex that is so busy it has its own donut shop right inside. People are in there morning till night."

"Hmm," he says. I can tell he's being polite. After a pause he shares with me his ideas on what the community needs. "But what about all the folks who don't have children? They want sidewalks, things like that, lower taxes. Hard to convince them to put all that money into something they don't use."

It's my turn to play the skeptic. "Seems those are the same people saying they don't feel safe on the streets, who are always calling for more police to control kids. But the more police we bring on the more the problems persist. I just don't think we're looking at this problem from the point of view of the kids themselves.

"Like last year they wanted to take that old rink, the one they just started tearing down, and make it into an indoor soccer arena." He remembers. "It's smack dab in the heart of the poorest part of the city, near to where we're having all the problems. Soccer, not hockey or football, is the most popular kids' sport now. Not like in your time, or mine. Different, isn't it? But that's the truth. Soccer costs nothing but a pair of shoes to play. About the same price as a bathing suit. Girls and boys get to spend time together. Kids get to mix with all sorts, kids who just arrived in this country, kids from families who can trace their roots back fourteen generations. Native kids. It's a sport that everyone can play. But we didn't come up with that money either."

"It would have been a half million, I think I heard, to get the building changed over."

"Yeah, but we're spending three million on updates to city hall. We spent another million on the gardens down by the waterfront. I hate to say it, but I think we're telling kids they don't count, loud and clear. Then we're up in arms that the tourists are getting swarmed, or panhandled. A rink, a pool, is not going to solve every problem, but they're a start in the right direction."

I could see the fellow wanting to tell me more about his ideas for civic reform. I don't think he was that used to listening. A late baby boomer, almost a senior, a long time resident of this community, he had grown up with the privileges of his time, his race and his gender. He's a good fellow, mind you, salt of the earth. He means well. But he wasn't going to change anything. He is caught in a 50-year-old myth about his community and those who lived there. He soon took his leave, with a joke about maybe we can get more young people out to vote. Nice enough fellow, I thought, just not what I was hoping for in a city councillor.

The Walls to Climb

The myths we hold about youth permeate our culture because we don't want to see the world from the eyes of those who are disenfranchised, those with less power than those who rule. We are comfortable with imagining the world as we adults want it to be. Though we like to think differently, we suffer from a generational amnesia.

The five strategies to help youth nurture healthy identities with their peers and families depend on access to the resources youth need to construct healthy identities. No matter how hard we work as parents and caregivers, social, economic, political, family, and personal issues will limit the opportunities some youth have to find what they need to be healthy. Think back to the young mariner introduced in Chapter Five. When the islands which populate a young person's ocean and to which he or she can drift are limited in number, or his or her boat not sufficiently seaworthy for the journey, an at-risk child is just as likely to give up sailing altogether and instead settle for whatever happens to be handy. If children and their parents live in cultures of poverty or abuse and their bank balances act like snares keeping them there, then it will be a struggle to offer those at-risk children all but a few choices for health. Even when economic barriers are not the issue, social expectations and a consumer driven culture that offers things rather than substance and meaning conspire to take from our children opportunities to explore the many options they may have for a personal story. Unless we address the barriers kids face to writing their own scripts, we sentence them to time in a virtual prison of missed opportunities.

Too often, manuals for parents and caregivers such as this overly psychologize children's problems, leaving the mistaken notion that all one has to do is to work with the child individually in order to succeed. While I talk about children making choices, I never forget that they do so within the confines of the communities to which they were born. Some oceans are easier to cross than others. Some are infested with dangerous creatures. Some are known for their storms and wild winds.

Formulas for raising a healthy teen, even those discussed in previous chapters, do not take place in isolation of the real world which challenge both us adults and our children.

Take for example a young Native youth like Jeff, who at sixteen had spent most of his life living off reserve in the city with his father and mother. In the summer the family would go back home to visit the rest of their family living on reserve. Jeff told me he used to be called an "apple" during those visits, his peers teasing him he was "red outside and white inside." I don't think Jeff knew what he was. Mostly he just tried to fit in with his friends in town who roamed the streets most evenings. Some of those kids were Native as well and together they would cope with the racist stories their community told about them. Though the racism was subtle, people there knowing better than to be openly impolite, they still didn't really trust Jeff and his Native friends the way they did the White kids. Gas-sniffing and property crimes had become a way of life for Jeff. It was sometimes difficult to know which came first, Jeff feeling excluded or his problem behaviours justifying his exclusion. Like the proverbial chicken and egg, it was a question without an answer. Understanding this didn't change the fact that it was painful watching this bright kid slipping into behaviours that further stereotyped him and his friends. It was as if there was something missing inside Jeff that may have made him resist what was being done to him by others. That spark of defiance unfortunately never ignited. He didn't believe that things would ever be better, or maybe it was that he had no desire to resist the flood of expectations on the part of those around him that limited what he could and could not be. He was, he once told me, "just another Native kid."

It was hard to know what to offer Jeff by way of a lifeline. He eventually died in a car accident, an accident that most who knew him figured was intentional. For the sake of his parents, the possibility of suicide was ignored. Before his death, a few of us thought he was making some headway, climbing out of his stark and depleted world. He had started a process of defining himself as something other than what his community told him he was. He had momentarily found a peer group of other children, all visible minorities, that seemed to offer him something different than more put-downs. Perhaps if he had made it into his twenties he would have found his way to some social activism and with it, better piece of mind. Perhaps then he would have learned better how to resist and win a place for himself where he was accepted.

But the script he lived day to day of a worthless addicted "Indian" was powerful and so all-encompassing in his life, he couldn't shake the identity which clung to him. His parents' solution had been to join with Whites and seek a truce. Why shouldn't they? They deserved the middle-class dream as much as anyone. But their son had gotten caught between two worlds. Without a guide, he had become lost between cultures.

The issue of race and one's identification or non-identification with a particular racial group is a powerful constraint on one's identity construction. It's all well and good to argue in favour of our children's search for competence, but real world barriers speak louder than their caregivers about what children can expect from life.

It's the same for other barriers children face. There is a pattern to the way these forces colour our children's lives. Peers and adults who typecast a child like Jeff, forever seeing him as an Indian, or poor, or as a drug addict, teenager, or child of this type of parent or that, are likely to believe he is limited in what he can be or do. Society conspires to erect systemic barriers against some children ever having an opportunity to express their talents. We needn't think hard to know this is true. It is only within our lifetimes that sports have been racially desegrated. It is only in the past dozen or so years that girls are being given many of the same opportunities to play male dominated sports such as hockey and rugby. While adults struggle with breaking through glass ceilings at work, kids just want to enjoy the right to have fun despite who and what they are. Though it's easy to see the problems, I am actually more optimistic than most of my colleagues in this regard. The fact is that kids like Jeff are being woken up to a different set of choices. And girls are now able to take automotive classes rather than being ghettoized by outdated ideas that they belong in home economics. It's a changing world and teens are both leaders in constructing these changes and victims of the world as it once was. We can be a great deal of help in this shift towards an expanded selection of health-enhancing options for our children. Peer groups teach us that a child who has some power to pick and choose an identity is the one who is on a path to wellness.

The relative worth we as a culture assign different behaviours is a complex dance of power and relationships. Why is one look, one genre of music or one sporting activity more valued than another? Thankfully we are at a time when the global village is creating many more options for youth, though communities still work to limit which options will be found acceptable. Young Latino singers are at the top of the pop charts, Black artists infuse White artists with rap and reggae lyrics. In the cosmopolitan mix of cultures we are experiencing there is more room for diversity, but there is still the threat of sameness that comes from fear and hegemony. The child who does not fit with the current mass hysteria for a particular cultural artifact is swept aside and told he or she is of less value than teens who conform. Fortunately, the ones swept aside are finding it easier and easier to connect with like-minded others. The problem is, however, we as their caregivers are seldom well-prepared to pass judgment on what is and is not good growth and development.

When we talk specifically about what is and is not mental health, the same danger exists: that those in power decide for everyone what will be seen as healthy functioning. As adults, we can help teenagers to fight back against a mental health system that puts them in boxes that don't fit. Think back to Mitch, the young man who spent days curled up on the floor in a locked cell, choosing to go "crazy" rather than deal with the dangerous environment to which he had been committed. For those who come in contact with the mental health care system, there is a tendency for professionals to confuse conformity with well-being. When a child acts differently and outside what is expected of him or her, we are inclined to say the child is sick or disturbed. We blame the victim of our expectations for not "getting with the program" and fitting in.

We can help our kids resist this pull to the centre. I marvel when I read in the Saturday Living sections of our newspapers how the promise of health is held out to those who just join that next therapy group, polish their self-esteem, and work a little more on their relationships. But this insistence on *fixing ourselves* to meet society's expectations of us leaves out anyone who is different or who doesn't have the personal resources necessary to fit in. We seldom see any hint in this mass-marketing of self-improvement that the system into which we are expected to fit may be fundamentally flawed. If we are to help our children find healthy identities, we may find we have to ask ourselves some tough questions about the institutions which are there to serve them.

For example, I have yet to see a group for school administrators that helps them look critically at the way their schools work. We want kids to contort themselves to fit with what teachers need, but we never stop to examine how we might design learning environments that better suit the needs of high-risk children and youth. Why are kids who are full of "piss and vinegar," as I once heard it said, made to sit for six hours a day learning esoteric details of the world which they will not need to know?

I have yet to see a community meet to discuss the needs of high-risk youth for recreational zones that provide the types of activities when and where these kids want them. Instead I see concerned citizens trying to find ways to give kids recreational opportunities valued by the wider community which only serve to make high-risk youth invisible or marginal. Skateboard parks, for example, are often relegated to industrial zones, or concrete jungles, and rollerblade hockey rinks to unused parking lots. Meanwhile tennis courts, basketball courts, ice hockey rinks, soccer fields, and bike lanes are built for the needs of youth who are safely immersed in the mainstream culture. True, these same public spaces could be used just as readily by youth with problems, but are we willing to put up with their occasionally disruptive behaviours? Are we willing to understand that sometimes, despite the opportunities, kids are stuck in patterns that bolster their self-esteem at the price of social acceptability?

If we were really thinking of the needs of kids who are on the street we might begin to look at opening school gyms for midnight basketball, turning ice hockey rinks into year-round indoor soccer arenas, making tennis courts adaptable to rollerblade hockey, and putting skateboard parks where kids can strut their stuff in very public forums.

In my travels I have seen many of these ideas work. I know midnight basketball draws kids off the streets. I know of a community that put their skateboard park right on the commons, at a major intersection where all day long there is a steady flow of traffic from the nearby downtown district. Kids love it. As they swoop up and down the concrete and wooden platforms they have a constant audience whom they can impress. Another community built a fabulous indoor aquatics complex. Saturday and Sunday afternoons and evenings there is a steady stream of young people with one eye on their friends, the other on whomever catches their fancy. And I haven't even begun to mention the many drop-in centres, art programs, special programs to give at-risk youth summer jobs, alternative schools which are less structured and allow kids to pace themselves, vocational programs that teach work skills, supports for parents, and outdoor concerts. I'm fond of musing that "we have the technology" but not the will to implement the solutions that would make high-risk kids feel a part of their communities.

Alliances

A child cannot address these forces alone. When confronted with systemic racism, agism, classism, sexism or any other form of prejudice, is it any wonder that youth band together into paramilitary groups of "warriors" or "gangs" in order to assert their power? What else can they do? Buried deep within the culture of these groups is the same struggling spirit that is ours as well. Our children search through their chaotic behaviour for the tools of resistance which can make their worlds more bearable places in which to live. I'm not so sure that I always approve of the way at-risk youth resist the problems in their lives, but I know now that assuming that their solutions are any better or worse than mine gets me nowhere. If I am to help, I need to build an alliance with them founded on mutual respect and trust. Sadly, that's not usually how kids experience offers of help from those with power over them.

"There's nothing *you* can do to help. Really, nothing." I've been told this same thing bluntly, rudely, politely, and arrogantly by any number of different teens. I've seen their parents told it as well. Our kids don't really believe that we adults can help them as long as we are trapped believing we have the right answer and that their acts of resistance are nothing but the signs of a troubled youngster.

A while ago I met a young woman, Janice, who was nineteen at the time. She'd been through group homes, foster homes, an abusive family home, and jail. She explained, "The best thing people could have done to help me was leave me where I was. Nobody did anything that helped. All the moves, all the professionals, just made things worse than if I'd been left at home."

"But you were being abused," I protested.

"And like all those moves and being torn away from my family wasn't abuse?"

She had a point. The system's solution to her problems had been no better than what she might have come up with herself. At least that was her view. I, of course, struggle to rationalize leaving an abused child in an abusive home. But maybe what Janice is telling us is that nobody asked her what she wanted.

To cope, Janice told me, "I just hung out with other kids like me. It was like if the world said I was a bad kid then I was going to be a really bad kid. We were all like that, playing it up big time. But it wasn't really what I wanted. What I wanted was to be back home in my own place. But they wouldn't let me do that. They just didn't listen. It was like I was this young girl and they weren't going to take anything I had to say seriously. Nobody should be treated like that."

We prejudice ourselves with the blinders of age, gender, race and ability. Instead, we need to help fight our children's fights on their terms. We can help when we align ourselves with them, instead of against them.

My 8-year-old son struggles to have a positive relationship with the 10-year-old bully, Justin, who lives on our street. Scott is learning lots of new language and interesting things about human anatomy he needn't have learned until he's older, thanks to the language he hears Justin using. But despite it all, my son keeps going back for more punishment. I'd rather he didn't. The problem, as he understands it, is that he wants to do the exciting things that the whole group of kids down the street do. He loves that little boy energy which is found in games of war, hide-and-seek, and figuring out how to make rockets. Though he's outsized, and outsmarted at times, he is convinced he has few other choices to experience the same excitement he encounters when playing with Justin and his little group of friends. So I offered Scott a solution that I thought might turn the tables and give him a bit more power, while recognizing all the good things he gets from spending time with Justin. I built him a tree fort. The fort changed the power dynamics between Scott and Justin. Now my son is on his own turf and the kids come to our yard to play where we adults can help monitor the foul language. My son's status in the group is a bit higher, and he can set the pace a bit more.

This wasn't the first solution I tried. When the bullying started I talked with the bully's parents. That worked for a few days, but it still left my son appearing to need help to solve his own problems. I next tried redirecting him toward other children, more his own age. That also helped a bit, but he still missed the rough and tumble of his chosen peer group. So I thought, let's help him set the tone in the group. Let me make the kids a place where they can play in ways that we all will like. It's not a perfect solution but it is a step in the right direction. It was also an idea which grew from my respect for the way the neighbourhood kids were already relating to each other. In other words, the solution worked because the building of a tree fort fit with what my son's peer group already valued.

Jobs and More Jobs

Our hope is that children develop healthy identities that we can all live with. Employment can play a big part in that development for older children. Despite an economy which for many is doing quite well, depending on where you live, there are likely large numbers of youth distinguished either by race, gender, how much their folks earn, how much schooling they have, or whether they live in the city or in rural areas, who never benefit from economic upturns. It's always these "other" kids who don't get to share in the abundance we see around us. For them, jobs are scarce or poorly paid. It's as if each place I've lived has an invisible checklist that says which youth fit the description of the ones likely to succeed, and which do not. If a child's on the "B" list, then there is little he or she can do alone to change that. We like to believe otherwise. "Work hard and you'll succeed," we're told. But the truth is that unless children have an exceptional talent they will not overcome many of the systemic barriers laid in their paths.

Low academic achievers get pushed into vocational training for which there is a steadily shrinking job market. Even then, try being a janitor or even a farm hand today without a grade twelve education and one quickly finds many doors remain closed. While overall I see a trend toward things getting better, I am disheartened that in our rush to embrace the information revolution we are leaving a large number of youth behind.

These are the kids who used to find satisfying, good paying jobs for themselves as general labourers, apprentices in the trades, clerks, secretaries, maintenance workers, and as the heart and soul of many primary industries like fishing, farming and forestry. Many of these kinds of jobs are gone, or demanding more and more qualified people. We are progressing quickly, but leaving a hapless crew of dispossessed youth in our wake.

When youth do find work after high school, then sadly much of it is part-time and temporary, or so low paying and with so few possibilities for advancement that kids make the "sensible" decision to quit.

Kids need opportunities to work if they are going to create healthy identities that are more widely accepted than those they find among their peers. As adults we can fight for a more flexible education system which celebrates the many different ways our children learn. Every child deserves an education. It's the law. We just haven't been very good at looking critically at the type of education we are providing. Does it serve well the needs of our most vulnerable children?

A Crisis Needing Action

We invest very little in the infrastructure which could offer what I see as transitional spaces where youth can come in off the streets and explore their many and varied talents. We make decisions every day which either bring our children and their peers into positions of acceptance or relegate them to the status of second-class citizens.

My community is still fighting for an aquatics centre and an indoor soccer arena. I like the slogan we're using to promote both, "Build it and they will come." We still need, however, to give some thought to who it is we want there and how we will make them feel welcome when they arrive.

My real hope is that we redirect dollars away from an ever expanding police budget. The more police on the street the more kids feel like criminals and take on that identity. I can still remember the reaction of many youth to the increased foot patrols and bike patrols in our downtown core. "The cops are nice enough," the kids say, "but if they're gonna be on our case like then we'll just have to show them